Teaching Adult ESOL

Developing Adult Skills

Series Editors: David Mallows and Wendy Moss

The *Developing Adult Skills* series is written to support Developing Adult Skills professionals, particularly those who are studying for the new Developing Adult Skills qualifications. Each book offers strategies and practical tips as well as helping to link theory and practice. The editors and contributors are all experienced practitioners and researchers who share their experiences of meeting the diverse needs of learners.

Titles in the series:

Teaching Adult Literacy: Principles and Practice

Nora Hughes and Irene Schwab

Teaching Adult ESOL: Principles and Practice

Anne Paton and Meryl Wilkins

Teaching Adult ESOL

Principles and Practice

Edited by Anne Paton and Meryl Wilkins

Series editors: David Mallows and Wendy Moss

National Research and Development Centre
for adult literacy and numeracy

The views expressed in this publication are those of the authors and do not necessarily represent the decisions or the stated policy of the Institute of Education.

Open University Press
McGraw-Hill Education
McGraw-Hill House
Shoppenhangers Road
Maidenhead
Berkshire
England
SL6 2QL

email: enquiries@openup.co.uk
world wide web: www.openup.co.uk

and Two Penn Plaza, New York, NY 10121—2289, USA

First published 2009

A catalogue record of this book is available from the British Library

ISBN-13: 978-0-33-5237388 (pb) 978-0-33-5237371 (hb)
ISBN-10: 0-33-52378-X (pb) 0-33-523737-1 (hb)

Typeset by Kerrypress, Luton, Bedfordshire
Printed and bound in the UK by Bell and Bain Ltd, Glasgow.

Fictitious names of companies, products, people, characters and/or data that may be used herein (in case studies or in examples) are not intended to represent any real individual, company, product or event.

The McGraw·Hill Companies

Contents

List of contributors

Vivien Barr is a writer of educational materials, a teacher-trainer and a teacher of English and English for speakers of other languages (ESOL) to post-16 students and adults. She has written a number of ESOL books and materials in partnership with Clare Fletcher. Her current role is in widening access to higher education.

Sue Colquhoun is the continuing professional development (CPD) Strategic Adviser at the Institute for Learning and in her previous position she was Programme Manager for Post Compulsory Education and Training (PCET) at the University of Greenwich, responsible for initial teacher education and training. Her subject specialist area is in English for ESOL and she has led on the design of various curricula for the ESOL subject specialist qualifications at level 4 and the additional diplomas.

Jo-Ann Delaney has worked in English-language teaching (ELT) and teacher education for over 15 years. She has taught English as a second language in a number of different countries and has worked in the UK since 1995. She has extensive ESOL teacher-training experience and worked on the curriculum development of the new ESOL teacher-training courses. Currently she is a senior lecturer and skills for life course director in the Post Compulsory Education Department at Canterbury Christchurch University.

Clare Fletcher is a teacher and trainer in ESOL and English as a foreign language (EFL). She has a long-standing writing partnership with Vivien Barr, ranging from the ESOL classic topics and skills in English in 1983 to television scripts and the ESOL core curriculum and skills for life materials. She is a former chief examiner for Cambridge DELTA.

Anne Paton has taught on the post-graduate certificate in education (PGCE)/ certificate in education adult literacy and ESOL at the Institute of Education, University of London, and on Cambridge ESOL DELTA and CELTA courses. She has also worked for London South Bank University and the University of Portsmouth, and has substantial experience of both EFL and ESOL. Currently she teaches ESOL and works freelance as a teacher-educator.

Marina Spiegel was born in Argentina and has taught modern languages and ESOL since the mid-1970s in secondary schools, and further, adult and higher education. She worked at the LLU+ at London South Bank University, as a teacher-educator and is co-author of several publications, including *Chart Your Course in English,* with Meryl Wilkins; and *Writing Works* and *Teaching Basic Literacy to ESOL Learners,* with Helen Sunderland.

Helen Sunderland is Head of ESOL for LLU+ at London South Bank University, where she manages educational projects and a programme of ESOL teacher education. Her curriculum interests are in teaching literacy and in dyslexia. However, work on government projects has generated her interest in policy and its implementation, and in the often unintended consequences of policy decisions.

John Sutter is a senior lecturer in the ESOL division of LLU+ at London South Bank University, where he teaches on the MA teacher-education programme. Before joining LLU+, he worked as a teacher and teacher-trainer in the UK, Greece, Poland and Ecuador. His current interests include multimodal literacies, discourse/language and power, and critical approaches to teacher education.

Efisia Tranza has taught ESOL and literacy for over 20 years. She now works as a senior lecturer for LLU+ at London South Bank University, where she teaches on the combined ESOL and Literacy DTTLS programmes. Her main curriculum interest at present is in teaching basic literacy to ESOL learners.

Mary Weir has worked for many years as a teacher of English and French in a range of settings including schools, community classes, FE colleges and universities. She gained an MA in Language Teaching from Leeds Metropolitan University in 2004. Her current role involves ESOL teaching and teacher education.

Meryl Wilkins has many years experience as an ESOL teacher and teacher-trainer. She was involved in the development of the *Adult ESOL Core Curriculum* and a range of teaching materials, including those developed for Skills for Life. She has taught on DELTA, Level 4 ESOL subject specific courses and Training the Trainers courses.

The National Research and Development Centre for Adult Literacy and Numeracy (NRDC) aims to make a difference to policy and practice in post-14 literacy, language and numeracy. We have been working since 2002 to generate knowledge and transform it into practice. We undertake research and development activity in adult literacy, numeracy, ESOL and closely related fields. For more information visit www.nrdc.org.uk.

INTRODUCTION

Anne Paton and Meryl Wilkins

This book focuses on the English language learning of adults who have come to live in the UK. Work with these learners is usually known as ESOL (English for speakers of other languages), and is referred to as such throughout this book.

ESOL in the UK is informed by experience developed over many years, in particular since the 1970s, when adult ESOL became more widespread. It draws on expertise in related areas, in particular general English-language teaching (ELT) which takes place in a range of contexts and in most countries of the world, and on applied linguistics. It also draws on the experience of ESOL in other English-speaking countries such as Australia, and on adult literacy and the field of adult education in general.

There are some very good publications, both books and journals, which discuss the needs of this group of learners, but they are few. Much of the available literature, though relevant to a greater or lesser extent, does not directly address this specific language learning situation. This book acknowledges a range of sources, while maintaining its focus on the learners who concern us here.

All the writers have substantial experience in ESOL in the UK, both as teachers and as teacher-educators. All have been involved in developing and delivering the Level 4 qualifications for subject specialists in ESOL and/or training in the use of the *Adult ESOL Core Curriculum*. They have also all written teaching material for use in ESOL classes and/or articles on the subject of ESOL in the UK.

Who did we write for?

The book is intended to support teacher-training courses leading to a subject specific qualification in teaching ESOL to adults.

You will find this book useful if you are working in ESOL in a voluntary or paid capacity, and intend to develop your career in this area. If this is your first experience of English language teaching, you should read the book alongside other books which address ELT in general, as these will go into more detail on issues such as language analysis, language acquisition and general language teaching methodology. Relevant reading is recommended at the end of each chapter.

If you have already taught language in another context such as English abroad, or other languages in UK schools, and are now teaching or intending to teach ESOL, you will find this book useful in adapting your previous knowledge and experience to the new situation.

If you are not an ESOL teacher but are teaching adults in the UK, and many of your learners have a first language other than English, you will find Chapter 12 of this book is written with your situation in mind.

If you are teaching ESOL in another country where English is an official language and is needed extensively in everyday life, you will find much in this book that will interest you. However, there will be some references, for example to the UK Skills for Life agenda, that you will find less directly relevant, though hopefully still interesting.

The partner volume

The book has a partner volume – *Teaching Adult Literacy* – which is about working with learners who are fluent speakers of English but who wish to improve their reading and writing in particular. They may also wish to improve their use of spoken English, for example by comparing formal and informal language use.

Many learners in adult literacy classes have a first language other than English, and it is not always easy to decide whether a particular learner should be in an ESOL class or in an adult literacy class. Learners whose spoken English is very fluent might be better served by adult literacy classes, although they might also need to work on some similar aspects to those covered in ESOL classes, such as grammar. If you have this kind of learner in your classes, you could benefit from referring to the adult literacy book.

The contents of the book: an overview

Chapter 1, 'ESOL learners', begins by exploring some distinguishing features of the language learning situation which this book addresses, making a comparison with other contexts for language learning. We register the challenge presented by the variety of life experiences, cultures and educational backgrounds found in many ESOL classes, while suggesting that these same factors can present rich learning opportunities when learners' real-life needs and purposes for using English are recognized and addressed. The centrality of learner purpose in ESOL teaching is a key notion which informs the whole book.

Chapter 2, 'ESOL in the UK education system', locates the subject of our book in its political context, outlining the development of ESOL provision over time, and the way government policy has influenced and responded to it. In particular, we focus on the Skills for Life strategy (2001) and its impact on ESOL provision.

In Chapter 3, 'Language and context in ESOL teaching', we focus on the integration of language and thematic content in different ESOL teaching contexts. There is an outline of the language skills and systems involved in communication and their role in facilitating it. We then discuss thematic content in different course types, including vocational, citizenship and topic-based courses where linguistic content is embedded.

Chapter 4, 'Second language acquisition (SLA) and the contexts of UK ESOL practice', relates sociolinguistic realities of ESOL learners to current theories of SLA. Taking a critical view of certain concepts in SLA theorizing, we support calls for a 'social turn' in SLA theory and stress the need for ESOL practice to take account of learners' existing linguistic resources and repertoires; their uses of language and literacy both in English and their other language(s); and their developing social identities.

Chapter 5, 'The spoken language', opens with a discussion of language variety and accent in relation to ESOL learners. We go on to outline some aspects of phonology which are significant in developing speaking and listening skills. Learning materials and classroom practice are then considered in the light of ESOL learners' contexts and purposes for using English, and their need to develop and express a social identity. The role of negotiation for meaning (NfM) in developing language skills is briefly considered.

Chapter 6, 'The witten word', begins by noting the multimodal and socially situated nature of literacy, discussing its purposes and recognizing challenges which learners may face when developing literacy in another language. We identify skills involved in reading and discuss ways of developing them, including critical reading, genre approaches and strategies for active reading. Turning to writing, we look at process and genre approaches before considering the particular needs of learners working at a very basic level of literacy.

Chapter 7, 'Developing accuracy', opens by discussing the relationship of accuracy to fluency. We identify some aspects of accuracy in both lexis and grammar, and discuss different approaches to developing lexicogrammatical accuracy. In recognition of the prevalence of fluent but inaccurate users of English in many UK ESOL classes, a section of the chapter is concerned with the issue of developing accuracy with these learners.

Chapter 8, 'Developing and adapting resources', establishes principles for selecting and developing learning materials. We scrutinize resources from different media and subject areas, focusing on evaluating them and making adaptations which improve their suitability and accessibility for ESOL learners. Consideration is given to general English-language teaching (ELT) course materials, adult literacy resources and materials for vocational studies, as well as to authentic material. A second important focus of this chapter is on creating your own purpose-designed materials.

Chapter 9, 'Planning and assessment', concerns relationships between planning, assessment and learning, stressing the role of evaluation and reflection – by both teachers and learners – in this continuous and cyclical process. We consider the role of consultation and tutorials in planning for group and individual learning and take a fresh look at the role and potential of Individual Learning Plans.

Chapter 10, 'Differentiation', is about tailoring strategies to the needs and preferences of individuals, in a learning context of group diversity. We acknowledge possible tensions between the groupwork so fundamental to ESOL learning and the need to differentiate, suggesting ways of responding to this issue in a principled and practical way. Key elements of this chapter address differentiation in listening and speaking activities, the role of differentiation in teacher talk and differentiation in oral feedback.

Chapter 11, 'Inclusive learning', concerns the accessibility of ESOL learning to people with all kinds of disabilities. We examine different ways of thinking about disability and then outline important legislation which teachers need to know about. Moving on to practical issues, we discuss assessment; different kinds of support; the importance of consultation with learners when organizing support; and inclusive classroom practice.

Chapter 12, 'ESOL issues for teachers in the lifelong learning sector', has been written for teachers who are not ESOL specialists, but who teach some learners with an ESOL profile. It may, if wished, be read as a stand-alone section. It will also be of interest to ESOL teachers collaborating with teachers of other subjects on embedded courses. We describe the circumstances in which ESOL learners may have settled in the UK and introduce key thinking about levels of language expertise and about the process of language acquisition. We then look at strategies for helping these learners to participate fully, and for supporting the continued development of their language skills.

Tasks

Throughout the book you are invited to develop and apply your knowledge and understanding through reflective tasks, which can be done individually or as a group. A commentary is provided after the task whenever this is appropriate.

Part 1

ESOL and society

1 ESOL learners

Anne Paton and Meryl Wilkins

Introducing ESOL learners

> My husband have a problem with the Government, then he came about two and a half years here ... My house or anything I have in Iran finished and then I came here, because children – I have three children ... must see their father.
>
> (Naima from Iran)

> I am living in London three month ago. Actually I am living with my husband ... I marry in Peru, Lima Peru in October. I move with my husband ... my husband is English.
>
> (Dalia from Peru)

> My country have been at war for last about twelve years. We didn't have any chance or no school or nothing about learning. Every time we go outside we scared ... That's big reason I come this country.
>
> (Hawa from Somalia)

In the above quotations three different English for speakers of other languages (ESOL) learners give the reasons why they are now living in the UK. Hawa, Dalia and Naima were among a group of learners in South-East London who agreed to take part in a video recording, called *I Came to England*.[1] In this they describe and discuss their experiences of making a new life in the UK. The group on the recording consists of nine women and two men from Ecuador, Iraq, Iran, Kosovo, Morocco, Peru, Somalia and Vietnam. They have lived in the UK for between three months and 23 years. Their educational background ranges from PhD level to very little schooling. Most of them have children in London schools and all of them would like to find a new job at some time in the future. This book is about the English language development of learners such as these. The learners we are concerned with can be described as:

> minority ethnic adults living in a different culture and learning its dominant language
>
> (Pitt 2005)

They have come to live in an English-speaking country for a variety of reasons: to escape persecution or prejudice; to escape from situations such as war, famine or natural disasters; to find work; or to marry or join family already settled there. They are not staying in the country primarily because they want to learn the language, so their study of English is a consequence of their being in an English-speaking country, rather than the reason for their being there. We will refer to them as ESOL learners and to the field as ESOL throughout this book.

Learners in ESOL classes

Looking at the reasons for ESOL learners being in the country, it is clear that, to some extent, the ethnographic composition of ESOL classes will reflect immigration patterns. At the same time, it is necessary to recognize that *by no means all* learners in ESOL classes are recent arrivals in the country, so it is not always possible to look at current tendencies in immigration and predict the countries of origin of a group of learners on an ESOL programme.

The group of learners who appear on the video *I Came to England* represent a snapshot of the ethnic groups that made up the population of ESOL learners in a part of South-East London in 2004. This snapshot is viewed through the lens of a particular ESOL provider which has crèche facilities, with the result that a certain category of learner, that is women with children, is very well represented. The picture will not necessarily be the same in other parts of the country at other times.

TASK 1.1

1 Consider the makeup of different ESOL classes in your area; if you aren't sure then find someone to ask. Consider the following factors:
   - Country of origin of learners.
   - Language(s) spoken by the learners.
   - Age range.
   - Gender.
   - Educational background (in the UK and outside the UK).
   - Reasons for being in the UK.
   - Reasons for being in the class.
   - Any learners with specific requirements, e.g. a disability.
2 What changes have you (or the people you consulted) seen over time, and what do you think are the reasons for the changes?

COMMENT 1.1

We put these questions to two ESOL teachers, one in London and one in Leeds.
   The London teacher explained that four years earlier the vast majority of learners were refugees and asylum seekers. Some came with families, some were

single; there was quite a range of educational backgrounds and most were unemployed but wanting to work. There was a mix of men and women, but often large groups of single men, particularly from Kosovo.

In the ensuing years, she had noticed four major changes:

- There were many more learners from Eastern Europe, especially Poland. They were of all ages, including some older men, and they were normally in work.
- The refugees who attended were no longer new arrivals to the country but tended to be women who had been in the UK for some time.
- Her college was concentrating more on younger learners, often from countries such as Eritrea and Somalia. Some had spent time in British secondary schools, others were just leaving the care of Social Services.
- Her college was more aware of the need to provide for learners with disabilities, and as a result it was much easier for these learners to attend classes.

We can see how quickly the profile of ESOL learners in a particular area can change. There are a number of factors which may contribute to this at any one time:

- *Political decisions affecting rights of immigration*: in this case, the entry of Poland and other Eastern European countries into the EU.
- *Political decisions internal to the UK*: the teacher quoted above suggested that the reduction in numbers of asylum seekers in London may be due to a policy of 'dispersal' where asylum seekers are directed to different parts of the country. Obviously this will lead to an increase in the numbers of asylum seekers in other parts of the country.
- *Educational policy*: there is currently a trend in further education to increase provision for younger learners. Some learners who enter the UK with little English might be directed to further education rather than to schools. This can happen with learners as young as 14.
- *Policies designed to enable people with disabilities to participate in classes*: although this will not radically change the composition of a class, it can lead to the inclusion of a wider range of learners. As many ESOL learners have lived through war and other traumatic experiences, we can surmise that there will be a number of potential learners with physical or mental disabilities who will be encouraged to join ESOL classes if the appropriate support is provided. We will look at this and other issues of inclusion in more detail in Chapter 8.

An ESOL teacher working in Leeds discussed the challenge that ESOL teachers face in adapting to the wide range of learners and to frequent changes in class profile. She explained that ESOL classes in Leeds traditionally catered for settled communities from countries such as Pakistan, Bangladesh and China. In recent years there have been larger numbers of Chinese learners from Hong Kong as well as learners from the EU and refugees.

ESOL organizers and teachers have to respond swiftly to the new groups of people entering the UK and coming to classes. The same teacher in Leeds pointed out that: '... the arrival of large numbers of migrant workers from the EU and refugees with good study skills and high ambitions affects the class profile and influences the way tutors teach'. She went on to express concerns about the impact that such learners might have on existing learners with a different educational profile: 'Some of the new arrivals are very assertive and can displace more traditional ESOL learners, those perhaps from long established immigrant communities. They may claim places in crèche facilities more quickly, for example.' These concerns highlight the importance of catering for the needs of *all* the learners in a group, rather than allowing those of one very visible or vocal group to dictate the strategies we adopt.

Motivations for joining a class

In the video recording *I Came to England*, Hawa describes the frustration of being unable to speak English when she first arrived: 'Every time I go to doctor, I have to sit couple hours because someone have to translate my language.' She goes on to explain that, after four years attending ESOL classes, she no longer needs an interpreter in situations such as going to the doctor, and that she is now learning English with a view to getting work: 'I never worked anywhere before. Now I want to have something different. I want to become classroom assistant or something different ... Even other jobs, it doesn't matter, I want to see how work's like and how the people feel when they work.' Hawa explains that she wants to improve her writing in particular, in the hope that that can help her to find a job.

Learners' aims when they enrol for an ESOL class can be very varied. We asked a group of 18 ESOL learners in Portsmouth what they hoped to gain from their ESOL class. Some of their responses are shown below.

Why do you come to class?

To make life easier.

To speak English like I speak Farsi.

Doctor, anything, bank, work, talk to teacher and other learners.

I want to live in England and continue my old job as teacher. So I must speak.

I need speak with my family and one day get a good talk and job. My husband don't speak my language.

Because I'm not work and I want find one job.

To help my son in school, homework.

Language for cooking.

I want to take the Citizenship test.

English is everyday part of my life. I would like to speak it fluently and read newspapers, and understand everything with people.

Because I'd like to join the university next year and study computing.

I was a surveyor in my country and I want to work as a surveyor here.

I am a nurse but I have to take IELTs exam to work here.

To communicate, to make friends, to make a career.

In particular, understanding the spoken language and the street language because it is really hard to understand. People use slang, bite ends of words …

How to say things politely because I am a polite person. If you speak simply, people think you are stupid or uneducated.

To support myself and my son, because without English speaking I think I'm nothing in this country.

They spoke of their motivation in general terms. Many of them stressed the importance of English for communicating in every aspect of their lives, telling stories of the frustrations they had experienced as new arrivals. One learner related how she had come back from the shops with three different canisters of fiery red powder before she finally managed to get hold of the mild-tasting spice she wanted, paprika.

More specific aims, such as feeling more confident when visiting doctors, dealing with their children's schools, helping with their children's homework, applying for jobs and developing their careers were evident. One learner expressed a wish to apply for UK citizenship. More people have been motivated to join ESOL classes in order to meet the revised requirements for citizenship introduced in November 2005, and for settlement in April 2007. This is discussed in more detail in Chapter 2.

Finally, one man, who has been studying in Portsmouth for several years, spoke of the sense of friendship and support he gained from his English class, and the network of friends he had made in the different classes where he had studied: 'English is improving but class will help you in different ways. I have no family here but I have friends from class. My class is half my life, my class friends are like my brother.'

ESOL is not only concerned with new arrivals to the UK and it is by no means unusual to find learners attending classes after living in the country for a substantial length of time. Some were not able to attend in the past, perhaps because of childcare commitments, the demands of a job or personal problems in general. Others may have achieved a degree of ability to communicate in English which met their needs for a while, but later, as they want to start work, to change jobs or to apply for promotion, they find they need to improve their English, either in general or in relation to a particular skill such as writing.

ESOL and the field of ELT

We have noted that there may be substantial differences between learners, but in spite of these differences, there is a commonality of experience among all the learners we are considering. They are all learning English while living in an English-speaking country and they are learning it *because* they live in an English-speaking country. We shall now attempt to compare this particular language-learning situation with others.

David Block in *The Social Turn in Second Language Acquisition* (Block 2003) describes three language-learning contexts which language acquisition research has focused on:

- In the *foreign language context* the learners undertake formal classroom study of a language which is not 'the typical language of communication in their community' for example learning English in countries such as Albania, Brazil and Poland. The term normally used to describe this situation is EFL (English as a foreign language), a term which may also be applied to learners who have come to the UK on a temporary basis for the main purpose of studying English. Another example of the foreign language context is when speakers of English learn French, German or Spanish in school, or when English-speaking adults choose to study one of these three languages, or another language such as Arabic or Japanese, for the purposes of business, tourism or simply interest in language learning.
- The *second language context* also involves classroom study, but in a 'classroom situated inside a community where the target language is spoken'. This may apply to English language learning in countries such as Sri Lanka or South Africa. It definitely applies to English language learning in the countries where English is the dominant language, including the UK. In defining this context, Block suggests that the learners have 'potential multiple opportunities of contact with the target language outside the classroom'.
- The *naturalistic context* as described by Block 'involves no formal instruction and the learning of a language spoken in the surrounding community'. In this case, the learners are living in a country where the language is spoken and they have 'picked up' the language while going about their daily lives. Block suggests that, in order to do this, the learner 'must rely on her/his background knowledge, learning strategies and intuitions to get by'.

It is clear, in looking at these three contexts, that it is the second language context which is most closely applicable to the work of the ESOL teacher. However, it could be argued that ESOL learners are simultaneously learning in the naturalistic context, and that part of the role of the ESOL teacher, as well as providing classroom tuition, is to encourage the development of strategies which will enable their learners to continue their learning outside the classroom. In other words our learners are, and should be, both second-language learners and naturalistic learners.

Comparing learning situations

To consider what is specific to the situation of learning a language while living in the country where it is the dominant language, and how it differs from the foreign-language-learning situation, we can compare and contrast the experiences of two hypothetical language learners: an English speaker learning Spanish and a Spanish speaker learning English.

Adam

Adam is a monolingual English speaker living in the UK. Although he has now forgotten most of it, he enjoyed learning French at school and was sorry when he had to give it up to do science A levels. Now in his forties, he works as a chemistry teacher and is married to an accountant, Sandy. Sandy can 'get by' in Spanish and has used it on family holidays in Spain. She recently persuaded Adam to join a salsa dancing class, which he was surprised to find he enjoyed, and the two of them are developing an interest in Latin American culture. Now that their teenage children are losing interest in family holidays, Adam and his wife hope in the future to travel farther afield, perhaps to Latin America. He has enrolled on a Spanish class, partly to revive his interest in language learning and partly to be able to use the language on trips abroad.

Bernardo

Bernardo is a Spanish speaker from Latin America who now lives in the UK. He is monolingual in Spanish, but learned French in school and felt at the time that he had an aptitude for language learning. He and his wife, Gloria, are in the UK because they had political problems in their country of origin which made them feel it was safest to leave. They are now living in temporary accommodation, looking for a permanent home and trying to sort out secondary schools for their teenage children. As he cannot follow his profession (maths teaching), at least for the time being, Bernardo is working as a kitchen assistant in a Tex-Mex restaurant, a job he dislikes very much. Up until now he has had to rely on the (limited) English-language skills of his wife, who is an accountant but is not working at the moment. Now Bernardo is determined to make time to go to English classes and learn to speak the language himself.

TASK 1.2

List the factors which Adam and Bernardo have in common and those where they differ. Consider:

1   Background.
2   Reasons for learning.
3   Conditions for learning.

COMMENT 1.2

1 *Background.* On the surface, both Adam and Bernardo have a remarkable amount in common: they are similar in educational background and have the same profession, as do their wives; they are both speakers of European languages; have learned another European language; and have had a good experience of language learning. They are also similar in age, family situation and at least some aspects of their social background.

2 *Reasons for learning.* The difference between them is most noticeable when we consider what they need to do with the language; the urgency with which they need to learn it; and its place in their lives. Bernardo will need English to find more congenial and better-paid work (unless he works for a Spanish-speaking employer) and to get back into his profession. He also needs to use English for all the things he and his wife have to do regarding housing and schooling for his children. In addition, English will be essential for other kinds of official, social or casual contact, and it is needed immediately. It is not appropriate to try to learn English first, with a view to using it later. In contrast to this situation, Adam is learning for interest and for possible use in a tourist context. He can develop his Spanish quite substantially, and at leisure, before he needs to use it in Latin America.

3 *Conditions for learning.* Bernardo is very likely to be experiencing a high degree of stress. He has left his home country, and has a range of problems to deal with in key areas of his life. These are likely to affect his language learning, both in terms of concentration and the time available for study. Of course, Adam might also go through a period of intense stress, but if he does, he is free to stop learning Spanish (and salsa dancing) without any major adverse effect on his life.

We can see that Adam and Bernardo's backgrounds are very similar. What's more both have many advantages for language learning, particularly the connections between their first language and the target language, their educational level and previous positive experience of language learning. However, similarity of background can not be taken as an indicator that there will be similarity of experience overall. Reasons for learning and the conditions for learning will also play a significant part in the language development of ESOL learners, so that even learners whose background gives them certain advantages will find the experience of learning English while using it for everyday life different from the experience of 'foreign language' learners.

A range of background factors

Bernardo is an ESOL learner with an advantageous linguistic and educational background. However, this is far from the norm.

- Many ESOL learners do not speak a European language or even a language belonging to the Indo-European language family; e.g. Arabic, Somali, Chinese and Albanian belong to other language families and are structurally quite different from English.
- The phonological system of many languages, e.g. Chinese, can make the pronunciation of English especially difficult.
- Speakers of other languages, e.g. Arabic, may need to work very hard at reading and writing in English, as their own language has a writing system which goes from right to left and uses a completely different alphabet from that of English.
- The problems faced by educated learners whose own language uses a different writing system will be compounded for those who have not learned to read or write in any other language. Some ESOL learners have had little or no previous formal education before coming to class in the UK. The reasons for this are very often connected with circumstances such as war or famine.
- As well as finding the language and writing system very different from their own, many ESOL learners find the cultural context unfamiliar. This can affect all aspects of life, whether dealing with officialdom, socializing or attending classes to learn English. On the *I Came to England* video, Ravira from Kosovo describes her feelings on first coming to England: 'I felt alone, I felt foreign, because it's a different country from my country, it's a different language, a different style of life.'

Defining the ESOL context

In summary, it is suggested that there are two principal factors which distinguish ESOL from foreign language learners. ESOL learners are learning at the same time as living in the country where the language is used. They are normally aware of specific situations in their lives for which they need to use the language they are learning, and it is not an option to wait until their language is more developed before they go into these situations. Indeed they often have no choice but to use English in conversational transactions which strain their linguistic resources to the limit and beyond. In addition, they may have a lot of stress in dealing with difficult areas of their life, which is compounded by the need to use English in those areas.

There is a strong likelihood, though it is not the case with all learners, of difficulties in learning based on differences between the first language and culture, and the target language and culture. It is also fairly common for learners to have little previous experience of education, though this again does not apply to all learners. The result is likely to be that members of the same class can vary widely in educational profile. The challenge which often faces ESOL teachers is that learners with vastly different backgrounds and experiences might attend the same class: a person with a PhD may be sitting next to a person who had no previous schooling.

However, this need not be viewed negatively. This kind of class profile, frequently encountered, presents us with opportunities for a rewarding exchange of linguistic and cultural knowledge which can be very productive. A vital factor in making it so is to address the learners' real-life needs and purposes for using the language, where learners will find they have a lot in common, as well as drawing on the strengths of all the learners and being aware of the variety of approaches to learning which can be taken and with which some learners may be already familiar.

The common experience of all English language learners

We have attempted above to define some of the factors in the language-learning situation which are specific to the type of learner we are concerned with, and to contrast these with the situation of other language learners. However, we do not wish to suggest that the language-learning experience of ESOL learners in the UK is radically different from the experience of other learners of English.

While it can be useful to use categories such as 'foreign language', 'second language' and 'naturalistic' to help us to discuss the finer points of the language-learning context, it should be noted that these are not always discrete categories, and there is often substantial overlap in a person's language-learning history.

Some learners now attending classes started learning English in a naturalistic setting, and may have spent years in the country, using the English they have learned in this way, before attending classes. Others arrive in the UK having already studied English, often in a country where English is taught as a foreign language. They may bring with them expectations of the learning process, both positive and negative, based on their experiences as EFL learners. Sometimes they feel that the English learned in the foreign-language situation, whether they learned it as children or as adults, has not prepared them for having to use the language in everyday life, and they need the ESOL class to provide what their previous learning could not give them. One of the learners who took part in the video recording *I Came to England*, Amina from Iraq, explains how her own needs as a learner of English have changed since she became a permanent resident of the country: 'Before I came here to England to study, get a PhD – 1980 to 1985, I get a PhD in biochemistry, then I went back to Iraq, teaching in the University. My English is not ... as science it's OK, but for the life, normal life, it's not very well.'

We can see from Amina's situation that a person can change from being a learner of English in one context to being a learner in another one. With some other people, it is not at all easy to say what their context for learning actually is. For example, some people who initially came to the UK with a view to spending a short time studying English, then returning, find that events in their life have led them to stay longer than intended, eventually becoming resident. Other people may have come to live and work in the UK on an open-ended basis, with an additional aim of developing their English-language skills, but without a clear idea of how long they will stay. These people do not fit neatly into either the 'second-language' or 'foreign-language' categories.

So, when we refer to different language-learning contexts, we must not forget that whatever the differences in circumstances and motivation between the different categories of English language learner, and indeed the different individuals within those categories, they are working towards a common goal of learning English, and face many of the same linguistic challenges in doing so. The distinctions we have drawn, though significant, are not rigid or exclusive. There is fluidity between the different language-learning contexts and this is one reason why we should not see the language-learning situation of ESOL learners in the UK as being divorced from other English-language-learning contexts.

There is a wealth of published material aimed at the field of English-language teaching (ELT) worldwide. This includes books on the English language, on language-teaching methodology and language acquisition, course books and supplementary practice activities as well as classroom material for use with learners. At the end of each chapter we have identified a number of key texts that we feel you will find useful and we recommend that you make use of these.

However, most of the ELT material attempts to address a wide range of English-language learning situations across the globe; the purpose of this book is to discuss the specifics of one such situation – ESOL in the UK. You should use this book to help in considering the particular needs of this group of English-language learners, and approach other texts thoughtfully and critically, with the situation of these learners at the forefront of your mind.

Note

1   *I came to England* produced for the Skills for Life Quality Initiative in video or DVD format and available from Rosa Allen, LLU+, London South Bank University, 103 Borough Road, London SE1 OAA.

2 ESOL in the UK education system

Helen Sunderland

Global contexts for ESOL

This chapter will describe ESOL in what is called the lifelong learning, post-compulsory or post-16 sector, though, as mentioned above, this sector can sometimes provide education for ESOL learners as young as 14. The development of ESOL (also previously known as ESL/E2L and subsequently EAL in the schools sector) in the English education system demonstrates an interplay of demography, economics, social attitudes, applied linguistics, educational reform, government policy and global politics. Perhaps to a greater degree than any subject, its fortunes illustrate the complexity of educational provision.

Among the factors leading to immigration and the consequent demand for ESOL are the following:

- Periods of colonialism by Britain and other European nations were inevitably associated with huge imbalances in the geographical distribution of wealth. Despite a number of 'false starts', colonized nations have generally been unable to reach living standards considered common in the West, and their comparative disadvantage is being compounded by pressures resulting from globalization. Despite tight border controls being introduced in wealthy countries, the temptation to seek economic success elsewhere is increased by the relative ease of communication, combined with media images of Western consumerist lifestyles.
- Civil strife and political repression from around the world continue to create large numbers of refugees, although it should be remembered that only a small minority of refugees succeed in reaching Western Europe.
- The relaxation of restrictions upon working in member states of the EU has led to freedom of travel; its expansion to the relatively poorer countries of Eastern Europe in recent years has created an enlarged EU whose citizens have the right to work, travel and access education within the EU.
- Post-war reconstruction involved the recruitment of workers from the commonwealth. The recent period of economic growth in the UK, along with a low birth-rate now insufficient to replace the workforce, created a need for skilled and unskilled labour, particularly in areas such as the south-east.

- The unprecedented growth of English as an international language has also played a part in making the UK attractive for economic migrants.

National contexts for ESOL

These global developments have had an impact on patterns of migration to the UK and this chapter will look at these and the responses of government, media and ESOL providers in the post-compulsory sector.

Though migration to the UK is not a recent phenomenon and the first documented case of refugees coming to this country was in the twelfth century (Rutter 2000), the first adult ESOL learners, as we understand the term now, were migrants from the Commonwealth who came to contribute to the post-war economic growth and eventually brought their families to join them. By the late 1960s and early 1970s, the economic downturn meant that many adults needed to seek new jobs which required more sophisticated skills in the English language. Work-based learning started in the late 1960s and the Centre for Industrial Language Training (CILT) was set up in 1974[1] as a response to the growing need for ESOL (then called English as a second language or ESL) at work. Also during the 1950s and 1960s, migrants' families had started to join them in large numbers, and their children attended English schools, leading to the start of ESOL in the school, adult education and voluntary sectors (for a detailed history of ESOL, see Rosenberg 2007).

Some of the first refugees who were to make use of government-provided ESOL started to arrive soon after, in the 1970s; first from East Africa, then Chile and, eventually, from countries around the world: Iran, Vietnam, Poland, Eritrea, Somalia, Colombia, Angola, Afghanistan, Iraq and many more. The number of asylum applications fluctuated, depending on global conditions, and peaked at 84,130 in 2002, falling to 49,405 in 2003, 33,960 in 2004, and 25,710 in 2005.[2] Provisional annual 2008 figures show that there were 25,670 applications for asylum in the UK, higher than 2007 (23,430), but still continuing the fall from the peak in 2002. Europe has also provided a steady stream of migrants and this has increased considerably since the Accession countries[3] joined the European Union in May 2004. Unlike many other countries in the EU (for example Germany), the UK opened its doors to migrants from the expanded EU, and this resulted in large numbers joining the workforce, particularly in the building, agricultural and tourist industries. Between May 2004 and June 2006, 447,000 people from the Accession countries registered to work in the UK – if we include self-employed workers, this number is probably closer to 600,000.[4]

That recent growth had a cautious welcome by business, the government and some media sectors. An *Independent* headline claimed that 'Foreign labour helps Brown to meet targets on growth'[5] and the same paper quoted Minister Liam Byrne as saying the new workers were 'benefiting the UK, by filling skills and labour gaps that cannot be met from the UK-born population'.[6] However, the government was still nervous about unrestricted growth and the government's five-year strategy for asylum and immigration, 'Controlling our borders: making migration work for Britain' (Home Office 2005) announced new restrictions on migrants who need to satisfy a points system.[7]

Media attention

While media coverage of immigration has never been particularly positive, it does appear to have become more hostile over the last 20 years. By the mid-1990s the term 'economic migrant' had begun to be used as a term of abuse among certain sections of the press. In the same way the term 'asylum seeker' was and still is used by these sections of the media as pejorative. While this may not have a direct impact on ESOL teaching, it does set the context for the increasingly racist and hostile climate in which ESOL learners have to live and study.

Patterns of settlement

Since the 1970s, ESOL has mostly developed in urban areas where refugees and migrants have tended to settle, often among established immigrant communities. In the post-war period and until recently, the main exceptions to this trend were Ugandan, Asian and Vietnamese refugees who were 'dispersed' around the UK by the government, but who tended to move back to their communities in the urban areas in secondary resettlement. Outside these urban areas, small numbers of migrants often joined literacy courses or were catered for through open learning. However, in 1999 the government brought in a policy of dispersal, and asylum seekers (i.e. refugees who have not yet received a decision from the Home Office) were required to settle wherever cheap accommodation could be found for them.[8] This led to a demand for ESOL in small towns such as Great Yarmouth, where no ESOL had previously existed. The expansion of ESOL that followed dispersal was further encouraged by the arrival of migrants from the expanded EU who are working outside the major conurbations in the agricultural and tourist industries. Educational and training organizations have had to respond very rapidly to this new demand, with varying results and often without the necessary infrastructure of, for example, trained ESOL teachers or appropriate teaching and learning resources. At the time of writing, the economic downturn means that many of the EU workers are returning home again, demonstrating the volatility of the ESOL sector and its need to respond rapidly to changing events, in the UK and globally.

ESOL and citizenship

In 2005 the government brought in new requirements for immigrants wishing to apply for citizenship, following recommendations of an advisory group on citizenship chaired by Sir Bernard Crick (2003). This advisory group was held in the context of an increased interest in and concern about the role of citizenship education in promoting community cohesion and alongside the introduction of a citizenship curriculum for all schoolchildren.

From November 2005, would-be citizens are required to show that they either:

- have improved their English language skills in the context of citizenship by studying an ESOL with citizenship course and achieving a Skills for Life Certificate in Speaking and Listening at Entry 1, 2 or 3 (see below for an explanation of the levels); or
- already have a certain level of English (Entry 3 or above) and some knowledge about the British way of life by passing the Life in the UK Test which is administered in English.

ESOL with citizenship courses are required to use or adapt materials specially prepared for ESOL and Citizenship (NIACE and LLU+ 2005). These include topics such as 'what is citizenship'; 'community involvement'; 'human rights'; 'knowing the law'; and 'the parliamentary system' (for more information on the ESOL and citizenship initiatives, see Taylor 2007).

In April 2007, the same requirements came into force for anyone wanting to apply for settlement.

ESOL in post-compulsory education

There is huge variety in both quality and quantity of ESOL provision in different settings and in various parts of the country. It appears to be a matter of luck if a new learner arrives at a course that meets for two or 30 hours a week; with a trained or an untrained teacher; in a well-equipped computer suite or in a Church Hall. The Skills for Life strategy (see below) has brought some overall consistency, but there are still many variations around the country and even in the same neighbourhood.

The range of opportunities open to ESOL learners will vary from place to place, and cities with large numbers of potential ESOL learners will have a very wide range of provision, offering a good choice of courses to meet different needs. This provision may be organized by, for example, further education (FE) colleges; sixth form colleges; adult and community learning centres (ACL); prisons; voluntary organizations such as refugee or church groups; vocational training providers (private or through the FE system); the workplace; or universities (HE). These courses will receive funding from a variety of sources, all of which have different requirements. In many urban areas, ESOL provision exists in all of these sectors, and, at the time of writing, there is very often little coordination between the various providers. This means that two organizations, such as a college and a training provider might offer intensive ESOL within a mile of each other, while there is nothing at all four miles down the road. The length of the courses can vary, as can the number of hours; organizations offering ESOL under the training for work umbrella are often short-term but full-time, for example 30 hours per week for 13 weeks, while ACL may run 30-week courses but for only four hours per week. This may change with the requirements from September 2009 for greater coordination on the part of local authorities.

The actual classes might take place in college buildings, schools, workplaces, community centres, hospitals or any venue that potential learners can reach easily. There are also opportunities for online learning. Provision may be graded according to level, or might be mixed-level. Classes may be offered to anyone who can benefit from them, or they may target specific groups, such as women only, speakers of a particular language, people in a particular type of work or young people. Classes for younger learners sometimes target the 16–19 age group or may include learners below the age of 16.

TASK 2.1

Consider the area where you live and/or work, and find out as much as you can about the providers of classes suitable for ESOL learners, the venues in which teaching takes place, and the type of classes available.

1   Who are the providers?
- FE colleges.
- Adult education services.
- Voluntary organizations.
- Religious and community organizations.
- Training agencies.
- Prisons.
- Workplaces.
- Other.

2   What venues are used?
- College buildings.
- Schools.
- Community centres.
- Workplace.
- Training centres.
- Hospital.
- Other.

3   What types of class are offered?
- Graded classes.
- Mixed-level (all comers).
- Women only.
- For speakers of a particular language.
- Work-related.
- For younger learners.
- Other.

In many organizations, ESOL has never been altogether recognized as a specialist curriculum area in its own right with its own specialist knowledge and pedagogy. It maintains a rather uneasy position somewhere between EFL (see Chapter 1) and literacy with management never quite sure whether it is a basic skill or a modern language.

ESOL professionals are fond of saying that ESOL is not a subject as such but an access route to other things such as work, different social and cultural worlds, and further study. English across the wider curriculum is not a new concept and has been around for a long time. In the 1970s the first 'linked skills' courses started running – these were where English was studied at the same time as another skill such as childcare or computers. In the years that followed, 'linked skills' turned into 'language support' or 'language development'. The language and other subjects were sometimes taught together but more usually they were delivered separately, with the ESOL support being given in small workshops or on a one-to-one basis. ESOL and other subjects are now coming together again in 'embedded' ESOL courses in which ESOL is incorporated into vocational or academic courses. These courses are offered in many colleges and training providers (Roberts et al. 2005) and imply that ESOL teachers need to work with teachers of other subjects to plan and learn from each other, each contributing what has been referred to as 'complementary expertise' (Casey et al. 2006). ESOL teachers need to analyse the language needed on the vocational or academic course so that they can plan the ESOL scheme of work, while teachers of other subjects on the course need to consider the language needs of their learners. Courses with embedded ESOL may be just for ESOL learners, or may consist of mixed groups of ESOL learners and native or fluent English speakers. In some parts of the country, where there is a very small ESOL population, of necessity the learners will be integrated with fluent English speakers. In other cases integration is the result of a deliberate policy of inclusiveness, and is one example of the range of approaches to providing for the needs of ESOL learners.

Most ESOL providers also offer some ICT, some offer maths and other subjects alongside ESOL, and many ESOL courses now incorporate citizenship. In ACL, ESOL may be combined with family learning. At the time of writing, all providers funded by the Learning and Skills Council (LSC) are required to ensure that at least 80 per cent of their courses lead to SfL qualifications.

Some ESOL courses are free, from September 2007 others have had fees attached for some learners; the situation is complex and can be difficult for advisors and learners to understand.

TASK 2.2

The work of an ESOL teacher involves more than just teaching. As well as assessing, planning, teaching, and marking, teachers need to work closely with other professionals. Read the case studies below and consider whom the teachers will need to liaise with in order to carry out their job successfully.

1   A full-time teacher in a typical urban FE college may have a weekly timetable that looks something like this:
   - Six hours of ESOL to a group of 16–18-year-olds at Entry 2 on a full-time course.
   - Eight hours (plus being course tutor) to a group of adults on a part-time course at Entry 3.

- Eight hours of language support – four on an embedded hairdressing course and four with four different learners in the hair & beauty department.
2 A full-time trainer with a training provider might have a weekly timetable that looks something like this:
    - Two hours per week with a local employer, concentrating on work-related English that the employees need for their job.
    - Eight hours per week with the NHS, working on ESOL at a range of different levels.
    - Twenty hours per week on an E2E programme with 16–18-year-olds, preparing them for work and Skills for Life examinations.
3 A part-time tutor in ACL may have a timetable that looks something like this:
    - Four hours per week with a mixed level group in the local mosque, a class for women.
    - Two hours per week of basic literacy in one of the adult education centres, working with learners who normally attend Entry 1 and Entry 2 classes on other days.
    - Two hours per week in a local nursery school, working on a family learning course.

COMMENT 2.2

The teachers would need to liaise with:

1 *Other teachers who share responsibility for the courses they are teaching, either ESOL or subject teachers*: Teacher 1 only teaches for six hours of a full-time course. She will need to liaise with the others on this course. Teacher 2 will need to liaise with the family learning teacher.
2 *Professionals in the community*: Teacher 3 will need to liaise with community workers in the mosque and teachers in the nursery school.
3 *Professionals in the workplace*: Teacher 2 will need to liaise with managers, training officers and union learning representatives in the workplace.
4 *Parents*: Both teachers working with younger learners will need to liaise with parents, over their child's progress and for permission to do certain activities.
5 *Administrative staff*: Teacher 2 will need to liaise with staff in the exam board, Teacher 1 will probably need to liaise with admissions staff.

Skills for Life

The Skills for Life strategy was born out of the Moser (1999) enquiry which found that: 'Roughly 20% of adults – that is perhaps as many as 7 million people – have more or less severe problems with basic skills …' In the Skills for Life strategy document (DfEE: 2001a) the statements concerning ESOL were unequivocal: 'It is essential that the specific literacy and/or numeracy needs of these learners are not seen as secondary to the needs of English-speaking adults.'

The strategy has brought considerable resources to ESOL and a coordinated approach that includes a national curriculum, national qualifications for learners, recognized qualifications for ESOL teachers, teaching resources and research and development through a series of national pathfinder projects and the National Research and Development Centre (NRDC). To read more about the NRDC and download any of its many research reports, visit the NRDC website.[10] To get hold of any of the many documents created for Skills for Life, see the Skills for Life Improvement Programme website.[11]

The *Adult ESOL Core Curriculum* has had a considerable influence on current ESOL teaching and learning. The *Adult ESOL Core Curriculum* document is based on the literacy standards: common standards for both literacy and ESOL learners. These standards are divided into levels which fit into the Qualifications and Credit Framework (QCF).[12] This Framework is concerned, among other things, with the equivalence between various qualifications. The framework categorizes qualifications from Level 1 (for example GCSE grade D or E) up to Level 8. Skills for Life is concerned with Levels 1 and 2, and with the level below Level 1, which is known as Entry. Because so much of Skills for Life is at Entry level, this level has been divided again, into Entry 1, Entry 2 and Entry 3. You will see references to these levels in this book.

For more information about the *Adult ESOL Core Curriculum*, see the revised e-version at www.excellencegateway.org.uk/sflcurriculum

More than a language: the report of the NIACE Committee of Enquiry into ESOL

The NIACE Committee of Enquiry (2006) on English for Speakers of Other Languages met over the course of a year and produced its report in October 2006. The report gives a considered and detailed overview of ESOL in 2006 and makes 39 recommendations for changes to provision, management and funding of ESOL and ESOL teacher education. These were welcomed and broadly accepted by the Minister for Lifelong Learning and Further and Higher Education, Bill Rammell, in his speech at the launch. However, the report was overshadowed by the announcement, just a few weeks later, of the introduction of fees for 'those able to pay' and restricting access for new asylum seekers from September 2007 (LSC 2006).

While noting the obvious benefits in terms of increased funding and improved infrastructure that the Skills for Life strategy has brought, the NIACE Committee of Enquiry also highlighted some challenges including the following:

- Setting targets for achievement of qualifications at Entry 3, Level 1 and Level 2 has meant that some local funding bodies and educational organizations are cutting down on non-target bearing provision, mostly courses at lower levels.
- The emphasis on qualification bearing courses (80% of Learning and Skills Council funded provision) impacts on the most vulnerable, those who cannot attend frequently enough to obtain a qualification in the time specified. They are likely to be learners with a very low level of previous education, few literacy skills in any language, possibly living on isolated estates and with caring responsibilities.
- Quality and accountability procedures introduced under the Skills for Life strategy, in line with similar developments in other public services, have led to an emphasis on assessing, recording and monitoring of learners' progress, increasing the burden of paperwork on teachers (Baynham et al. 2007).

Notes

1 www.lancs.ac.uk/fss/projects/edres/changingfaces/profdevtimeline.htm
2 www.statistics.gov.uk/cci/nugget.asp?id=261
3 Cyprus, the Czech Republic, Estonia, Hungary, Latvia, Lithuania, Malta, Poland, Slovakia and Slovenia.
4 BBC News online 22 August 2006, quoting Tony McNulty from the Home Office.
5 *Independent*, 25 October 2006.
6 *Independent*, 22 November 2006.
7 www.icar.org.uk/?lid=6002#footnote26745
8 The Immigration and Asylum Act 1999.
9 www.ind.homeoffice.gov.uk/lawandpolicy/immigrationrules/part5
10 www.nrdc.org.uk/
11 www.sflip.org.uk
12 www.ofqual.gov.uk/51.aspx

3   Language and context in ESOL teaching

Meryl Wilkins

What do ESOL teachers teach?

Clearly ESOL teachers teach the English language and in planning course content, they consider language, described in terms of grammar, vocabulary, language function, etc. However, teachers of the type of learners described in this book usually recognize a need to teach 'more than just language' and like all other language teachers nowadays, they teach the language within meaningful contexts of use. The thematic content is often described in terms of situations or topic areas, for example:

- The situations in which the learners have to or want to operate, such as job-seeking, socializing with neighbours, travelling by train and seeing a doctor.
- The topics which people need information about, such as how to access services, and their rights under Employment Law.
- Topics of interest, such as sport, food, current events and traditional customs.

The choice of thematic content is clearly important in all forms of language teaching, as teachers and materials developers wish to demonstrate language use in realistic contexts which will motivate their learners. However, it can be argued that the choice of thematic content has a more central role when teaching people resident in an English-speaking country, as the topics themselves may form important teaching points.

The job interview

The relationship between language and content may differ according to the teaching situation. The following examples show the way three different types of course might focus on the same situation – the job interview.

Example 1: English language teaching worldwide

In many materials for teaching English worldwide, there is an example of a job interview, even though the learners are never likely to go for an interview in English. The purpose of the material is not to prepare them for attending job interviews, but to provide a realistic context as a vehicle for introducing specific language points. Look at the model dialogue below:

Interviewer: How long have you been in your present job?
Interviewee: I've been there for 6 years, before that I worked in an advertising agency.
Interviewer: And have you used desk top publishing programmes?
Interviewee: I have. I used them when I worked in …

This could be introduced to contrast the use of present perfect with the simple past to talk about past experience. It demonstrates the use of present perfect for situations which continue from the past into the present and are still true ('I've been there for six years') and the use of simple past for situations which are finished ('before that I worked'). It also gives an example of a question and answer sequence in English.

Example 2: A job-search course for unemployed people

This example considers courses for people who are fluent speakers of English and will definitely seek work within the UK system. They may be long-term unemployed people, women returning to work or young people seeking work for the first time. In addition, they are likely to be speakers of English as a first language or competent speakers of English as an additional language.

In preparing for interviews, they will all need to be aware of the overall picture regarding the current job search situation and the place of the interview within the system. They will need to know, for example, about what employers are likely to be looking for and it will be useful for them to know something about their rights under employment law. They might learn about the process of short-listing and selecting applicants, and about the way the interview questions relate to the job description and person specification. In addition, some participants might want to discuss such matters as appropriate dress, and some might need to work on their time-management skills.

They will also need to be aware of the conventions governing the way the interview is conducted and be able to conform to them. For example, they will need to know about the tendency to invite questions at the end of an interview. They can discuss what type of question it is suitable to ask and can practise listening to an interview carefully, so that they don't ask a question they have prepared if it has already been answered. They can predict difficult questions and work out ways of answering them. Those who have little work experience will need to evaluate their other life experiences and learn how to present them so that they appear relevant to the job applied for. Those who have been unemployed for a long time will need to consider how to present their time out of work in as positive a light as possible.

The emphasis of the course is clearly on more than just language. Although language will be a component of the course, there is unlikely to be a grammatical focus such as that seen in the first example. With participants who already speak English fluently and competently, the emphasis is likely to be on the way talk is conventionally constructed within the interview and on what language is considered appropriate, for example the level of formality expected or suitable ways to show politeness.

Example 3: ESOL learners resident in UK

It is clear that any ESOL learners who are currently seeking work or who might in the future seek work will have much in common with the group described in Example 2, and will probably need to learn similar things. They are, after all, likely to be competing for jobs with competent speakers of English. At the same time, they will have the specific language learning needs of the group described in Example 1. It is therefore essential to combine aspects of language work with aspects of what they need to know and do to prepare for the actual situation.

Analysing language

Before further considering the content of ESOL courses overall, it is useful to examine the ways in which language can be analysed for the purpose of planning for ESOL teaching. At this stage, we will introduce key terminology, which will be used and expanded on in later chapters. The examples provided all relate to the job interview context described above.

When analysing language for teaching purposes, it is useful to consider language skills, language systems and functional language.

Language skills

An analysis in terms of skills considers the 'four skills' of listening, speaking, reading and writing, and learners often have varying abilities in these skills. For example, some learners can read and understand English reasonably well, but want to develop confidence in speaking, while others can listen and speak quite easily, but need a lot of help with writing. The skills are often categorized in one of two ways:

- Spoken versus written language.
- Receptive versus productive use.

Spoken and written language

There are often significant differences between spoken and written English. These differences are largely due to the fact that written language needs to be more explicit than spoken language, which can rely on immediate context and body language to aid understanding. There is also an issue of formality, with written language on the whole likely to be more formal than spoken, although there is a continuum between formal and informal varieties of both written and spoken language.

Some features of informal spoken English are listed in the *Adult ESOL Core Curriculum*, for example markers such as 'anyway, well, right, now, OK', grammatical ellipsis as in 'sounds good' for 'that sounds good' and purposefully vague language such as 'or so, sort of'.

Teachers need to consider how the language they are teaching is likely to be used in both spoken and written English, and provide realistic examples for either variety.

Receptive and productive language use

In analysing language for teaching purposes, a teacher has to make a distinction between what learners need to understand and what they need to produce. With this in mind, listening and reading are described as *receptive* skills and speaking and writing as *productive* skills.

Normally all language learners understand more language receptively than they can use productively. So, it is not realistic to expect learners to be able to produce all the language they can understand when reading or listening. Teachers need to decide whether the language being introduced in a session is for receptive or productive use.

Some ESOL learners who have learned English in a natural setting have extensive receptive understanding, and there is a bigger than usual gap between this and their productive ability. If teachers recognize where this is the case, they can draw on this 'passive understanding' in developing their learners' productive skills.

Integration of skills

Having considered language use in terms of the four skills, it is important to remember that the skills are rarely used in isolation. For example, when attending a job interview, a person will read anything sent in advance, read notices directing them to the right place, maybe sign a visitors' book, listen and respond to questions, and most probably take part in further spoken communication after that.

Language systems

The most commonly referred to language systems are grammar, phonology, lexis and discourse. Language analysis is considered in more detail in Chapters 4, 5 and 6, and there are also a large number of excellent books and resources available that look at language from the perspective of a learner of English and from that of an English-language teacher.

Grammar

The study of grammar is normally divided into *syntax* and *morphology*. David Crystal (2003), in *The Cambridge Encyclopedia of the English Language* defines *syntax* as 'the study of sentence structure' and *morphology* as 'the study of the structure of words'.

Syntax includes such items as the order of the parts of a sentence. For example, the English sentence 'Ali teaches maths' would be rendered in Urdu as 'Ali maths teaches'. The way the question is formed is also a feature of syntax, and question formation is an important element in preparing learners for a job interview.

Morphology deals with changes at word level, such as the addition of 's' to a noun to form a plural or the addition of 'er' to an adjective to make the comparative form.

Linked with this is the idea of *word class*, where words are categorized as nouns, verbs, etc., according to their function within a sentence.

While it is important that as teachers we know about the syntax and morphology of English grammar, these aren't terms that are used in the classroom. That isn't to say that grammar is not of great importance in any language classroom it clearly is, rather that we need a more learner-friendly way to approach the teaching of grammar in the ESOL classroom.

As a general rule teachers need to contextualize any new language items they introduce, this is particularly important for verb tenses, which form a large part of any grammatical syllabus. The contextualization helps the learners to understand the *meaning* of the grammatical item and to explore its *use*. When these have been established the teacher can then focus on *form*, the way the particular structure being studied is made up, for example the present perfect tense ('I have been to the USA three times') is made up of: subject + to have + past participle.

Grammar is discussed in more detail in Chapter 6.

Phonology

Phonology is concerned with the pronunciation of English. Teaching pronunciation can focus on *phonemes*, the individual vowel and consonant sounds of English. It is important to make sure that learners can perceive the sound that you want them to work on before you ask them to produce it. Some phonemes are more important than others for particular first-language speakers. For example, a speaker of Arabic or Somali might have difficulty distinguishing between the sounds /b/ and /p/.

The placing of *stress* is also important. Incorrect *word stress* can cause problems of comprehensibility, for example if a learner stresses the first syllable of the word *eme*rgency rather than the second em*e*rgency. *Sentence stress* refers to the choice of which syllable to stress in a longer utterance, for example 'What do you *want*?' As opposed to 'What do *you* want?' Stress is linked closely with *rhythm*. The rhythm of English is based on the regular occurrence of stressed syllables, and this is not the case with all languages.

Intonation, which links closely with stress, is sometimes referred to as the 'melody' of the language. Intonation plays an important part in indicating the type or function of an utterance, for example it can help to distinguish between a statement and a question, or between a request and a command. It also has a role in conveying attitudes such as politeness, and inappropriate use of intonation by learners can lead to them being considered rude when that was not their intention.

Learners preparing for a job interview will need to work on whichever areas of phonology are impeding them from being 'comfortably intelligible'. These are likely to be individual or related to their first language, and may involve work on phonemes or stress and rhythm, for example. All learners will need to check they can pronounce key words such as 'employment', placing the stress correctly, and they will need to be able to use intonation to convey attitudes of politeness and interest.

Lexis

A lexical item may consist of a single word or a phrase functioning as a single word. For example, the phrases 'of course' or 'on the whole' need to be taught as single items and not analysed as separate words. To be able to understand and recall new lexical items learners need a lot of information about them. This information includes:

- *Meaning*: this is, of course, central, and learners need to be given lots of help here through questions that clarify the core concept of the lexical item, examples, pictures, etc.
- *Use*: two words often have the same referential meaning but carry additional information about the speaker's attitude. This is known as *connotation*. For example, if I call someone 'slim' I'm making a positive comment whereas if I call them 'skinny' I'm being negative. Learners also need to know about the *register* of a lexical item – 'Hiya' and 'Hello' are both greetings but we use them in different contexts.
- *Pronunciation*: particularly word stress for longer words.
- *Grammar*: for example, the plural form.
- *Common collocations*: the way in which individual words co-occur with others is known as 'collocation'. For example, we can talk about 'heavy rainfall' and 'strong winds', but not 'strong rainfall'.

Words and phrases may be said to belong to the same *lexical set* if they are likely to occur in the same contexts, for example judge, jury, defendant, prosecute, plead all form part of a courtroom lexical set.

Discourse

The term 'discourse' normally refers to whole stretches of language, larger than the sentence level, and the term 'discourse analysis' refers to ways of discussing these larger units. This is illustrated by the following quotation: 'The traditional concern of linguistic analysis has been the construction of sentences; but in recent years there has been an increasing interest in analysing the way sentences work in sequence to produce coherent stretches of language' (Crystal 2003).

Coherence

A written text or stretch of spoken language is likely to be considered coherent if it hangs together in a way which helps to achieve the purpose of the writer or speaker. In composing a report, a writer has to decide on the order in which to present points. Similarly, a person telling a friend a long story about something that happened to them will make decisions about the ordering of information, although this decision making will be done quickly and less consciously. Indeed, if the person telling the story is in a distressed state, the story might lack coherence and confuse the listener about what actually happened.

In an interview, people need to talk about their experience coherently, enabling the interview panel to follow easily. Coherence in the interaction will be demonstrated if they respond to the interviewer's questions in a relevant manner.

Cohesion

Cohesion refers to the specific features which help a text to hang together coherently. For example, *discourse markers* such as 'first', 'however', 'for instance' can be used to indicate sequence, contrast or exemplification.

Grammatical cohesion includes use of pronouns to refer specifically to what has gone before in the text. Effective *pronoun reference* means that it is clear which noun a pronoun refers back to. An example of ineffective pronoun reference might be 'Jane met Ann and she gave her the money'. Here it is unclear who gave the money and who received it.

Sometimes a text hangs together because words and phrases are repeated, or related words are used throughout the text. This is known as *lexical cohesion*. In a job interview, the repeated use of words and phrases belonging to the lexical set of 'employment' will help to make the discourse cohesive.

Discourse and the schemata of the language user

When a person reads a text, takes part in interaction or listens to spoken English, for example on the radio or TV, he or she does not approach the task 'cold'. According to schema theory, every reader or listener interprets what they read or what they hear in the light of the *schemata* they have developed based on their experience of life. For example, an English speaker from the UK could go to a small town in Australia and not fully understand a local newspaper because they do not have the background knowledge and experience to interpret it.

TASK 3.1

You are told someone lives in the suburbs. What type of home do you picture for them? What type of job do you imagine they might have?

COMMENT 3.1

If you pictured someone in a semi-detached house, working in an office or a professional job, then the schemata activated when you read the word 'suburbs' are based on the British idea of suburbia, e.g. the suburbs of London. If you pictured someone in a high-rise flat, working in a low-paid job or unemployed, then the schemata activated are based on the continental idea of 'suburbs', e.g. the suburbs of Paris.

It can be seen then that anyone approaching a text with the inappropriate schemata activated is likely to become confused quite quickly, however well they understand the actual language.

People also need to predict, when they are giving information, whether their readers or listeners have similar experience to them, that is if they share similar schemata. If they do, the communication is likely to be successful, but if not, the speaker or writer has to make more effort to contextualize the information they are giving.

When approaching a job interview, people need some understanding of what the interviewers expect. If a person has work experience in their country of origin, and is interviewed for a similar job in the UK, there is a risk that, during the interview, their schemata regarding the job will not be in tune with the schemata of the interviewer. It is therefore important that learners have an opportunity to find out about the interviewer's likely expectations regarding the job, so that they can approach the situation with the right kind of schemata activated.

Discourse and culture

From the example above, it should be clear that a person's schemata owes much to their cultural background, and that sometimes texts present difficulty, not because of the language but because learners lack the requisite background knowledge to understand them. In some cases, learners do have background knowledge, but their schemata are based on a cultural model which is different from the model in the mind of the writer or speaker, for example a person who has never been to a primary school outside their country of origin hearing someone talking about a British primary school. Without relevant background information, they might picture a very different scene from that pictured by the speaker and might be puzzled by reference to children working in groups with learning-support assistants. They will need information or experience to help them to adapt their schemata before they can participate fully in the conversation.

Understanding the requirements of the interview situation might, for some ESOL learners, be a matter of re-learning something they believe they are familiar with. For example, some of the cultural norms associated with the interview are very different from those in other countries, even countries where English is spoken. For example in the British context, it is expected that interviewees, when asked a question, will expand on the answer to that question, offering what is considered the right amount of additional information, not too much, not too little. In other cultures, by contrast, it might be seen as impertinent to go beyond a straightforward answer to the interviewer's question.

Besides the effect of culture on schemata, there are other ways in which culture and discourse interlink. In any form of communication or interaction, there will be an influence of cultural norms.

According to *genre theory*, written texts with a similar purpose will have a similar format and similar linguistic features. For example, instructions are normally written in lists with numbers or bullets, and include many examples of imperative or passive forms. Sometimes genres translate from language to language, but often they do not, for example the conventions of beginning and ending a letter. In a formal situation such as an interview, learners need to be aware of conventions such as making a general point followed by examples from their own experience. This may be different from the way they would conventionally be expected to recount the same events in their own language.

In interaction, cultural norms determine much of the way dialogue proceeds. For example, in Britain, when people meet, they often ask 'How are you?' but don't expect an answer beyond 'Fine thanks'. In some cultures, it is expected that greetings are accompanied by enquiries after the health of all members of the family before discussing other business.

Body language

Cultural norms in spoken interaction are closely linked with body language. While some aspects of body language are universal, some are dependent on cultural expectations. For example in some cultures two people will stand close together to talk, in other cultures they are expected to maintain a certain distance.

In job interviews in the UK, it is generally considered good form for an interviewee to maintain eye contact with the interviewer, whereas in some cultures it is seen as a mark of respect for the interviewee to avoid looking the interviewer in the eye, and learners need to be aware of the particular expectations of the situation they are in.

Given the range of backgrounds among ESOL learners, the question of cross-cultural communication, involving linguistic conventions and other conventions, is of prime significance in working in the ESOL field.

Functional language

One approach to language analysis which has been very influential in the field of ESOL is that based on *language functions*. A 'language functions' approach describes language in terms of the purposes for which it is used, for example making requests, inviting, describing, expressing wishes and hopes. Clearly, there is more than one way to do any of these, and teachers have to select the most appropriate forms to teach, bearing in mind learners' level of English. For example, if the language teaching point is 'requesting help', learners at lower levels will learn 'Can you help me?' This form is chosen as it is relatively simple grammatically, is frequently used and is transferable, that is it can be used in a number of common situations. At higher levels, learners will learn a range of ways of making requests, such as:

Could you help me move this?

I wonder if you could possibly help me?

Give us a hand, will you?

All of the above are *exponents* of the function 'making requests', that is the different forms of language which can be used for a similar purpose. They illustrate the fact that there is no one-to-one correlation between form and function.

TASK 3.2

How many ways can you think of to invite someone to a social event? Could you use them all interchangeably in any context? What factors would you have to take into account when deciding this?

COMMENT 3.2

You might have suggested something like:

- Would you like to come to ... ?
- Do you fancy coming with us to ... ?
- My husband and I would like to invite you to ...

Clearly these exponents of the function of inviting are not interchangeable. The choice of exponent is dependent on the context, including who the speaker is and who he or she is inviting; the relationship between them; whether the invitation is spoken or written; and what the interaction is about, in this case what event the invitation is for.

The term *'appropriacy'* is normally used to refer to the role of the overall context in making choices regarding language. The term *'register'* may also be used, often to distinguish between formal and informal use of language. If you look at a range of possible exponents of the function 'inviting', you will find that some are appropriate for spoken and some for written invitations, some are appropriate for formal and some for informal invitations.

An interviewee for a job will need to use language in order to greet, give information, ask for information, and express preferences and future wishes. The exponents chosen for these functions will need to be appropriate for formal, spoken English.

TASK 3.3

Look again at your examples, and decide, for each one;

- The likely overall situation.
- Whether the communication is spoken or written.
- The speaker or writer and the person they are addressing and the relationship between them.
- The type of event.
- The formality of the invitation.

Implications for teaching

The above sections consider the way language may be analysed and how this analysis can be applied in a specific context. Teachers select the language focus of lessons, without losing sight of the whole picture. It would clearly be overwhelming for both teacher and learners if an attempt were made to focus on all possible aspects of language at one time.

TASK 3.4

Examine the two lesson plans below. Both use a job interview as context and are suitable for a group working towards Entry 3. You will notice that the teacher of each lesson has focused on different language points, as detailed below.

In Lesson 1 the teacher has addressed:

- *Skills*: reading and listening critically for what is included and what is not, plus work on speaking.
- *Grammar*: the formation of direct and indirect questions.
- *Phonology*: intonation to show politeness, when asking questions.
- *Discourse and culture*: the kind of questions considered appropriate in a UK interview.
- *Knowledge of the situation as a whole*: the importance of preparing questions and adapting them during the interview if necessary.

In Lesson 2 the teacher has addressed:

- *Lexis*: useful interview phrases.
- *Coherence and cohesion*: use of discourse markers to structure a short talk.
- *Discourse and culture*: the amount of talk that is expected in answer to a question; different conventions of body language.
- *Knowledge of the situation as a whole*: understanding of the requirements for different jobs; ways of dealing with a 'very real' problem of having to talk about experience without having enough of it.

Read both plans and note the stages of the lesson where the above points are addressed. Note also how the teacher has incorporated opportunities for the learners to contribute their own experience and to share ideas.

Table 2.1 Lesson 1

Timing	Teacher activity	Learner activity	Materials
10 mins.	Elicit learners' experience of interviews and discuss questions they were asked and whether they asked any questions.	Discuss experience of answering and asking questions in interview.	
15 mins.	Give out adverts to groups.	Work in groups to look at job adverts and decide what info. is given and what not given – what questions they would want to ask about the job.	Job adverts from local papers.
5 mins.	Present list of topics to learners.	Check list of topics against their own list and discuss which ones are most acceptable to ask in an interview.	List of topics about which people might want to ask questions, e.g. opportunities for promotion, shift work.
10 mins.	Ask learners to write questions.	Learners work in pairs or alone to write questions they might ask, in any format.	

Timing	Teacher activity	Learner activity	Materials
15 mins.	Elicit some questions and write them up, asking class to correct where necessary. Elicit ways of re-formatting into indirect questions, e.g. 'could you tell me ...'	Provide example questions.	
15 mins.	Demonstrate how to convert direct questions to indirect. Monitor and check pair/individual work.	Work in pairs or alone (as before) to correct their original questions (if necessary) and convert them to indirect questions. Pass to another pair to proofread.	
10 mins.	Demonstrate use of intonation for politeness, using the examples already worked on. Drill the group and individuals.	Practise intonation for politeness as full class, then in pairs or groups.	
10 mins.	Elicit at which point in the interview the questions will come. Show list of topics again, and discuss whether to leave out less acceptable questions, or ask them after asking one or two other questions.	Discuss acceptable questions, in a full-class, teacher-led discussion.	List of topics (as above).
15 mins.	Ask learners to practise in pairs, responding to 'do you have any questions for us?' Ask them to think about question type, intonation and order of questions. Monitor pair work.	Practise in pairs.	

Timing	Teacher activity	Learner activity	Materials
15 mins.	Discuss usefulness of preparing questions to ask, but point out the danger of asking a question if the answer has been given during the interview. Show three questions; tell learners these are their prepared questions. Give a short information talk (live or on tape) and ask learners whether they still want to ask all three questions.	Listen and consider whether any of the three 'prepared' questions has been answered in the talk.	Three questions. A tape or a prepared talk to give 'live', in which one of the prepared questions has been answered.

Table 2.2 Lesson 2

Timing	Teacher activity	Learner activity	Materials
20 mins.	Ask learners to work in groups, drawing a spidergram of skills and experience needed for a particular job.	Work with people who have experience of or interest in a similar job to themselves. Draw a spidergram showing the skills and experience needed. Report back to the class.	
10 mins.	Elicit what work experience learners have. Show a resumé of own experience in note form. Raise the topic of what a person can do if they do not have relevant experience for a job – finding relevance in other life experience.	Take part in discussion.	Resumé of teacher's own work experience in note form.
15 mins.	Divide learners into groups – with/without work experience. Work with those who have no work experience to consider other things they can focus on in interview.	Discuss their own experience in pairs/groups and make notes similar to the teacher's resumé (those without experience work with the teacher on a similar activity).	

Timing	Teacher activity	Learner activity	Materials
15 mins.	Play a tape or show a video of three clips from interview. Lead discussion.	Listen/watch and fill in evaluation sheet. Discuss how much one is expected to say in interview in Britain, and compare with other countries, if appropriate.	Tape or video – one good interview, one rambling (irrelevant, talking too much), one saying too little. Evaluation sheet to fill in relating to relevance, how much said.
15 mins.	Play tape of the 'good' interview again, and give out the transcript, minus discourse markers. Show list of 'useful interview phrases' taken from the transcript. Lead discussion.	Listen and fill in the discourse markers on the transcript. Check using full transcript. Look at list of 'useful interview phrases' and find them in the transcript. Discuss how the discourse markers help structure the talk and discuss how the 'useful phrases' can be helpful, including for people who have little work experience.	Tape of the 'good' interview. Transcript of the 'good' interview, with discourse markers deleted, and another full version. A list of some useful phrases taken from the transcript and projected for all learners to see.
10 mins.	Ask learners to practise in pairs.	Learners work in pairs, with the notes they made earlier, practising talking about their experience, incorporating discourse markers and 'useful phrases'.	
5 mins.	Start discussion about appropriate body language.	Discuss appropriate body language for an interview, and possible cross-cultural differences, e.g. eye contact.	
20 mins.	Set up role-play and monitor. Organize feedback.	Work in groups of three, taking turns – two to role-play, one to evaluate with a checklist. Take part in full group feedback.	Checklist, covering amount said, relevance, use of discourse markers and useful phrases, body language.

Consideration of the thematic content

We have seen in the example lesson plans how one or more specific language features can be focused on within a single communicative context. Language teaching should not be divorced from the contexts in which the language is used, and in ESOL, learners are often learning language whilst learning something else. There are two principle approaches to the relationship between language and other lesson content depending on whether the starting point for planning is the language or the content. These approaches are known as 'embedded' and 'contextualized'.

Embedded ESOL

When a course takes an embedded approach to ESOL, the starting point is the thematic content. Three of the most common types of ESOL course which use an embedded approach are vocational ESOL, ESOL and citizenship, and topic-based ESOL, and we shall now discuss some of the issues involved with each of these.

Vocational ESOL

The introduction to the 'Skills for Life Materials for Embedded Learning Project'[1] states that: 'Embedded teaching and learning combines the development of Literacy, Language and Numeracy with vocational and other skills. The skills acquired provide learners with the confidence, competence and motivation necessary for them to succeed in qualifications, in life and at work.'

Vocational ESOL often relates to a particular vocational area that the learners either already work in or would like to work in, e.g. 'English for engineers' or 'English for working in the NHS'. However, it can also be more general, focusing on such things as reading a contract, attending an appraisal, etc., which are common to most jobs. It can also focus on job search skills for people who are looking for work. Whatever the focus, it is the content which is the starting point – the rationale for any language work is based on how the language is used at work, in training or in seeking work. For example:

- Construction workers have to be able to talk about dimensions and qualities of material. This will involve using language for comparison, such as: 'longer than', 'not as big as', 'too heavy', 'not strong enough'.
- Care workers in a residential home sometimes have to write reports on incidents involving residents. They will need to be able to structure a short narrative using past tenses and have a range of lexical phrases connected with minor accidents.

Vocational ESOL usually draws on the expertise of both ESOL specialists and specialists in the vocational area concerned. These people may be involved at the level of teaching, course design, materials development or any combination of these three. For example, an ESOL teacher may work with a vocational teacher in a team-teaching situation; an ESOL teacher may use the vocational teacher's syllabus in order to assess the language that ESOL learners need to work on; a vocational teacher may supplement their own course material with material devised by ESOL specialists.

One view of this process is that, as learners study the subject matter, they will acquire English naturally, as long as the teacher makes sure the subject matter is comprehensible to them. Another view is that the teacher should focus on specific language items as they relate to the content of the course.

The latter view is taken with the DfES 'Embedded Learning Project'.[2] For example, in the 'Materials for international nurses' Module 1 – 'Admitting patients' – there is a focus on listening and speaking skills in terms of starting an interview, showing interest, using questions effectively and showing they are listening. Reading and writing skills are developed in terms of understanding patient assessment forms and recording patient information.

TASK 3.5

A figure X shows a page from the materials for bricklayers. The aim of this piece of material is to increase ability to read a diagram, including dimensions. If the learners using this material do not have English as a first language there may be a need for further analysis of the language involved.

What language do you think ESOL learners might need to focus on when working with diagrams like this?

COMMENT 3.5

Some suggestions are:

- Vocabulary for items such as 'socket', 'plug', 'pin', 'switch'.
- Ways to express dimensions in words, e.g. '12 metres by 12', '4000 mm long'.
- The relationship between the words such as 'long' and 'length', 'high' and 'height'.
- Prepositions and ways of expressing precise location, e.g. '1500 metres to the left of the door frame'.

ESOL and citizenship

Embedded language learning is often associated with vocational courses, but this need not always be the case. For example, courses with a focus on citizenship may also have content as a starting point. Courses designed for people who wish to take the citizenship test will be based around the topics covered in the test, for example the law, the political system, the Health Service. Language work will be integrated with the work around the topics, but will not be the starting point for planning the course.

Topic-based ESOL

Many ESOL courses take topic, rather than language, as their starting point. This may be because there is a particular area that learners have in common and want to focus on, for example they all have responsibility for children or they are all pregnant. Often, the reason for choosing a topic-based approach is practical – in community ESOL classes, not graded according to language level, it is often difficult to identify common language needs and easier to find common topics of interest. Learners might also be interested in short courses with a specific focus such as local history or understanding TV documentaries. All of these non-vocational courses can be seen as examples of embedded language learning.

Why choose an embedded approach?

Some reasons why an embedded approach may be more suitable than a contextualized approach with certain learners are:

- Instrumental reasons, such as learning a new vocational skill or preparing for the citizenship test.
- Organizational reasons, such as teaching a mixed ability group, where commonality of interest is easier to find than commonality of specific language learning needs.
- Some learners, especially those who have been attending classes for some time, may seem to have reached a plateau with language-focused work.
- Some learners might not be motivated by a class with a language focus and can feel much more involved with an embedded approach.

Contextualized ESOL

Contextualized ESOL has more in common with other forms of language teaching, such as EFL and the teaching of languages such as French or Japanese to English speakers. When language is contextualized for teaching purposes, a language point is chosen first and then integrated with content likely to be useful or interesting for the learner. With contextualized ESOL, the component skills or grammar points listed in the *Adult ESOL Core Curriculum* may be taken as a starting point. The Skills for Life ESOL materials, published in 2003, take a contextualized approach, for example:

- A component skill listed in the ESOL curriculum Entry 1 Speaking, 'ask for directions and location', is contextualized through learners asking where places are when walking in the street.
- The use of time markers in written English at Entry 2 is contextualized through writing about past education.
- Use of comparative and superlative at Entry 3 is contextualized through comparisons of countries and cities.

TASK 3.6

What other contexts can you think of for the language points?

COMMENT 3.6

There are many possible contexts, a few are suggested here.

1 Asking for direction and location:
   - Finding your way around a big building, such as an office or the local college.
   - Finding the right platform or meeting someone at a big railway station.
   - Finding the right aisle in a supermarket.
2 Use of time markers:
   - Telling your own life story or that of a famous person.
   - Describing a journey.
   - Talking about a significant day or event.
3 Comparative and superlative:
   - Shops and markets in the neighbourhood.
   - Styles of clothes worn by learners in the class/different cultures/nations, etc.
   - Famous people.

Why choose a contextualized approach?

There may be a number of reasons why it is appropriate to take language rather than content as a starting point, for example:

- *Institutional requirements*: an institution may have a policy of assessing specific language points as a means of deciding on progression routes.
- *The requirements of the accreditation process*: an exam syllabus may require attention to specific language points.

- *A perceived need for the learners to develop accuracy*: when learners can express themselves fairly easily, but inaccurately, in speaking and/or writing but lack accuracy. This is often a need identified by learners themselves who often give their reason for continuing with or returning to ESOL classes as being to 'improve grammar'.
- *Perceived gaps in the learners' abilities*: when diagnostic assessment identifies specific language points as areas for development.

Combining approaches

While it is clear that some courses need to take a contextualized approach and others an embedded approach, it is also possible to combine both approaches in a single course. Topic-based and project-based work can be very motivating and may serve as a way of prioritizing language work to be done on another occasion. Rather than seeing contextualized and embedded approaches as mutually exclusive, teachers, in consultation with learners, can work to the benefits of both approaches and successfully integrate language work with interesting content in their classes.

Choosing topics

Whereas with vocational ESOL and some other contexts for embedded language learning, the content is fairly closely prescribed, when using either a contextualized approach or the type of topic-based approach used, for example, in many community classes, there is freedom to select topics. With both of these approaches, selection of topic is a matter deserving of careful consideration.

In the 1970s teacher-training courses dealing specifically with teaching ESOL to adults were developed, and as a result there was some consistency of approach, which had not existed previously. It was very common at that time to find teachers taking a topic-based approach, focusing largely on the perceived everyday functional needs of their learners such as going to the doctor, talking to a child's teacher, buying a train ticket, shopping or returning faulty goods to a shop. There is clearly great value in working on language that learners will find immediately useful in difficult day-to-day situations. However, there has since been much criticism of this approach with its focus on day-to-day problems, as it seems to suggest that learners are people who need help to cope with the difficulties of life in the UK, and fails to recognize their wider experience and aspirations. The term 'deficit model' is used to describe any approach to ESOL teaching which appears to present this type of restricted view of the learner, the learner's life and the learner's potential future. It is possible that the citizenship agenda can help to resolve this dilemma by providing a broader framework in which to situate the work on everyday language use.

The citizenship agenda

Currently, applicants for UK citizenship whose level of English is insufficient to take the citizenship test, are required to show that they have studied English in the context of citizenship. In addition, the handbook and materials linked with the citizenship test address topics which may be of interest to any ESOL learners, regardless of whether or not they wish to apply for citizenship, for two principle reasons.

First, they can help to develop background knowledge about UK systems. This is important to help learners access reading material and to understand speech. As we have seen previously, it is important that readers and listeners can approach texts with the appropriate schemata activated. If this is not possible, then they need to be able to access information or have experiences which will help them to form new schemata. Background knowledge is particularly important to help learners access authentic materials such as newspapers, which can play a large part in ESOL classes. For example, a news item about a court case will be better understood with some basic understanding of UK systems, for example what the 'Old Bailey' is and what the roles of the main players are in a courtroom. Many ESOL learners will need to be given relevant background knowledge before they can be expected to read a news article about a trial at the 'Old Bailey'. In another example, people can more effectively read news items about events around the UK if they have some knowledge of UK geography. This knowledge might also be useful when they listen to a weather report on the radio or if they have a conversation with someone who tells them about various places in the UK they have lived.

Second, an understanding of the UK system can link closely with work on how to use English in daily life. The citizenship agenda can be seen as a way of re-visiting topics and situations such as health, education and transport, which have been used in ESOL for a long time and which are of great immediate use to learners, while at the same time broadening the syllabus to include topics such as geography, local history and political systems.

In re-considering work on situations such as 'making appointments', 'talking to the doctor', 'talking to a teacher', we need to think of ways to avoid implementing a 'deficit model'. The situations in which learners have to use English in order to carry out fairly formal transactions, frequently referred to as *gatekeeping* encounters', involve an imbalance of power. Although teachers and learners cannot alter the fact of this power imbalance, teachers sometimes find they can move the emphasis from 'coping' to 'empowering'. For example, if work on talking to the doctor is limited to describing a problem, listening to what the doctor says and following the doctor's instructions, this can be seen as learning to 'cope'. If, in addition to these points, learners are encouraged to ask the doctor questions, the work becomes more 'empowering', that is it enables learners to take some control of the situation and to consider what they want from the interaction.

Another important point when preparing learners for 'gatekeeping encounters' is to maintain an awareness of the likely reality of the interaction. For example, when asking for an appointment, people are often told they will have to wait longer than they want to, or when phoning an organization to ask for information, people often have to listen intensively and press the right keys on their telephone pad before they can expect to speak to an operator. Practice of the language for the situation needs to take account of this reality, prepare the learner for the unpredictable and include discussion of strategies for dealing with different issues that could arise. Clearly, this will be done most effectively with learners at higher levels, but even at Entry 1 learners can be equipped with strategies such as asking for repetition and clarification.

The background knowledge which the citizenship agenda can provide is essential for participating fully in these 'gatekeeping encounters'. If we return to the question of making an appointment with the doctor, we note that people cannot always get an appointment when they want one. While it is useful to equip learners with the language to explain why they need an early appointment, it may be more practical for learners to know about alternatives, for example phoning NHS Direct or going to a pharmacist. In this case, knowledge is empowering as it offers choices and gives a basis for decision making.

Finally, it is important to remember that, although some learners may have a lot to learn about UK systems such as the NHS, others will already have extensive knowledge and experience. Many will fall between these two extremes, but all are likely to have opinions, based on experience either in the UK or in other countries, and opportunities for the learners to express themselves on these issues should both be planned by the teacher, and taken when they arise naturally. Even learners whose use of English is very limited can make their voice heard if they feel strongly enough about something.

Drawing on the learners' experiences

Concentrating too much on the citizenship agenda can mean that the classroom focus is always on something about which the learner does not know. This can potentially lead to a new kind of deficit model, in which learners are seen as people who lack knowledge about the country in which they live.

It is a guiding principle of adult education that learners' own experience is a valuable resource for the teaching and learning process. In his book *Teaching Adults* Alan Rogers (2002) is referring to any adult learners, not specifically those learning English language:

> Each of the learners brings a range of experience and knowledge more or less relevant to the task in hand. New learners are not new people; they possess a set of values, established prejudices and attitudes in which they have invested a great deal of emotional investment. These are based on their past experience. Knowles suggests that, for children, experience is something that happens to them; for adults, experience serves to determine who they are, to create their sense of self-identity. When this experience is devalued or ignored (e.g. by the teacher), this implies a rejection of the person, not just of the experience.

Rogers' reference above, to self-identity, has particular significance for ESOL learners, all of whom are adjusting to a life situation which involves a central role for a language other than their own. They are in the process of forming a new 'language identity'. In *The Social Turn in Second Language Acquisition,* Block (2003) describes a study by Norton of five immigrant women in Canada. One of the women, a Polish woman named Eva, worked in a restaurant, where she was ignored in conversation and given the most menial jobs.

> However, through social contacts with her fellow workers outside the confines of work, she came to be seen in a different light, in particular as someone who did have an interesting life, who knew about Europe and who spoke Italian. Feeling more legitimate as a co-worker and human being, Eva began to lose her self-consciousness about speaking English and eventually engaged in many more interactions in English, both on and off the job. Eventually, she was able to carve out an identity as a fully functioning co-worker who was 'worthy to speak and listen'.

It can be seen here that part of carving out an identity in the new language is to be able to see oneself as 'worthy to speak and listen' when using that language. Block also suggests that before making the social contacts that she did, Eva did not feel completely legitimate *as a human being*. Teachers who encourage the expression of learners' experience, feelings, beliefs and opinions may be assisting the process of developing this feeling of legitimacy when using English. In addition, the typical ESOL class, with its multilingual composition and consequent need for English as a communicative tool between learners, can be an essential first step in the process of learning to see oneself and to be seen as a person 'worthy to speak and listen' when using English.

ESOL learners bring with them a vast and varied range of experience, with huge diversity in terms of country of origin, cultural background, profession, length of time in the UK, etc. Drawing on this experience in class can lead to rich and interesting exchanges, from which both tutor and learners can benefit.

Project work

One of the ways in which teachers link learners' experiences with language work in class is to organize project work. This can draw on both present and past experience and enables learners to have new experiences in an English-speaking environment.

For example, a group of learners might undertake a joint planning exercise, such as planning an outing to a museum. This can involve finding out about the museum, its opening times and how to get to it, jointly agreeing on a date and going to the museum. Once there, learners can agree what each of them will investigate, and they might each prepare a short talk to give in class.

Another way is to ask learners to undertake a simple research task on a topic such as the NHS, the local council or the geography of the UK. Learners can work in teams, using the Internet, the library or interviews, and present their findings either in a talk or in writing. This can be a very dynamic way to engage learners with those areas covered by the citizenship agenda, and simulate the way they might use English outside the class.

Content outside the learners' experience

We have considered content related to life in the UK (the citizenship agenda) and content drawn from learners' own experience. However, we do not intend to suggest that content should be limited to these areas as there is a wealth of other content that ESOL learners can enjoy reading about and discussing. Whilst recognizing the value of drawing on people's experience, we must also remember that content which helps people *forget* their own experience can be very stimulating and can be a relief for those whose experiences have been traumatic. To a large extent, this content is likely to be provided by ELT materials published for worldwide use and by authentic materials such as magazines.[3] Obviously, it is not always possible to predict exactly what will grab learners' attention, so an element of trial and error may be involved.

Screening content

It is sometimes necessary to screen content to make sure it is suitable for all learners. When it is not suitable, this is usually for one of two reasons. First, learners' life experiences, interests, background knowledge, etc., might not facilitate relating to particular topics. Second, some topics might cause offence or distress to some groups.

Screening – schemata

As we have discussed already, learners need to have the appropriate schemata activated before approaching a topic. This is particularly noticeable with the receptive skills of listening and reading, where learners may find considerable difficulties in understanding a text if they lack the relevant background knowledge. When deciding whether to use a particular text, for example one found in an ELT course book, a teacher has to try to predict the extent to which their learners will have the required background knowledge. If they are not likely to have this knowledge, the teacher then has to decide whether to provide information and help to activate the schemata for accessing the text or whether it is best not to use that particular text.

Before reading a text, teachers normally have some discussion or other pre-reading activity to activate the appropriate schemata in the learners. With the following extract taken from the Skills for Life materials at Entry 3, some learners might have substantial background knowledge, and others very little.

From public enemy number one to most popular man in Britain

In 1998 Beckham was losing popularity fast. Then came the disaster of the World Cup match. After the referee sent him off for tripping up Argentina's Diego Simeone, everyone blamed him for England's defeat in the match. His fast, luxurious lifestyle and marriage to Victoria ('Posh Spice') made him even more unpopular.

Perhaps the most effective pre-reading strategy is to elicit background knowledge from the group, without nominating individuals and allowing people to remain silent if they want to. By asking the group if they've heard of David Beckham and showing a picture of him, it is likely that some members of the group who have the background knowledge will be happy to contribute while those who don't can learn from listening to their peers and to the teacher's reinforcement of the points made. Other key areas of schemata here include football – if learners don't know much about football they might have difficulty imagining why a World Cup match may be so significant. There are also assumptions about knowledge of celebrity – who is Posh Spice? Why is she famous? And why does she have such a lifestyle?

TASK 3.7

You are teaching a group of young learners and you think they would enjoy and benefit from participating in a quiz. You have found some quiz questions, but they tend to be Eurocentric in content. Your learners are a mix of Europeans, Latin Americans, Asians and Africans, and you do not want to risk making some of the learners feel inadequate because they do not have the background knowledge of some other learners. Does this mean you have to abandon the idea of a quiz?

COMMENT 3.7

Two possible solutions are suggested here:

1   Make up a quiz of your own based on a theme, such as 'the area where we live' or 'the topics we have discussed in class this term'. This approach has the benefit of putting everyone in the same position. It can also help to increase knowledge of the local area or provide revision of the non-linguistic content of classes.

2   Divide the class into teams, making sure that each team reflects the same mix of backgrounds. Give out the quiz questions you have found, with answers. Ask teams to write their own questions, based on their own background knowledge and using the questions you have given them as a model. During the quiz, make sure that teams can confer and pass the question to the person most likely to be able to answer.

This approach can have a number of benefits – learners get practice in forming questions, people get a chance to feel positive about bringing their own background knowledge in to class, learners will learn more about each others' culture and country of origin, and may feel more respect for each other.

Screening – potential distress in learners

ESOL learners come from a large range of backgrounds and have come to the UK for many different reasons. Some have come as refugees and asylum seekers, and may have suffered trauma. Teachers need to know enough about their learners and their countries of origin to understand which topics should be approached sensitively. This does not necessarily mean that these topics should be avoided, but teachers do need to be aware of how certain individuals might be feeling when the topics are raised.

For example, discussion of 'family' can cause extreme distress to someone who has lost all or most of their relatives at war. At the same time, it is not practical to avoid such an important topic and it is likely that the majority of the learners in a class will be very motivated to talk about their own families. Some principles that can be followed in this situation are suggested here:

- Illustrate and practise the language of 'family' using an imaginary textbook family or the teacher's own family.
- Encourage learners to talk about their own families if they want to, but accept silence if someone prefers not to speak.
- Avoid direct questions to individuals, such as 'Have you got any brothers?' unless you already know that this is not a sensitive question for that person.
- When it comes to tasks, offer choice, e.g. 'Look at this family tree, and write about the family. If you prefer, write about your own family. Choose your group according to what you will write about'.

Sometimes, teachers encounter topics in ELT course books or in exam syllabi which would be very interesting for some learners but which could cause discomfort in others, and they need to adapt them to suit all.

TASK 3.8

You have a group of learners who all live in the same area, but some have their own homes and others are living in sub-standard temporary accommodation. How would you adapt this speaking and writing task to avoid any discomfort some learners might feel?

'Describe your home. Tell another learner where it is and what it is like inside'.

COMMENT 3.8

Two possible solutions are suggested here:

1　Give a choice about what they actually describe, e.g. 'Describe a home. This can be the place where you live now or a place where you lived in the past or a place you have visited'.
2　Learners work in groups to draw a plan of their ideal house or flat, being as imaginative as they like. They then describe this place to learners from another group.

Screening – offensiveness

Whereas topics like those exemplified above should be approached with sensitivity and adapted as necessary, it is usually neither easy nor desirable to try to avoid them entirely.

With topics which could cause offence, the case for avoidance is perhaps stronger. However, a simple dictum such as 'avoid the topics of politics and religion' does not allow for the richness of experience, belief and opinion which ESOL learners can bring to class. People often want to talk about a religion which is central to their lives, or the political events which have affected them. In addition, ESOL learners have often had experience of racism in the UK and may want to talk about it. However, whereas a group of refugees may be very keen to talk about attitudes to asylum seekers in the media, a single refugee in a class of non-refugees might feel very uncomfortable with this topic.

Perhaps the solution is to amend the dictum 'avoid the topics of politics and religion' to 'avoid those aspects of the topics of politics and religion which could cause offence until you and your learners know each other better'. The teacher's task then is to facilitate a group dynamic where all learners interact with each other and have plenty of opportunity to share experiences and to take an interest in each other's background and opinions. In this way, class content based on personal experience, combined with class-management strategies which encourage all learners to interact with all other learners, will pave the way for a class atmosphere where learners can express themselves more freely and may lead to possibilities of broaching more contentious topics.

TASK 3.9

You are teaching a group of learners with mixed cultural and linguistic backgrounds. The different groups are not communicating well with each other, and you sense a lack of understanding of each other's background and culture. What can you do to help create an atmosphere in which learners can express themselves and listen to each other?

COMMENT 3.9

Some possible solutions are suggested here:

- Prepare questions about different cultural backgrounds, e.g. 'What is the most popular food in your country?', 'What is the national dress of your country?' Learners can prepare their answers together with people from the same country and then take a partner from a different country and exchange information.
- At higher levels, learners might prepare a short talk to give to the class, alone or in pairs, on the country they come from, focusing on whatever aspect they want to, e.g. climate, geography, social customs or political problems.
- At low levels, learners can circulate round the class asking everyone the same questions, e.g. 'Where do you come from?' and 'When is New Year in your country?' Learners would need to make sure they speak to every single other person in the class.

Involving learners in choice of content

Understanding the needs of learners is of fundamental importance to successful teaching. Nunan (1991) describes two kinds of data to collect about learners in order to carry out a needs analysis:

> 'Objective' data is that factual information which does not require the attitudes and views of the learners to be taken into account. Thus, biographical information on age, nationality, home language, etc. is said to be 'objective'. 'Subjective' information, on the other hand, reflects the perceptions, goals, and priorities of the learner. It will include, among other things, information on why the learner has undertaken to learn a second language, and the classroom tasks and activities which the learner prefers.

The trend throughout adult education is to consult the learner about course content. In ESOL, consultation with learners is often centred around choice of topic. At higher levels, this may be done through discussion, whereas at lower levels, learners are often given pictorial cues to help them to make choices, and in some cases translation may be used. However, learner consultation does not have to be only about topic, and there is a growing tendency to consult on language work, particularly the balance of reading, writing, listening and speaking, and on types of activity and learning methods.

There are, however, occasions when consultation is very difficult, principally when working with learners at very low levels. In this case, teachers have to take a more 'objective' approach and predict learners' language needs. To do this, they need to know not only about the learners' lives but also something about the community the learners are living in. There is sometimes a risk of making assumptions about where people need to use English, and knowing about the community can help to avoid this. For example, in some communities there are plenty of doctors and other professionals who speak the learner's language, so that it is not so useful to learn to talk to a doctor in English.

Although it may be necessary to make assumptions about what learners should work on when they first arrive in a class, either because their level of English is low or because they appear resistant to a consultation process, it is both possible and desirable to move to a more consultative approach over time. Alan Rogers (2002) considers this idea in relation to adult learners in general:

> some adults, re-entering education after some time away from school, expect to be treated as children. The expectations of 'being taught' are sometimes strong, and if these expectations are not met in some way or other, once again learning is hindered. However, experience suggests that even the most docile group of adult learners, happy for much of the time to be directed as if they were in school, will at the right time rebel against their teachers when the affront to their adulthood becomes too great. It can be a great help to provoke such a situation when we feel the time is right to break up the more formal atmosphere and secure greater participation by the learners in their own learning process.

One way to move from teacher control to the greater participation of the learners is to begin with a retrospective review of lessons already experienced, moving from that to the discussion of content of future lessons. Learners whose previous experience of learning has been in a different cultural context will need to know what is on offer before they can participate in the planning. It is also very useful if teachers make a point of equipping learners with the language they can use to take part in consultation, for example:

- *Expressing preferences*: 'I prefer to read the text silently'.
- *Expressing opinions*: 'I don't think it's useful to learn about X'.
- *Making comparisons*: 'Learning about X is more important than Y'.
- *Making requests*: 'Could we have a lesson about ...?
- *Making suggestions*: 'Why don't we put our writing up on the wall?'

Summary

In summary, the following principles should be applied in selecting content for classes with adult ESOL learners:

- Make an attempt to know as much as you can about your learners and their communities, so that you can plan for them adequately.
- Always integrate language work closely with the contexts in which the language is used.

- Select content that will be useful and interesting.
- Take care never to marginalize a learner or a minority group of learners when selecting content.
- Pay attention to background knowledge needed (e.g. if teaching how to buy a train ticket, learners need to know that prices vary according to the time of travel).
- Emulate real-life language use. Be aware of differences between spoken and written language, and provide realistic examples.
- Emulate the realities of communication outside the classroom (e.g. making an official phonecall is rarely straightforward, so it should not be portrayed this way in classroom practice).
- Emulate the resources encountered outside class, by using authentic material as much as possible.
- Emulate real-life tasks in the classroom (e.g. by organizing project work).
- Consult learners as much as is feasible about lesson content, and invite their evaluations.

Notes

1   CfBT 2005 available at: www.dfes.gov.uk/readwriteplus/learning_material/
     reports/tranche41_batch3.doc
2   www.dfes.gov.uk/readwriteplus/embeddedlearning/
3   Use of teaching resources is discussed in more detail in Chapter 9.

4 Second language acquisition (SLA) and the contexts of UK ESOL practice

John Sutter

Having considered the contexts in which ESOL learners live and learn, we will now go on to look at how these contexts interact with current theories of language acquisition and consider the implications for ESOL teaching and learning.

Before we do this, let's briefly revisit the idea of a 'context' of language learning, in particular the notions of ESOL versus EFL contexts – where typically, a crucial difference is seen to be the presence or absence of a 'host community' of target-language speakers. Block (2003) provides a quadrant diagram to illustrate the contexts generally recognized and considered by SLA theorists and researchers (see Figure 4.1):

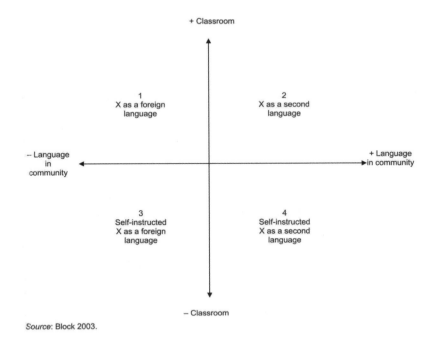

Source: Block 2003.

Figure 4.1 A quadrant diagram of recognized SLA contexts

TASK 4.1

Think about your own language learning experiences, and try marking them onto the quadrant in the appropriate place: do they fit neatly into the individual quadrants?

As we saw in Chapter 1, a crude division between ESOL and EFL is an oversimplification – as soon as we look at real so-called 'foreign-' or 'second-' language learners we find that there can often be as many similarities between them as there are differences. For instance, although ESOL learners are by definition living in the 'target-language community', they may have little – or even no – opportunity to use the language they are trying to learn outside of the classroom: 'We wake up in the morning and we don't know where to go, sometimes we spend the whole day at home' (learner cited in Roberts et al. 2004: 30). And when there are opportunities to use the new language, these are often not the most conducive to language learning: Barton and Pitt (2003) cite research by Perdue that found that:

> adult immigrants typically have to use the target language in environments which promote anxiety and marginalisation rather than opportunities for language learning ... most of their everyday use of the additional language is within asymmetrical interaction (such as when they are clients, customers and interviewees).

> (Barton and Pitt 2003: 11)

Just as these contextual categories – *EFL* versus *ESOL*; *classroom learning* versus *naturalistic acquisition in the community* – appear inadequate to account for the diverse real-life contexts and experiences of many language learners, so too do the keynote terms of SLA theory: 'second', 'language' and 'acquisition' (Block 2003). In fact there is great tension between this terminology and the social contexts and sociolinguistic realities of UK ESOL learners; for this reason, we will first briefly examine the problematic nature of SLA terminology.

Bilingualism/multilingualism – second language?

Block (2003) points out that it is highly inaccurate to talk about English as a 'second' language for many learners: a great number will be bilingual or multilingual before they begin learning English. For many, this will have been from birth, and such learners may have a problem identifying their so-called 'first' language. Yet SLA assumes that language users should have a 'first' language, and places a high value on 'native speaker' status: it therefore has some difficulty accounting for the experiences of language users who are from a multilingual background (and it should be pointed out that such learners are in the majority). This, according to some theorists, indicates a *monolingual bias* in SLA; in other words, SLA is a field of study with a profoundly monolingual worldview. As Kathy Pitt puts it,

There is an unexplored assumption in much of SLA research that a learner has acquired one language from birth and, now that she is living in another country with a different language, she will gradually acquire this additional language and assimilate to 'native-speaker' norms. The two languages are seen as separate and stable entities.

(Pitt 2005: 67)

Indeed, Harris (1997) coined the term 'romantic bilingualism' to describe the process by which language users who are actually multilingual, and who may find it difficult to say which language is truly their 'first' language, come to be *essentialized* as speakers of language X or Y, having particular *allegiance to* or *expertise in* that language despite the fact that their knowledge of their so-called 'first language' may in fact be quite limited. This, of course, makes such speakers easier to categorize within a monolingual worldview – such learners are 'romantically' reclassified simply as 'bilinguals', but is also highly inaccurate.

This is more than an academic debate. There is some research to indicate that *third* language acquisition, may be a rather different process to *second* language acquisition. It may thus be important to find out whether learners are already bi- or multilingual. In particular, learners who already speak two or more languages are less likely to have monolingual perspectives on social aspects of language learning – they are likely to be swifter to notice and accept cultural differences and mores. And as they are likely to already have a broader range of cultural and linguistic repertoires than monolingual speakers, they are less likely to feel threatened by different interaction patterns, politeness routines and all the other 'culture-bound' features of a language.

Many UK ESOL learners may be using several languages in their daily lives. In her study of Panjabis in Southall, Saxena (1994) gives the example of a family whose members use English, Hindi, Panjabi/Gurmukhi, Panjabi-Hindi, Hindi/Devanagari according to function and context. Such learners may thus be using English only in a narrow range of functions: the question is whether they wish to improve their English only for a particular narrow range of functions (with obvious implications for the syllabus) or whether they have aspirations towards using English in a broader set of contexts (and if so, which ones). The point being that ESOL teachers have to cater for learners who are truly *multilingual*, and who wish to maintain their uses of their other languages, and who consequently may not see English as ever being their sole, or even main, language of daily communication.

Language varieties – second language or languages?

Just as there has been a tendency to essentialize speakers of other languages, we might argue that 'English' speakers are often similarly essentialized as speakers of a particular variety of English – 'Scottish', 'Estuary', 'Mockney', 'Black' or 'Standard' English, for example.

In fact, we all have a repertoire of varieties – and these are not clear-cut, but shade into each other in our day-to-day lives. ESOL learners, in particular, will very likely meet many varieties of English in their daily lives, in addition to the 'standard' English they probably find in most teaching materials, especially in the highly multicultural settings of many big cities and towns. They will certainly encounter vexations should they try to define 'English' or identify what exactly *is* the language they are trying to learn!

It is quite probable that many UK ESOL learners will use English, albeit to perhaps quite a limited degree:

- At work.
- In local shops.
- With neighbours.
- To deal with institutions.
- To watch television.
- To read a variety of types of text.

They will therefore, as we have noted above in relation to *varieties*, be exposed to many *styles* or *registers* of English, though they may not be especially sensitized to any differences between them (in terms of, pronunciation, lexis, grammar, level of formality, perceived status, and so on). They will almost certainly need eventually to have a repertoire of such styles rather than just one.

Acquisition and learning

One persistent legacy of Krashen's (1978: 153) work on SLA has been the acquisition/learning dichotomy: 'Language acquisition is a subconscious process. Language learning, on the other hand is a conscious process, and is the result of either a formal language learning situation, or a self-study program.' As Block (2003: 94) observes, it is a distinction that is popular with language teachers, as it: 'resonates with their day-to-day experience of ineffective classroom language teaching'. It appears to correlate with the classroom contexts in Figure 4.1 above: learners *learn* in the classroom, and *acquire* in naturalistic contexts. However, a moment's thought shows that this is not the case: learners clearly will process language consciously and unconsciously in both contexts. In a naturalistic context they may consult dictionaries and reflect on the form of language they have encountered; in the classroom they may be inattentive to form-focused teaching, or simply engage in 'normal' conversation with a teacher or classmate.

Krashen maintained that the two systems – acquisition and learning – were entirely separate; this is called the *non-interface* position. Learning, therefore, would not lead to acquisition. This, of course, would explain the 'ineffective classroom language teaching' referred to in the quote from Block above. However, although this position is largely discredited now, there remain competing accounts of how conscious attention to language, or conscious processing, eventually result in unconscious processing and use, and we will examine some of these accounts below. The question Block (2003) raises though, is whether second language acquisition is simply a matter of *processing* or whether wider social factors also play a role. This again, as we shall see below, is of particular relevance to the contexts of ESOL learning.

Applying SLA theory to ESOL

SLA as a field of study is currently in a state of considerable flux. At the end of their review of current theories in SLA, Mitchell and Myles (2004: 257) state: 'we are left with a reinforced impression of great diversity ... We find that new theoretical perspectives (such as connectionism or socio-cultural theory) have entered the field, without displacing the established ones (such as universal grammar)'.

However, in spite of this great diversity, it is possible to group many of these theories according to their general approach. In many ways, the current situation in SLA mirrors a divide in linguistics generally, which can perhaps best be described as the competing claims of *internal* and *external* factors. In general, linguistics *internal* factors refer to a Chomskyan interest in the *mind* of language users, *universal grammars*, and *competence* or knowledge about the structures of language. *External* factors refer to a Hallidayan focus on the *contexts* of language use, the *social factors* involved and *performance* or actual real-life instances of language use. In SLA, an interest in the *internal* has produced theories driven by psycholinguistic or cognitive factors and linguistic structures. More recently there has been an increasing interest in the *external*. This is behind calls for a 'social turn' in SLA: the idea that the examination of social contexts and social factors can cast light on how languages are learnt. For a more detailed examination of social and individual factors in SLA, good follow-up reading would be of the book referred to above – David Block's (2003) *The Social Turn in Second Language Acquisition*.

Internal and external factors, or theories based on either of these, are not, however, necessarily opposed. Indeed, they could be seen as complementing each other, and many researchers are now looking at possible ways of synthesizing these two perspectives. Further, there are claims that the categories 'internal' and 'external' are a false dichotomy: minds are not purely internal phenomena, and so-called 'social factors' are not outside individuals. These factors only come to have meaning in relation to the minds of individuals or groups of individuals (Rogoff 1990, 1995).

However, leaving this aside for the moment, the claim often made by researchers interested in the external is that the *social* has often been overlooked in favour of the *individual*, and this omission creates, at best, a partial account of language, language use and language acquisition, and at worst, an account that is deeply warped. We have already highlighted the special importance of the social contexts that ESOL learning takes place in; a good understanding of these external and social factors in relation to language learning or acquisition is thus of particular significance to the practice of ESOL teachers.

Given the multiplicity of SLA theories alluded to above, we will not attempt here to outline individual theories in any detail (for a good overview, see Mitchell and Myles 2004). Rather, we will examine *concepts* from SLA that have particular significance for the contexts of ESOL learners, and examine what the implications might be for classroom practice.

Acculturation – Schumann, Alberto and identity

One of the earliest attempts to recognize the importance of social factors to SLA theory was Schumann's (1978) study of a single learner, Alberto – a Costa Rican immigrant to the US. Alberto was not a particularly successful language learner, which Schumann attributes to two key groups of factors: *social* and *psychological distance*. Alberto's membership of a low-status, low-income group (Spanish-speaking immigrants) who are relatively isolated from the host community gave him social distance from speakers of the target language. His low motivation to integrate with the host community, and the stress and anxiety of his daily life separated him *psychologically*. Schumann called this the *acculturation model*.

Whilst the significance of Schumann's inclusion of social factors in a model of SLA is now universally acknowledged, Norton (1995) points out that the model 'essentializes' concepts such as community, motivation, group identity (echoing Harris's point about the 'essentialization' of language allegiance and expertise, above), and fails to recognize the social complexities of learning contexts such as Alberto's. Rather than being recognized as a unique and complex individual, Alberto is firmly classified as a 'Costa Rican' or 'Latino' trying to become 'American'. It is blandly assumed that Alberto identifies himself fully and completely with a distinct and definable 'community' of other Costa Ricans or 'Latinos'. In fact Alberto may see himself rather differently (perhaps as a Costa Rican *émigré*, or even a 'citizen of the world'), and the Costa Rican 'community' may well be a more diverse, less definable and less unified than the terminology suggests. Mixed marriages and partnerships, geographical spread, internal distinctions of class and allegiance will all have a bearing on this.

Factors such as membership of low-status and low-income groups, or high levels of stress and anxiety in daily life are certainly features of many present-day ESOL learners' experience, but in Schumann's model the onus on doing the 'acculturating' seems nonetheless to be firmly on Alberto. Schumann's conclusion also seems to imply that Alberto is unwilling to learn, and that he is almost too comfortable in his Spanish-speaking community. In fact, as we have seen earlier, and as is borne out by research such as that of Bremer et al. (1996), immigrant second-language learners may have very little opportunity to use the new language in anything other than official or gate-keeping encounters (such as dealing with government agencies or visits to the doctor – encounters which might determine access to goods or services, often characterized by unequal power relations between participants), and will therefore find it extremely difficult to enter into social relations, or negotiate their position with regard to social or psychological distance from the 'host community'. The NRDC's case studies of ESOL provision do indeed cite the strong motivation of many ESOL learners to learn English in order to integrate and develop more independence in their lives. But motivation is not simply a *personal* characteristic of this or that learner – it is highly context dependent; having to do a disproportionate amount of work for limited rewards will eventually undermine the most motivated learner.

Social practices

Learning an additional language is not just a matter of learning linguistic content in the form of grammar, lexis and phonology. It's also about learning, and participating in, the social practices that *contextualize* the language. Two examples might be *leave-taking* and *talking to strangers*. Leave-taking, at the end of an informal conversation, or a telephone call, is not simply a matter of saying 'Goodbye': there are particular routines and features – both physical and linguistic – that characterize it in English. Final 'goodbyes' are usually preceded by phrases such as ' … anyway' '… OK … well …' that indicate the conversation is to be drawn to a close. Sometimes the intention to end the conversation is stated more clearly – though still euphemistically – with phrases such as '… I'd better let you go/get on'. These will probably, in the case of a face-to-face conversation, be accompanied by a small step or two away from the other participant(s), or small physical movements indicating imminent departure (e.g. picking up a bag).

Different cultures will have different practices in talking to strangers, which constrain the type of situation or context in which strangers might typically strike up conversations. In Britain, one context where it does seem legitimate to 'talk to a stranger' is at a children's playgroup. However, there are still certain conventions appearing to govern this, for instance:

- Such 'stranger talk' will normally be adult-to-adult.
- Where it is adult-to-child, it will normally have been initiated by the child.
- Adult-to-adult interactions will often commence with a comment or question about their children or the children at the playgroup.

Language, behaviours, and context are thus very tightly bound. Context shapes the types of behaviour and language that will occur, and much of this appears to be a matter of 'convention' – convention being one aspect of 'social practices'.

Wenger uses the metaphor of a river and a mountain to describe this. Does the river carve its way through and down the mountain, or does the mountain shape and mould the river and its course? Well – both: the river and the mountain shape and constrain each other. So it is with the relationship between the individual and society, or between language and context. For the ESOL learner, then, part of the job of learning language is to learn the 'contours' of the landscape – and these 'contours' are really what is meant by 'social practices'.

TASK 4.2

What are the elements of the social practice of job interviews that ESOL learners in the UK would need to be aware of?

COMMENT 4.2

Preparation for a job interview would involve more than the study of typical interaction patterns and language functions and forms that occur in these, it would also involve looking at other elements of the context such as the typical physical positioning of participants, body postures, dress codes, levels of formality, turn-taking, the importance of giving detailed answers and of 'selling' oneself to the interview panel. Like the linguistic elements, these too may differ from culture to culture; indeed they are often the very things that most puzzle and fascinate people who have moved into a new society.

So a 'practices' view of social interaction and language is one that does not attribute fixed meanings to decontextualized interaction – it regards all meaning making as highly context-bound, and 'meaning' itself as something to be socially negotiated. 'Making meaning', therefore, is a *communal* rather than individual activity in which the participants' various expectations, linguistic resources, individual histories and social backgrounds will have great bearing upon the outcome. And for ESOL learners, one key site of this communal meaning making will be the ESOL classroom itself. The 'class' therefore, is more than just the collection of individuals in it, it is a primary contextual feature of the meaning-making process.

Communities of Practice

Communities of Practice (Lave and Wenger 1991) has been applied to many fields and holds special relevance to ESOL. Eckert and McConnell-Ginet (1992) define communities of practice as:

> An aggregate of people who come together around mutual engagement in an endeavour. Ways of doing things, ways of talking, beliefs, values, power relationships – in short practices – emerge in the course of this mutual endeavour. As a social construct, a community of practice is different from the traditional community, primarily because it is defined simultaneously by its membership and by the practice in which that membership engages.

Becoming a member of particular communities of practice is therefore a key element of learning – essentially it is a 'licence to participate' in a particular endeavour.

TASK 4.3

What 'communities of practice' do you belong to? What 'communities of practice' do you think your ESOL learners might belong to, or aspire to belong to?

Clearly, the ESOL class itself may be one of the most important communities of practice to which a learner may feel they belong. Indeed, in many cases, it may be the only one in which they can use English, or even the only group of any sort that they have access to:

> For many learners the classroom is their main reference group, sometimes the most motivating aspect of their lives – what helps them to get up in the morning.
>
> (Roberts et al. 2004: 14)

> We wake up I the morning and we don't know where to go, sometimes we spend the whole day at home
>
> (Learner cited in Roberts et al. 2004: 30)

It is therefore worth analysing what exactly this community of practice is, and what is involved in belonging to it. The quote from Eckert and McConnell-Ginet (1992) above talked about 'ways of doing things, ways of talking, beliefs, values, power relationships' – these undoubtedly exist in ESOL classrooms.

TASK 4.4

What 'ways of doing things, ways of talking, beliefs, values and power relationships' can you identify as being a part of ESOL classroom practices? Where might difficulties lie for ESOL learners?

COMMENT 4.4

> In a language class, the classroom group together not only freshly evolves the new language (the content of lessons), but also together jointly constructs the lessons (the social procedures of teaching and learning)
>
> (Breen 2001: 132)

> ESOL classes are 'not only a vital learning environment but also an important social space which is enriched by the resources and life experience, informal support systems and desire to learn that ... learners and their teacher bring to it
>
> (Roberts et al 2004: 31)

1 *Ways of doing things*: ESOL methodology could be highlighted here: pairwork, groupwork, 'even' participation, are typically features of classroom life that learners encounter and to which they will have greater or lesser difficulty adapting. Some learners may find it difficult

to adjust to some classroom methods because of personality factors (they may be shy) or learning style factors (they may favour lots of auditory input over writing; and find using a textbook quite difficult), or because of their past educational experiences. Some learners (and teachers) will have experienced classrooms as places where teachers talk and learners listen and write; they may consequently find pairwork very challenging indeed). Some learners may not have experienced classrooms at all.

2   *Ways of talking*: Again, ESOL classrooms typically involve a lot of cooperative talking; and 'talk is work' here too (Roberts et al. 2004). Levels of formality may present challenges (for instance, does the teacher nominate learners to speak or do they 'self-select'? Do learners raise hands if they wish to speak? How are learners expected to speak to each other? Is L1 permitted?).

3   *Beliefs and values*: This is potentially one of the most difficult areas. ESOL learners tend to come from a great diversity of backgrounds – many may find this diversity difficult in itself. It is common to have learners from countries nominally in conflict sharing the same class. In addition, many of the 'values' of an ESOL class are currently 'imposed' in some sense: the 'liberal' values of the West, which manifest themselves in the classroom in the form of equal opportunities, for example, or concepts like 'tolerance', are enshrined in legislation and the general practices of educational institutions. These values may conflict with learners' own belief systems. Teachers have a very difficult job here to negotiate some sort of shared classroom values.

4   *Power relationships*: This is another potentially difficult area. Learners may expect particular power relationships between themselves and the teacher. They may for instance expect every mistake they make to be corrected, and to be explicitly told how to perform every single task they undertake. Learners may challenge power relationships that do not seem appropriate to them; ESOL teachers often find it difficult to devolve responsibility to learners, who may wish for a greater level of direction than current language-teaching ideologies, such as 'learner-centredness', or 'self-correction', promote. Learners may find the teacher's ethnicity or gender problematic; they may not be used to what they perceive as being in a subordinate position to a woman, or they may regard a non-white teacher as not being a speaker of 'real' English.

Equally, power relationships between learners may be problematic – issues of ethnicity and gender may again come to the fore here. Losey's (1995) study showed how Mexican-American males participated in an adult literacy class on an equal basis with Anglo-American males: however, though they comprised nearly half the class, Mexican-American females hardly participated at all. Losey concludes that they were effectively powerless – positioned as a 'double minority' in terms of both ethnicity and gender.

> The transformation of a diverse group of individuals into a community who 'come together around mutual engagement in an endeavour' – in this case language learning – is clearly not an overnight affair, but a more drawn-out process that can take more or less time according to context and the individuals involved. It does seem though, that learners feel that they have an important stake in what 'ways of doing things, ways of talking, beliefs, values, power relationships' eventually come to exist in their classes, so explicit discussion of these may help: for instance, Montse, a Spanish learner of English cited by Block (2003), complains about the irregular attendance patterns of her class-mates – she feels this has slowed down the development of a 'real' class that would learn faster and more effectively: 'I'd rather have a lesson with five people maximum, but always the same ... the thing is is that if it is a group of nine, ideally everyone should be there. I don't know why but the people seem more disconnected ...' (Montse, quoted in Block 2003: 111).

It is important for ESOL teachers to try to discover what communities of practice their learner encounter, belong to or aspire to belonging to. Teachers will also have to be aware of what kind of language and what kind of practices occur in such communities; this will in turn highlight language areas that would benefit from classroom work:

> Understanding good language learning requires attention to social practices in the contexts in which individuals learn L2s. As well, we have argued for the importance of examining the ways in which learners exercise their agency in forming and reforming their identities in those contexts. We see this dual focus as necessary to understand good language learning.
>
> (Norton and Toohey 2001: 318)

'Input' – the raw 'stuff' of language learning

Stephen Krashen (1976) famously proposed that 'input' of the target language was a *necessary condition* for language learning, though not the only one. It seems to be a matter of commonsense that you won't learn a language unless you are exposed to it in some way, whether by hearing it spoken or by reading it. Although Krashen's theories have now been generally rejected or superseded, 'input' remains a widely used concept in SLA. He is today, according to Block (2003: 94), 'more respected for putting input on the research agenda in SLA than he is for providing a workable theory of SLA'. 'Input' is also an important part of what has come to be known as the *Input–Interaction–Output* (IIO) model of SLA. There are several different versions of this, but it is perhaps the single most 'mainstream' framework for accounts of SLA (Block 2003).

It is therefore pertinent to ask what 'input' do ESOL learners receive – what language are they exposed to?

TASK 4.5

Make a list of all the different sources of English your ESOL learners might be exposed to during the course of a single day.

COMMENT 4.5

Unlike learners in a 'foreign-' language learning setting, ESOL learners will probably encounter the language they are trying to learn throughout their daily life. Even very low-level learners might:

- Listen to radio/TV.
- Receive a variety of texts in English in the post (e.g. junk mail, official letters, bills).
- Look at magazines or newspapers.
- Overhear conversations in shops, at bus stops.
- Engage in transactions in English in various settings.
- Browse the Internet.
- Read billboards and other advertisements.
- Talk to their classmates before and after class.
- Listen to their children using English.
- Speak to neighbours.

They will consequently be exposed to far more English than just that which they encounter during their language class. In addition, learners who are beyond beginner level will very likely be engaging in conversations in English; both *transactional* – where the primary communicative objective is to get something done (e.g. in shops) – and *interractional* – where the primary communicative objective is to maintain social relationships (e.g. informal conversation with neighbours). This will expose them to many varieties of English (e.g. local dialects, 'non-native' English), some of which are discussed below.

Obviously, learners will be able to make more sense of some chunks of this input than others, and it is the input that is in some sense 'comprehensible' which is of most use to learners. This doesn't mean that they have to make sense of *all* of it, or understand it completely – but they have to be able to somehow work on this input to make meaning, or to use it as a basis for learning (for example, by noticing grammatical or lexical or phonological elements of it). Input, on this account, needs to be comprehensible to be of value: so, two immediate implications for classroom practice are that:

1   Teachers can help learners make sense of texts which they might encounter in their daily lives, and which might be useful to them, by selecting such

texts for analysis and use in the classroom – or by asking learners to bring in examples of such texts (spoken or written).

2   Teachers can set learning tasks which help learners to 'notice' key elements of such texts – which in effect helps turn 'raw' input into comprehensible input. Thus, for ESOL learners, it is generally better to set *tasks* graded to the learners' level than to grade (or oversimplify) the *text* itself. (For instance, with lower level learners, gas bills – which are quite complex texts – might be used with tasks set to identify key numbers; most of the other language in the text could be ignored).

TASK 4.6

Look at the excerpt below from the Jamaican folksong, *Evenin' Time*. What grammatical, phonological and lexical features of Jamaican English might you notice?

> Come Miss Claire
> Tek de bankra off yu head mi dear,
> Evening breeze a blow,
> Come dis way Miss Flo.
>
> Evenin' time,
> Work is over now is evenin' time,
> Wih deh walk pon mountain,
> Deh walk pan mountain,
> Deh walk pan mountain side.
>
> Meck we cook wih bickle pan dih way,
> Meck wih eat an sing,
> Dance an play ring ding
> Pan dih mountain side.

(taken from www.jamaicans.com)

COMMENT 4.6

You might have noticed the following:

1   Grammar:
   • 'a blow' similar to 'is blowing'.
   • 'a' marks 'presentness'.
   • 'yu' = possessive 'your'.
2   Phonology:
   • 'th' sound becomes /d/.

- Some final consonants dropped ('evenin' 'an').

3   Lexis:
- spelling is not always consistent (e.g. 'pon/pan', 'we/wih') perhaps a result of trying to accurately represent phonological differences.
- We can deduce that 'bankra' and 'bickle' are nouns, without knowing meaning (a 'bankra' is a 'big basket', 'bickle' means 'food').

Of course, 'noticing' features of Jamican English, which has great similarities to British English, is a rather different proposition to ESOL learners' ability to notice features of English when their first language is a very different one: but the 'decoding' element is the same – letting your attention be drawn to particular features, spotting patterns and making connections.

Affordance

Language learning is highly unpredictable. A common observation of ESOL teachers is that in any given lesson, what the teacher is teaching and what the learners are learning is rarely the same thing. Learners may come away from a lesson that was ostensibly all about the present perfect tense with little new understanding about it, or ability to use it, but instead with several new items of vocabulary or improved reading skills. Unsurprisly then, the term 'input' has been critiqued (by van Lier 2000, among others), as being based on a mechanistic and computational metaphor for the mind, and thus being too linear to account for the complexities of language, language learning and the mind itself. Van Lier (2000), proposes instead the term 'affordances', in other words opportunities for learners to engage with language. This may seem a trivial difference, but there is a major implication for the classroom. With the 'input' model, in planning a lesson, the teacher is, among other things, selecting texts as 'input' for the learners. This gives rise to notions such as 'target language', where particular structures, forms or patterns are designated as content for noticing and study. An affordance model is less directive; the teacher might still select texts on the basis of linguistic or other interest, but would have a lower expectation of what features of that text learners might end up noticing. This at least acknowledges some of the unpredictabilities of language learning.

As we have observed, most language teachers and language learners have anecdotes about classes in which particular items for study were presented, but in which something completely different was actually learnt. 'Affordance' suggests that the focus of a good ESOL lesson, in terms of 'target' language, can be less narrow than a traditional structural syllabus might follow (i.e. the teaching of a single 'form' in a lesson). The aim of the lesson would instead be for all the learners to encounter affordances appropriate to their individual language abilities and their idiolects. The role of the teacher is therefore to manage classroom interaction, and to provide a wide range of 'learning opportunities' (Allwright and Bailey 1991). The teacher will thus be occupied more with the 'quality of classroom life' than with the efficient teaching of particular target forms (Ivanic and Tseng 2005). This is differentiation[1] writ large, and requires that teachers have excellent language awareness and language-analysis skills, as they need to be ready and able to help learners make the most of 'affordances' as they arise.

This also fits well with the findings of the NRDC's Effective Practice in ESOL project, which described effective teachers as '*bricoleurs*' (literally, handymen) – able to use whatever was to hand to create learning opportunities, highly responsive to learners and able to plan on the spot (Baynham et al. 2007).

'Affordance' also chimes well with the haphazard and serendipitous learning opportunities that learners may have outside class, and goes some way to explaining how people learn languages in naturalistic settings. For instance, a language learner who happens to pass an advertising billboard for a theme park holiday destination, featuring graphics of wild animals and a roller-coaster along with the text, 'Wild animals and wilder rides' might notice a number of different things:

- The correspondence of lexis and images ('animal'/'rides'); this might afford an opportunity for vocabulary acquisition.
- The comparative 'er' form of 'wilder'; this might afford some raised awareness or consolidation of comparative structures.
- Adjective/noun word order.
- The incomplete sentence structure: for an advanced learner this might afford an opportunity to reflect on or further notice how common such elided forms (where part of a sentence or phrase is deliberately omitted – here: 'there are' or 'we have') are in advertising language.

'Automaticization', 'restructuring' and connectionism

Two important concepts derived from cognitive SLA theory are 'automaticization' and 'restructuring'. The first of these, 'automaticization' refers to the move from short-term memory (i.e. controlled and conscious processing) to long-term memory, so that conscious attention is no longer needed. When a piece of new language is learnt, it at first requires considerable conscious attention on the learner's part to actually use it; the learner has to make an effort to recall and think about the pronunciation, for instance, or grammatical form, or syntax, or all three. As time goes by, and with repeated use, it becomes easier and easier to use the new language and less of a conscious effort is required. Until at last, the new language is fully integrated into the learner's repertoire, and is 'automaticized'.

Restructuring is, in Block's (2003: 96) words, 'a two-way process of assimilation and accommodation ... the incorporation of the new ... [and] the destabilisation and eventual reforming of old knowledge'. This recognizes the fundamentally cyclical nature of language learning. That is, the need for teachers and learners to regularly revisit items of language in order to help learners achieve a fuller understanding of them. It is why, typically, grammatical forms such as tenses are taught not once, 'all in one go', but are revisited many times over. ESOL teaching materials often present just one use or function of a grammatical form at a time – for example the use of the present perfect to talk about experiences – 'I've been to Quito'. The learner will later go on to discover other uses for this form such as talking about present results/effects of past events – 'Someone's spilt coffee all over the rug – it's ruined!') and will 'restructure' their understanding of it.

So, on the one hand, teachers can help learners with the move from conscious to unconscious processing (automaticization) by providing regular analysis and practice of relevant items of lexis, grammar and phonology. The classroom is an ideal place for this, providing the space for both analysis and repetition in a way that the real contexts of language use in the outside world don't. On the other hand, given the exposure of many ESOL learners to English(es) outside the classroom, it is important to select linguistic items for this kind of treatment with an eye on their usefulness and frequency in the 'outside world'. For instance, it may be useful for ESOL learners to pay particular attention to lexical chunks of the kind they might encounter or use in their daily lives. For instance, it might be useful to analyse the following examples of language used to talk about changing plans, or 'hedge', in social situations and teach them as lexical chunks with a characterisitic structure:

- I was intending to go to the library, but I'm not sure if I've time now.
- I was planning to get a little work done, but I'd love to go for a coffee!
- I was hoping to get one in blue or black, but if you've only got silver …

I was intending/planning/hoping to + infinitive (+ clause) *but* + clause

In any case, the twin concepts of automaticization and restructuring suggest that teachers should divide their time between helping learners pay attention to linguistic items in conscious study, and providing opportunities for practice which help learners 'automaticize' their language use. These linguistic items should be contextualized in ways which reflect the way they are likely to be used by learners in the real world.

However, a view of learning which only focuses on these cognitive processes is a very narrow one; as we indicated in relation to 'input' above, it follows an essentially mechanistic and computational metaphor. There are also some similarities with behaviourism. It is thus no surprise to note that some of the favourite teaching techniques of a behaviourist approach also seem to fit approaches which try to establish automaticization of information processing: oral drilling; 'lockstep staging' – where all of the class are doing the same thing at the same time in a tightly controlled series of steps; intense repetition and highly controlled practice of linguistic items.

A less linear account of language learning is provided by connectionist theories: here, learning a language – or learning anything – is not seen as the sequential acquisition of a set of rules, but as a process of constant restructuring. The trajectory of a learner's developing interlanguage is influenced by many interacting factors; progress and backsliding in equal and unpredictable measures is the norm rather than the exception. There is also interaction between the language forms in a learner's system; when a learner starts to learn a new form, formerly 'mastered' forms may become destabilized. Likewise, seeing a new 'rule' in a new context can temporarily destabilize the learner's understanding of that rule.

TASK 4.7

Many English-language teaching coursebooks for beginner to intermediate learners present the following typical uses of 'will':

- To talk about the future.
- To make predictions, promises, threats and offers.

How do you think a learner makes sense of the following use of 'will' when they first come across a sentence like the one below?

If you come to college by bus you will have noticed the police roadblocks on Gliddon Avenue this morning.

COMMENT 4.7

At first sight this is quite destabilizing. The sentence contains no future reference and is in fact about past time, which appears to contradict the typical use of 'will' for future time. However, on closer analysis, a learner may come to see that the utterance does fit with the use of 'will' for predictions; odd though it may seem at first, this sentence is in fact a prediction about past time, about the unknown, to the speaker, but guessable experiences of the addressee. The learner, in coming to understand this, will experience some 'restructuring' of their concepts of 'will' and of what is meant by 'prediction'. (For an excellent, and fuller, analysis of this, see *The English Verb* (1997) by Michael Lewis.)

A broadly connectionist view of language acquisition may thus explain why learners learn different things from the language they are exposed to; different learners will make different connections depending on the sum of all their language experiences and exposure, both within and without the classroom. And as 'constant restructuring' is by definition an ongoing process, with the raw clay of language constantly being reshaped and reinterpreted as the learner tries to make sense and meaning, there is also great benefit in teachers explicitly linking learners' experiences of language in the classroom with their 'outside' exposure to it.

There is also a clear link to the notion of 'affordances', discussed above. Teachers, therefore, need to be casting their nets quite widely in order to provide learners with the maximum possible opportunities for learning – and this may mean conflicts with a fixed curriculum: 'Much of the language visible in ... classrooms cannot be neatly tied to curricular objectives. It cannot be dismissed as incidental, since it assumes it is a sideline to the main project; the ordered acquisition of language' (Roberts et al. 2004: 14).

Accommodation theory

Bremer et al. (1996) found that when ESOL learners have opportunities to talk to native speakers they do a disproportionate amount of the conversational work in terms of maintaining mutual understanding; the onus appeared to be on them, not the 'native speakers', to keep the interaction on track. Accommodation theory may go some way to explaining these difficulties and may also account for some phenomena in language use of particular relevance to ESOL learners. During any interaction, language users are constantly adjusting elements of grammar, lexis and phonology to 'accommodate' towards, or away from, their interlocutor(s). This is known as convergence or divergence. Speakers converge when they want to show solidarity with, or sympathy towards, their audience. The former British Prime Minister, Tony Blair, often varied his pronunciation. Speaking in formal situations, his accent could broadly be described as standard 'Southern' middle or upper-middle class, betraying his public-school background. But in settings perceived as more informal because of the nature of the audience, such as an appearance on a TV chat show, or during a speech to factory workers, he frequently deviated towards a more lower-middle-class pronunciation common around London called 'Estuary', using glottal stops and dropping consonants (Sylvester 1998). What we don't know is whether this convergence towards his perceived audience was unconscious or deliberate on his part, or indeed whether, as with many politicians, he was coached in it.

Divergence, on the other hand, occurs when speakers wish to create some social distance between themselves and the audience – as in the example of factory workers using stronger vernacular forms when in the presence of temporary learner vacation workers, whom they perceived as being 'posh' (Holmes 2001). Divergence can be a matter of receptiveness in interaction as much as of production. Studies of interaction between speakers of related languages (such as Czech and Slovak, or Swedish and Danish) have consistently found that although the languages appear to be mutually intelligible, speakers of the language of the economically *richer* nation will more regularly claim not to understand speaker of the language of the *poorer* nation.

TASK 4.8

1   Think of some instances when you have converged or diverged from other speakers, or when they have converged with or diverged from you – can you explain these accommodations?
2   In what ways do you think ESOL learners might experience convergence and divergence?

COMMENT 4.8

The first point to make here is that ESOL learners may not always realize when their interlocutors are diverging or converging, or, just as any language user, when they themselves are doing the same. They will also be likely to attribute conversational breakdown to their own 'failures'. ESOL learners are quite likely to encounter divergence in relation to their 'foreign' pronunciation; interlocutors may simply make very limited efforts to understand or claim not to understand at all. In extreme cases interlocutors may understand very well, but refuse to acknowledge this. In such situations, learners are likely to blame their own pronunciation, rather than seeing that the real issue, the factor that is actually causing the divergence, is their perceived 'foreignness', which may have been identified by their dress or skin colour as much as by their pronunciation.

ESOL learners are quite likely to converge towards the pronunciation of those they interract with, or to the variety of language they hear most around them. This may have important implications; most learners will not be at the stage of learning where they can necessarily recognize the social register of language they hear. They may therefore converge towards highly vernacular, informal pronunciations without recognizing these as such. Many ESOL teachers will have encountered learners who have in this way acquired forms such as 'innit?' but who do not necessarily appreciate the social implications of the use of such forms and may consequently use them in quite formal and inappropriate situations. This is not to suggest that such forms or vernacular pronunciations are at all 'wrong', but ESOL teachers clearly have an important role in helping learners to recognize the relationships between language variety and context, and to be self-aware in terms of the language they are using.

Identity

SLA researchers and theorists who have taken what Block calls the 'social turn', in that they regard social factors as legitimate (and crucial) objects of study, are forced to considerations of *identity*. In particular, studies of literacy acquisition have high-lighted how learners may encounter conflicts of identity. Brian Street (1995) critiques views that regard language and literacy as merely *functional* or a set of 'skills' which can be unproblematically taught or given to those who lack them. Such a view, he suggests, fails to recognize the true importance and centrality of language and literacy practices in people's lives, and hides the way non-mainstream (or foreign) language and literacy practices are marginalized by 'dominant' ones. The ideological nature of dominant language and literacy practices is therefore disguised.

As learners acquire new literacy or language practices, they may find conflicts with their existing practices: for example, a prestige literacy practice in Arabic relates to reading from the Koran, often in small groups, with particular heed being paid to precise interpretation of syntax and lexis. This may involve very detailed reading of individual sentences or sections, interspersed with discussions of their meaning. In an ESOL context, though, learners may encounter very different yet nevertheless prestige literacy practices – such as reading of academic or 'valued' text, perhaps in prepara-tion for an exam such as IELTs. Here learners will be told they need to skim and scan,[2] skills which both place a very high premium on *speed*. This requires, or produces, a very different orientation towards the text itself – and a learner who has acquired prestige literacy practices in their first language such as the example above, may find it difficult to approach an evidently 'valued' text in such an apparently contradictory way. Furthermore, such a learner may feel very disoriented and destabilized – this is not just a new 'skill' to acquire, it is a 'skill' that appears to call into question everything they have already learnt, and their self-image as a 'literate' person.

Scott Thornbury (2005) relates an encounter with a learner of his outside the class in downtown Cairo. The conversation ran as follows:

ST: Hey, Hamdi, where are you going?

Hamdi: I go to sporting club.

ST   [*Unable to resist a chance to correct*] Go?

Hamdi   [*Impatiently*] Oh, go, going, went!

He then asks how we should interpret Hamdi's 'outburst', offering five possibilities, reproduced below:

1   'Correction is for classrooms – the street is for communication!'

2   'You understood what I meant, so why the correction?'

3 . 'Search me. I still don't know the difference between go/going/went'

4   'Don't expect me to say what I mean and get it right at the same time!'

5   All of the above.

(Thornbury 2005: 31)

Interestingly, Thornbury doesn't question the appropriacy of the use of *English* in downtown Cairo in the first place; he doesn't mention whether he could speak Egyptian Arabic or not, and perhaps Hamdi, rightly or wrongly, was under the impression that Thornbury couldn't. He doesn't address identity or how the act of correction effectively positions Hamdi as a 'learner' even though this is outside the usual learning context. Hamdi might certainly have wanted to resist such positioning; he might regard himself as anything but a learner in such a context. Certainly, he might feel that if the situation merits teacher–learner positioning at all, it is Thornbury who is better qualified to adopt the *learner* role: after all, Thornbury is the foreigner, far less experienced in Egyptian life than he.

Many UK ESOL learners have experiences similar to Hamdi's; they find that they are positioned as 'learners' not just in the classroom, but in many aspects of their daily lives. Yet in many cases, such 'learners' may be highly experienced, highly qualified individuals; they may also find it rather troubling that many of their 'correctors' outside of the classroom appear to be less experienced or less qualified than themselves: 'Teaching and learning processes are different in classrooms where talk is work. Theories of language, teaching and learning are most responsive to learners when the significance of social relations and social identities is understood' (Roberts et al. 2004:16). It is important to bring learners' social relations and social identities into classroom practice. The most obvious way to do this is by allowing learners to talk about themselves and their own lives, and by providing them with opportunities to do so. Tasks from published materials, or from coursebooks can be *personalized* so that they address learners' own contexts more directly: 'The value of creating spaces for learners to talk about their lives relates directly to their language learning. Learning another language is partly about taking on a new voice, a new set of identities. However, it is also about making the new language real and meaningful to yourself and your life' (Roberts et al. 2004: 36). And, of course, teachers' identities are relevant here too: 'Adult educators need not only to be aware of the belief structures underlying their own philosophies or perspectives on teaching, but also to reflect on how their pedagogical "identities" are constructed in the social and political contexts in which they work' (Morton et al. 2006: 13).

Appropriation

'Appropriation' has usually been used in SLA theory to mean the process by which learners eventually bring new elements of knowledge and language skills into their consciousness. However, as Block (2003) points out, this is a very reduced sense of the original term, used in sociocultural theory, which Wertsch (1998: 53) defines as meaning 'to bring something into oneself, or to make something one's own ... taking something that belongs to others and making it one's own'.

Block describes appropriation as, 'not just the passing of the external to the internal; it is the meeting of the external and the internal to form a synthesised new state' (Block 2003: 103). This fits well with the links noted above between language and identity, and gives some sense of the process through which the emergent identities of language learners may be formed.

There is also something here of a parallel with the 'immigrant experience'; the 'external', the immigrant, meeting the 'internal' of the new country. UK ESOL learners then, may want to make English 'their own' as well as just learn or use it. They may want to 'appropriate' parts of English language and culture, and identity, for themselves: this may be part of their journey towards becoming one deemed 'worthy to speak and listen'.

Conclusions

It seems, then, that whilst SLA researchers and theorists try to find ways of bringing cognitivist and interactionist accounts of language learning together with social analyses, ESOL practitioners have to find ways of incorporating learners' complex and developing identities and their various social contexts into classroom practice. This involves ongoing processes of negotiation, discovery and accommodation. In particular, it means that ESOL practitioners have to find ways to mediate between:

- learners' existing linguistic resources and repertoires and their uses of English;

- literacy and language practices in learners' first/other languages, and literacy and language practices in English;
- learners' developing identities and their social positioning.

It also means that, at different stages of the teaching and learning process, teachers (and learners) will have different orientations to the subject matter, language, that they are addressing. They will, at different times, have a greater or lesser interest in,

- *Social and functional aspects of language use*: for instance, politeness routines or how cultural allegiances are expressed in language, and the social and interpersonal meanings created in interactions. These will help learners to focus on how they can 'do' things with language in the real social world, and how they can express and develop identities in the new language.
- *Analyses of form* (textual, grammatical, lexical and phonological): to help learners develop or restructure their understandings of the forms of language.
- Fluency: providing opportunities to automaticize language use, and to 'appropriate' the new language:

'A model of second language socialisation is more appropriate than second language acquisition in that it assumes that language is developed through social relationships and prepares learners for communicating in a community of practice. However, even this model cannot fully account for the different goals and identities which participating in complex urban environments entails (Kramsch 2002).

(Roberts et al. 2004: 14)

Notes

1   See Chapter 7 for discussion of differentiation.
2   See Chapter 5 for discussion of these reading skills.

Part 2

Teaching and learning ESOL

5 The spoken language

Anne Paton

Introduction

TASK 5.1

One of your learners, Ahmed, tells you that the language he is learning in class is not what he hears 'in the street'. He is a single Algerian man in his late twenties, who has been living in the same South-Coast town since he arrived in the UK three years ago. He was recently granted refugee status and is currently doing occasional work for a building firm whilst looking for a more permanent job. He attends a twice-weekly evening class, and is studying at Entry Level 3 of the *Adult ESOL Core Curriculum*.

What might be the reasons for Ahmed's perception? As his teacher, how do you respond?

COMMENT 5.1

There are several possible reasons for Ahmed's perception. One is that, as he assimilates into the local community, he is hearing and acquiring a language variety whose grammar and vocabulary differs in some respects from the one he has been learning formally in class.

Then there is the related issue of accent: the pronunciation Ahmed hears on the tapes his class is using, and perhaps the accent modelled by the teacher, may differ in significant aspects from local pronunciation, as will the accents of his fellow ESOL learners.

Another possibility is that what Ahmed hears in the street is not what is actually said. Incomplete understanding of the sound system of English can lead to mis-hearing, resulting in incorrect conclusions being drawn about natural language usage. For example, many learners do not hear the contracted form of the auxiliary verb '*am*' in a sentence like '*I'm* living at a friend's at the moment' so that when they attempt to use this verb form themselves they produce 'I living'.

On the other hand, Ahmed may be politely informing the teacher of a perceived lack of realism in the language taught and practised in the classroom.

Most people who have studied a language have been required to produce sentences which are improbable, illogical or untrue. This practice can be demotivating because it takes no account of the fact that the purpose of language is to communicate meaning.

All language teachers need to realize the importance of practising language in a way that mirrors natural usage and communicates something which is (a) true and (b) worth saying; we will return to this subject later in this chapter.

Varieties of English

In this book we use the term 'language variety' to refer to different ways of speaking the same language (influenced by geography, social class, age group and so on), to avoid the strong associations with regional varieties of language which the word 'dialect' has for many people.

Task 5.2

Consider the questions below:

- What do you understand by 'Standard English?'
- What other varieties are spoken in your local area?
- Do you think Standard English should be taught in the classroom or is there an argument for teaching another variety?

Standard English

Standard language can be defined as: 'That variety of language considered by its speakers to be most appropriate in formal or educational contexts' (Trask 1999). Trask goes on to point out that there are varieties that differ between regions but also differences between different social groups within the same community. For this reason sociolinguists speak of Englishes in the plural. However, one of these Englishes, Standard English, has special status. This is the variety associated with education, broadcasting and publications.

There are, of course, a number of standard Englishes across the world in speech communities where English is used as a lingua franca, such as in West Africa, as well as those where it is the principal language, such as in the UK or Australia. The speech of many ESOL learners is influenced by one of these as well as by standard and non-standard British varieties.

'Standard English' is the variety which most teachers of ESOL aim to approximate to in the classroom, even if they also speak another variety. Many ESOL learners who are aware of the high status associated with Standard English and/or of its wider currency will be happy with this situation. They may speak a prestige language or language variety as their L1 and want to do the same in English. Some may not feel a strong affiliation to their local area or community and, if they have acquired elements of a local variety (by learning in a naturalistic context), they may be keen to modify it towards a more standard variety of English, or to be able to do so when they choose. This skill is part of the repertoire of competent L1 speakers, who vary the way they speak according to the social context. ESOL learners already have this ability in their first language and indeed many habitually switch not only between language varieties but between actual languages in their country of origin. They will find it useful to develop the same skill in English.

However, some learners may prefer to learn the variety spoken by a social group to which they belong, or want to belong. They may have married a person who speaks it, have strong affiliations with a community that uses it, or work in a context where it is widely used. In any case, they will almost certainly acquire elements of that variety through being exposed to it. So whilst teachers need to acknowledge the role of Standard English in society and the value it might have for learners, we also need to recognize the role and value of other varieties, particularly those spoken by learners' friends, workmates or families.

Differences between Standard English and other varieties need to be dealt with sensitively, especially when giving feedback to learners on the accuracy of their speech. 'We done that last week', may be an accurate reproduction of the past tense form used by most of the people someone, such as Ahmed (see Task 1), meets in his or her day-to-day life; this use of 'done' is a feature of many language varieties occurring in British urban areas. If we correct his use of 'done' to the standard 'did' without acknowledging local usage, he may justly feel that a different (and perhaps less real?) kind of English is being taught in class. Ahmed needs to be aware that 'done' is an accepted past tense form in the local variety of English, but not in Standard spoken or written English. With this knowledge he is in a better position to make informed choices.

The terminology used in discussions of choices relating to language should recognize the validity of different varieties. In this book we use the term non-standard as, unlike the term 'sub-standard' (also widely used) it avoids any implication that other varieties are inferior, and we recommend that ESOL teachers do likewise.

Learners will encounter different regional and age-related varieties in their day-to-day life. Ahmed, for example, meets speakers of Indian English at Muslim community events and in the ethnic food stores where he buys the ingredients he needs to make North-African dishes. When he mixes with young British people at work or in his leisure time, he encounters various types of youth slang and will be excluded from social contact with certain groups if he does not understand their speech. So whatever variety he is acquiring himself, he needs to understand a range of others. This has implications for the teacher's choice of listening material, which should not be restricted to dialogues and monologues in standard British English. However, varieties do not usually differ enough from each other to make mutual comprehension a serious problem. It is accents which can be more problematic.

Language variety and accent

Some linguists, although not all, regard accent as an aspect of language variety or dialect, and obviously there is a strong relationship between the two: a person who speaks a Welsh variety of English is likely to have a Welsh accent. However, the converse does not always apply; many people with relatively marked regional accents use the grammar and vocabulary of Standard English some or all of the time.

Whether or not we regard accent as an element of language variety or dialect is not really important for language teachers. What is important is to recognize its significance for our sense of identity. A person's accent allows conclusions to be drawn, or at least informed guesses to be made, about their social background, age group and, except in the case of regionally neutral accents, the geographical area they are from. The regionally neutral accent (or group of accents) in Britain used to be known as BBC English and is now more commonly termed Received Pronunciation (RP).

Attitudes to regional accents have changed over time, as has the status of RP, now spoken only by a very small minority of L1 speakers estimated at something like 3 per cent. Regional accents and modified forms of RP such as 'Estuary English' are heard on the BBC and in other social contexts where RP might in the past have been more widely used than now. Even so, RP is still regarded as a norm for describing the pronunciation of British English. Most language learning and teaching materials for people wishing to learn British English are based on it, as are the phonemic transcriptions in British dictionaries.

A minority accent which is on the decline may not be a suitable model for many of our UK ESOL learners to aim at, particularly as most teachers do not speak RP. We will go on to consider what a realistic aim is, but first we need to look at some of the reasons why 'native-like' pronunciation of any kind, and not just RP, may not be an appropriate goal for learners.

Accent and identity

TASK 5.3

Do you think your own accent has changed much during your life? If so, what were the reasons for the changes?

Imagine you have settled permanently in another country. How 'native-like' would you hope for your accent to become, and why? (If you came from another country to settle in the UK you will not have to imagine anything!)

COMMENT 5.3

When a person is geographically or socially mobile their accent is likely to change, but it is noticeable that some people's accents change more readily and easily than others. Most of us know somebody who has moved from one area of the country to another and seems to have retained pretty much the accent that they always had, although of course these perceptions are subjective. Someone who lives in London but who has an accent which sounds 'Northern' to Londoners, might be teased about their 'Cockney' accent when they visit their old friends and family in Lancashire (and again, on their return, by their London-born children who find that Lancashire elements of their pronunciation have become more noticeable as a result of their trip).

It used to be assumed that all language learners aspired, or ought to aspire, to the accent of an L1 speaker, and some enthusiastic language learners certainly do. Their goal of speaking the language 'perfectly' includes mastery of its pronunciation system to the extent that they are indistinguishable from an L1 speaker. But this is by no means the goal of all learners. This may be because the learner's accent expresses their sense of identity, or because he or she is unaware of differences between the way he or she speaks and the target accent (which for many ESOL learners will not be RP). What's more some highly motivated learners with a keen ear for language often feel they would prefer not to lose their 'foreign' accent completely when speaking another language, even if that were possible. To do so might feel like denying a part of their identity.

In any case, for most people beyond the age of puberty the acquisition of a completely 'native-like' accent is not a realistic aim. Accordingly, we and our learners might as well recognize this limitation and set ourselves an achievable goal: an accent which is easily understood in the context(s) in which the speaker is operating. Some learners will want to go beyond this, but we can help those individuals to improve without setting such a high standard for the group as a whole that most learners will fail to achieve it.

Comfortable intelligibility

In thinking about realistic goals regarding pronunciation, we need to consider a number of factors influencing the accent any one learner is likely to develop. One of these will, of course, be the accent which learners carry over from the other language(s) they speak. Ahmed's English pronunciation, for instance, will be affected by the sound systems of both Arabic and French, as he speaks both languages. Other influences will be the teacher's accent, and local accents, which may not be the same as the teacher's. Then there are all the contexts in which the learner has heard and used English in the past, including classrooms elsewhere in the world. Well-educated Congolese learners, for example, will probably have been taught an African variety rather than Standard British or American, although they may also have acquired elements of other varieties as a result of influences such as the media.

In summary, then, every learner has a different starting point, but all can share the goal of being easily understood without imposing a lot of strain on the listener. This goal is often known as '*comfortable intelligibility*'. Of course, different listeners vary in how intelligible they find any individual's way of speaking. ESOL teachers, in particular, accustomed to hearing and interpreting different foreign accents, may find them more 'comfortably intelligible' than other people do. But although a subjective notion, 'comfortable intelligibility' is at least an idea we and our learners can understand and work with, so the next question we need to ask ourselves is this: what are the aspects of pronunciation which make a person's speech intelligible or otherwise?

Aspects of pronunciation

The branch of linguistics concerned with the study of sound systems of languages is called phonology. It is distinct from phonetics, the science which studies and describes human soundmaking in general, especially speech sounds. It is phonology which informs our practice when we teach pronunciation.

The main areas which are important for intelligibility are: *phonemes* (the basic sound units, both consonants and vowels); *stress* (the way some syllables are more prominent than other syllables within a word or a sentence); and *intonation*, the way the pitch of our voice varies as we speak.

An additional area which is particularly important for understanding spoken English, particularly L1 speakers, is *connected speech*. Individual words within a stream of language are not pronounced as they would be in isolation. Both vowel and consonant sounds in a word can be influenced by the other words surrounding them, and the boundaries between words are not clear (this applies to RP as well as to other accents, although many L1 speakers are not aware of it). It can be very difficult for listeners to decode a continuous stream of language, and this is why learners often observe that 'English people speak too fast'.

Word stress

It is difficult to overestimate the importance for comprehensibility of word stress. When words are misheard it is often because the L2 speaker has emphasized the wrong syllable. We need to ensure that we teach the stress pattern of new lexis (whether individual words or expressions) and train learners (a) to notice these patterns and (b) to record them in their notebooks, along with meanings and spellings. Both L1 and L2 speakers of English vary in their ability to perceive stress. If you find it difficult, make sure you understand how stress is marked in dictionaries and check it when preparing to introduce new lexis.

For a syllable to be heard as stressed, the syllables around it need to be unstressed, and the vowel sound in some syllables will be reduced. For example, in the word 'tomorrow', the middle syllable is stressed, the first syllable is reduced to the sound known as '*schwa*' whose phonemic symbol is / ə / and the final syllable is unstressed. In some accents, the final syllable of tomorrow is also reduced to a *schwa*, though not in RP.

Learners can be encouraged from the very beginning to produce schwa sounds as appropriate, and to notice them when listening for phonological detail. Those who are confident with Roman script often find it useful to learn the phonemic symbol for the sound.

Sentence stress

We also use stress to emphasize the most important content words when we are speaking. For example, in the suggestion 'Fancy a cup of tea?' the main, or *primary,* stress will be on 'tea'. On the other hand, the words 'a' and 'of', which do not carry lexical meaning, are pronounced with a reduced vowel sound (in both cases the sound is *'schwa'*).

Stressed and unstressed words combine in speech to give English its character-istic rhythm. When a person speaks English with an unfamiliar rhythm carried over from their first language, it imposes a strain on the listener. Teachers therefore need to work hard on sentence stress and rhythm. The key to this, as with all pronunciation work, is guiding learners to hear and recognize stress patterns before attempting to produce them. It follows that all materials used to present spoken English, such as recorded dialogues, should present realistic models of stress and rhythm.

It is also important that teachers do not distort the natural stress patterns of English in an effort to be more easily understood by our learners. It can be hard to avoid doing this when slowing our speech down, or repeating the same phrase many times, so teachers need to practise speaking slowly but naturally, and keeping stress patterns consistent, when leading controlled oral practice.

Hearing stressed words is an important aid to listening for general meaning and should be practised in class. Unstressed syllables, including words of one syllable such as 'a' and 'of' in 'Do you want a cup of tea?' can be hard to hear and may need to be guessed. In fact not hearing these syllables is probably a factor in Ahmed's perception of 'street English' as being different from classroom English.

A useful technique in developing the ability to hear unstressed words is to ask learners to listen to an utterance and count the number of words. Other valuable suggestions can be found in general ELT literature dealing with pronunciation.

Phonemes

When working on specific phonemes we need to concentrate on those which (a) affect particular groups of learners and (b) are important for intelligibility. Because there is so much variation in the way vowel sounds are pronounced in different but mutually intelligible L1 accents, they are generally much less problematic for intelligibility than consonant sounds. This is the case despite the fact that English has an unusually high number of vowel phonemes and most L2 speakers of English substitute other vowel sounds for some of them.

Many of the problems learners experience with particular vowel or consonant phonemes are to do with differences between English and their L1; we will consider three important differences. The first reason is that some phonemes do not exist in the speaker's first language. Cantonese does not have the sound /v/ (as in 'van'). A Cantonese speaker will tend to substitute the voiceless /f /, as in 'fan', which does occur in Cantonese.

The second problem occurs when a speaker can make a particular sound, but is only used to making it at the beginning of a word, or only at the end (an example of this is the phoneme / /, written as 'ng', as in si*ng*ing which never occurs in initial position in English, although it does in Vietnamese).

The third problem is consonant clusters. '*Spare*' has a cluster of two consonants at the beginning, '*Spr*ing' a cluster of three. As they are very rare in Cantonese, speakers of that language find English consonant clusters problematic. Even languages which have consonant clusters do not necessarily have the same ones as English, and even when they do, the clusters may not occur in the same places. In Spanish, /sp/, /st/ and /sk/ clusters do not occur in initial position, which is why speakers of that language tend to insert an /e/ before them in English, producing 'espare' and 'espring' rather than 'spare' and 'spring'.

There are many useful and enjoyable exercises for working on phonemes, both in general coursebooks and in books about pronunciation. They can be an excellent resource if used discriminatingly and with the goal of *comfortable intelligibility* in mind.

Intonation

We use intonation to express intentions and attitudes. Variation in pitch on a single word such as 'oh' can indicate a huge range of attitudes and emotions, such as joy, rage, sarcasm, contentment, dismay, shock or resignation. We also use intonation patterns at discourse level, for example to signal that we are coming to the end of a topic, or initiating a new one.

The wrong intonation pattern can convey to a listener an attitude that the speaker did not intend. As Kenworthy (1987) points out, 'the effect of intonation can be cumulative; the misunderstandings may be minor, but if they occur constantly then they may result in judgements about the attitudes, character, ways of behaving etc of a particular speaker'. From the earliest levels on, we need to encourage learners to notice and practise intonation patterns which express the attitude they want to convey. A speaker who does not use the appropriate intonation pattern when making a request may be interpreted as demanding or brusque, even if the words used are polite.

Understanding intonation patterns is also an important listening skill, allowing us to infer the speaker's attitude. At discourse level, changes in pitch allow us to predict the way the talk is going to develop. Teachers can focus on these aspects of phonology when using taped material with their learners.

Other aspects of connected speech

We have already looked at word stress, sentence stress and intonation, all of which are aspects of connected speech (as are contracted forms such as 'I've' for 'I have').

Another aspect of connected speech is that individual sounds are not pronounced the same way as they are in isolation. Learners like Ahmed may be puzzled by repeatedly hearing phrases like 'koshukan' ('course you can') or 'festival' ('first of all').

Awareness of the various features of connected speech can be raised through detailed listening. Some teachers find that working on active production of the features just identified helps their learners to interpret them correctly when listening. It is certainly valuable to work actively on stress, intonation, unstressed vowels and contractions.

TASK 5.4

1   What aspects of your learners' speech, or of the speech of other L2 speakers with whom you come into contact, can make it difficult for people from a different language background to understand them? Consider word stress, sentence stress, individual phonemes, intonation and aspects of connected speech.

2   If you have studied another language, can you identify any aspects of its pronunciation system which are problematic for you, for example sounds which you find it difficult to produce? Have you ever found it difficult to make yourself understood because of this?

Receptive and productive skills

We do not necessarily need the same language productively (i.e. when speaking) as receptively (i.e. when listening). On railway journeys we listen to announcements at stations and on trains, but (unless employed by a railway company) we do not make them. The same distinction applies to many face-to-face contacts.

As teachers, we need to distinguish between language which learners need to use productively and language they are likely to use only receptively, and this is not always the same for all the learners in a particular group. If learners have asked for a lesson about going to the hairdresser, then the main language skills required of the client in this situation are explaining what he or she wants done to his or her hair and making light conversation on suitable topics. However, if there is someone in the class who has worked as a hairdresser and hopes to resume that career, or who is interested in training as a hairdresser, it will be useful for that person to learn language which other people in the class will only use receptively. He or she could practise appropriate ways of making requests and enquiring about past cuts or treatments. He or she also needs to learn some language for explaining procedures and recommending products. In turn, those who plan only to be clients need to *understand* at least some of the specialized lexis used by hairdressers when explaining and making recommendations, and to be able to respond by asking for more information or by politely turning down suggestions. Of course, carrying out the role of hairdresser will make many additional demands on linguistic resources, and teachers embedding ESOL within a vocational course in hairdressing would need to discuss with the subject specialist the various roles carried out and identify the language needed.

The distinction between receptive and productive skills also applies to more general aspects of language. We do not need to produce the full range of accents, language varieties and discourse types we hear when watching television, listening to the radio and talking to the people we meet, but we need to understand them. When preparing lessons and courses, and selecting and devising materials, it is important to predict what language our learners are likely to use only receptively, and what they may need to produce themselves.

The importance of purpose and context

Learners need to practise and develop the full range of listening skills necessary to function well in an English speaking society (bearing in mind their personal circumstances, needs and preferences). Included in this range will be the skills required to understand different kinds of television and radio programmes. Those learners who opt for vocational or academic study will need to listen actively to, and take notes on, talks and lectures. There is good advice in general ELT literature about approaching this type of material in a way that recognizes the purpose of listening (for example, for entertainment or for information) and develops the sub-skills needed. These include both 'top–down' and 'bottom–up' skills. Top–down skills involve using knowledge of the subject (content schemata) and the genre, or type of discourse (formal schemata) to help predict the content of a stretch of spoken discourse. Bottom–up skills are used to make sense of the sounds we hear and attribute meaning to them. An example of a 'bottom–up' skill would be picking out a string of familiar words which give us the general sense of the topic of the discourse. The top–down and bottom–up skills just identified combine to help us understand the gist of a stretch of discourse, such as a news broadcast. Listening for grammatical and phonological detail are also important skills for general language development.

Real-life speaking and listening

As we have seen, the type of language we use productively and receptively depends on our relationship with the other person and our purposes in speaking to each other. In certain situations, such as service encounters, it is possible to predict the way the conversation is likely to develop. Traditionally, ESOL teachers have spent a lot of time practising this kind of *transactional* language, where the object of the conversation is to get something done (e.g. appointment made; car fixed).

In other situations, for example conversations between friends, family or workmates, the content of the conversation is less predictable and the range of possible topics much wider. The proportions of *transactional* language and *interac-*

tional language (where the object is to develop and sustain social relationships) will vary according to the type of relationship, the social setting and the purpose of a particular conversation.

It follows that, when teaching speaking and listening, it is vital to consider the situations in which learners will be using these skills; the relationships they will have with the people they speak to; and their communicative purposes in engaging in conversation.

TASK 5.5

Think back over some conversations you have had today (this can include very short ones such as an exchange of greetings with a colleague or neighbour) and consider:

- Why you talked to the other person.
- What you talked about.
- Your respective roles in the conversation.

You might like to ask some of your learners the same question. You could also ask which conversations they found easy and comfortable, and which challenged them linguistically, and why.

Learners acquire both *transactional* and *interactional* language informally as well as in class. We need to find ways of drawing on their experience of language outside the classroom and exploiting and building on this knowledge. For example, a learner who comes into class and greets his middle-aged, female teacher with a cheery 'All right, mate?' or 'Hello darling' presents an opportunity to explore the different greetings and forms of address which learners hear and use, and to learn more about their appropriacy. Clarifying whether and in what contexts language learned naturalistically might be suitable for learners' own productive use is one of the ways we can take account of their experience of language outside the classroom.

We also need to predict the language learners will really meet as they go about their daily business, and to recognize how this may differ from dialogues designed for classroom practice. To do this, we need to analyse the way certain types of conversations typically develop, the challenges they may present and the strategies learners can employ to help them to meet these challenges. The next section will focus on the type of dialogue which might feature in a class working at Entry 1.

Real-life and scripted language

Overleaf is an example of the kind of dialogue a teacher might find in a coursebook, or write and record him- or herself, in order to focus on and practise transactional language to use at the post office with an Entry 1 group.

Dialogue 1

Customer 1: Hi. Can I have a book of first class stamps please?

Clerk: Would you like twelve or six?

Customer 1: Six please.

Clerk: Here you are. That's ... please.

Customer 1: [*Gives money*] Thanks a lot. Bye.

Clerk: Bye.

Dialogue 2

Customer 2: Hello. I'd like to send this to Manchester, please.

Clerk: Could you put it on the scale please? Do you want to send it first or second class?

Customer 2: [*Puts letter on the scale*] First, please.

Clerk: That's 65p please ...

Customer 2: [*Customer gives the money to the clerk*] Thanks very much. Bye.

Clerk: Bye.

Practising these dialogues would provide learners working towards Entry 1 level speaking and listening with some useful language. They contain some key lexis for the context, such as 'stamps', 'book' (of stamps), and 'scale'. The dialogues demonstrate the way this type of conversation might be initiated, developed and concluded. Two widely applicable ways of making requests (DfES 2001b: Sc/E1.2a) are embedded within them, as are two alternative greetings (2001b: Sd/E1.1a) and two ways of thanking (2001b: Sd/E1.1a) in a register that seems appropriate for the context.

Other language functions from the Entry 1 curriculum are also included: in both dialogues, the customer responds to a request for more information (DfES 2001b: Lr/E1.4a); in the second dialogue he or she has to respond to a request to perform an action – to put the letter on the scale (2001b: Lr/E1.4a). The lexical phrase 'here you are' is also introduced.

The dialogue also incorporates some of the phonological features of spoken English: contracted forms are used appropriately and if the dialogue is well-recorded and skilfully exploited it can provide opportunities to notice and practise the stress on important content words, and the intonation patterns appropriate for greetings, requests, thanks and leave taking (DfES 2001b: Lr/E1.2d: 'listen for phonological detail'; and Sc/E1.1a: 'use stress and intonation to make speech comprehensible to a sympathetic native speaker').

Elements of schematic knowledge are also introduced. There are references in the dialogues themselves to the fact that stamps come in books of six and 12 and can be first or second class, and that heavy letters cost more and may need to be weighed. The dialogues could also act as a stimulus for discussion about the other services which post offices offer and the way they operate.

However, not all the features of real discourse are present in the invented dialogues, as can be seen when we compare them with transcripts of two real dialogues below, taken from *Exploring Spoken English* (Carter and McCarthy 1997).

Task 5.6

Compare the invented dialogues above with the genuine transcripts below. List the features which are present in the transcripts but not in the invented dialogue.

Extract 1

Speakers

<SO1> customer: male

<SO2> assistant: female

Transcript

1<SO1>   Right, send that first class please

2<SO2>   That one wants to go first class, right we'll see if

3   it is, it's not it's not 41, it's a 60, I thought it would be, I'd be in

4   the ... 60 pence [6 secs] there we are

<SO1>   Lovely thank you

<SO2>   Okay 70 80 whoops 90 100

<SO1>   Thanks very much

<SO2 >   Thank you

Extract 2

Speakers

<SO1> customer: female

<SO2> assistant: female

Transcript

<SO1>   Can I have a second class stamp please Les

<SO2 >   You can ... there we are

<SO1>   Thank you

<SO2>   And one penny thank you

<SO1>   That's for me to spend is it?

<SO2>   That's right

<SO1>   I bought a book of ten first class when I was in town today and I've left them at home in me shopping bag

<SO2>   Have you?

<SO1>   And I've got one left

<SO2>   Oh dear [laughs]

<SO1>   Bye

<SO2>   Bye

COMMENT 5.6

You probably noticed some of the following features:

- The first conversation was purely transactional. The second, where the speakers knew each other, involved elements of interactional (personal and social) language.
- Only one of the three ways of making requests (can I have ...?) which were introduced in the dialogues written by the teacher actually appeared in the real-life dialogue.
- Use of colloquial spoken language such as: 'this one wants to go first class' meaning 'needs to'; 'lovely' to mean 'good' or 'thanks'; the use of 'there we are' rather than 'here you are' when handing something over.
- Discourse markers: 'right' is used as a way of intitiating the conversation in the first dialogue rather than a greeting such as 'hello'.
- Non-standard language: 'me shopping bag' instead of 'my'. Carter and McCarthy (1997) point out that this usage is 'common throughout the Midlands and North of England and some parts of Ireland'.
- Ellipsis: oddly, the first conversation appears to start with an imperative. This would in fact be too direct in British English and, as Carter and McCarthy (1997) point out, 'send' is probably ellipsis of a phrase such as 'I'd like to send'. Part of the utterance is being left out because the speaker and listener both know what it would have been.
- Unpredictable turns in the conversation. In the first dialogue the clerk speculates about the weight of the letter and comments on her correct guess. She counts out the change, perhaps dropping a coin (at any rate, she makes some kind of mistake and says 'whoops').
- Interactional language interspersed with transactional language, a feature of many primarily transactional conversations: the second customer makes remarks that are not directly relevant to the transaction. She also makes a joke, saying 'that's for me to spend' when she receives her 1p change, and the clerk responds. This would be less likely if she did not know the clerk, but as small local post offices are often quite friendly places, many encounters there would have an element of personal interaction.

So, although the post office dialogues written by the teacher will certainly help in giving the learners the schematic knowledge, vocabulary and functional language they need to buy stamps and post letters, in real-life transactions they may also have to deal with colloquial language, non-standard language, friendly chit-chat, unpredictable developments in the conversation and the fact that there are many ways of carrying out any one language function, such as greeting or making a request.

At low levels it is right when teaching speaking skills to concentrate on language items which sound appropriate in a range of contexts, such as 'could you ...' and 'can I ...' . But we need to bear in mind that what comes back to the E1 speaker may not be what they have encountered in a scripted dialogue and to develop strategies for dealing with this when listening for gist.

The E1 curriculum identifies some of these strategies. Even at this early level, in order to *listen for gist and respond in a face-to-face situation* (DfES 2001b: Lr/E1.1d) a learner needs to:

> understand that much of the gist can be understood from context and non-verbal signals by the speaker

- be able to signal they are listening, by using markers, e.g. yes, OK
- understand that new language may be learned from listening actively and questioning
- be able to ask for clarification and repetition

Opportunities need to be provided to develop these skills in class.

Using the language class to prepare for real-life speaking and listening

Used with Entry 1 learners, the two genuine dialogues recorded by Carter and McCarthy (1997) would be a confusing introduction to the language used at the post office counter and would in any case introduce only one way of making a request and one way of greeting. There are three expressions for thanking, but most learners working towards Entry 1 already know 'thank you' and 'thanks', and the use of 'lovely' as a way of thanking is probably not something they should aim for themselves at this stage of language development (although they may well encounter it). For active production, it might be more useful for them to focus on some other expressions for thanking, such as the more informal 'thanks a lot' (included in the dialogue written by the teacher).

Scripted dialogues

It seems, then, that in this case the two scripted dialogues will be more suitable for the teacher's purpose than the real-life ones, but perhaps they could be made even more useful with a few minor adaptations.

When planning and organizing dialogue work, you can increase the real-life relevance in the following ways:

- Look for or write dialogue which incorporates some of the features of genuine spoken discourse. For example, in the invented post office dialogues we have already looked at, the clerk could count out the change, drop some money and say 'whoops!' or 'Cheers' (now widely used in service transactions) could be included as an alternative way of thanking.
- Try to find dialogues incorporating discourse markers which allow the listener to predict the development of the conversation. For example, 'goodness, is that the time?' often signals that the speaker will soon be leaving.

- Write or look for dialogues which (a) contain instances of back-channelling (indications that the listener is following, and is interested) such as 'yes, I see, uh-huh, mmm, OK' and so on); and (b) requests for clarification or repetition. Both these skills play a vital role in keeping communication going, and need to be modelled for learners.
- Get learners to back-channel by giving them a set of cards with suitable phrases on (such as those above) and ask them to make sure they use all the cards during a conversation which involves following an explanation – for example of how to carry out a particular procedure. The same techniques can be used to practise asking for clarification.
- When using a scripted dialogue in class, focus on the language functions incorporated in it (such as requesting, thanking, greeting and so on) ask about alternative expressions learners have heard, then talk about when they are and when they are not appropriate.
- Include information in the dialogues which will be useful in real life: for example, one of the dialogues could be about somebody posting an item to Poland.

Although the suggestions listed above are made with E1 learners in mind, the same strategies can be used, with adaptations, when working with higher levels.

Authentic material

Authentic materials (spoken or written texts not produced with language learners in mind) are also useful. Watch out for short TV or video clips which incorporate real-life features of discourse, for example in soap operas, and use these to practise listening skills and to focus on aspects of discourse, functional language, lexis and phonology. Doing this kind of activity in class encourages learners to 'notice' these features when watching TV or observing social interactions outside the classroom. The relative merits and uses of authentic and scripted materials are further discussed in Chapter 9.

Incorporating role-play in a lesson

Role-play is the usual name given to the 'acting out' in the classroom of a situation such as telephoning the college; making an appointment with a doctor; dealing with an angry customer in a restaurant; or returning faulty goods to a shop. This type of activity is most often used in a lesson sequence which also involves dialogue practice, the object being to:

- link the dialogue work with real world language use;
- give learners a chance to combine the language presented in the dialogue with other language they know.

Traditionally, role-play has often followed dialogue practice, the rationale being that learners first focus on and practise salient features of the dialogue and then they attempt to use them more spontaneously in a role-play, providing a rehearsal for a similar conversation in real life. This way of organizing the lesson is likely to be appropriate when learners have little experience of the situation they are rehearsing or when they have very limited linguistic resources.

Another way teachers use role-play is to begin with the role-play and follow it with dialogue work, focusing on features of the dialogue that the learners found difficult or were unable to complete. The relevance and usefulness of these features is thus clearly apparent from the experience of the role-play increasing learners' motivation to engage in the more controlled language work of the dialogue. This way of staging the lesson can work very well with learners who have more linguistic resources, and at least some experience of the situation.

Setting up role-plays

Role-play is not always as productive as it might be. Certain roles, particularly those learners have not played in everyday life, may present some people with too great a linguistic challenge, with the result that they give up after a half-hearted attempt, or subvert the activity in some way. A different problem is posed by the need to suspend disbelief. The participants (not, after all, professional actors) may find it difficult to imagine that they are in a crowded market talking to a stallholder, and not in their English class. Teachers need (a) to pitch the role-play at the right level of challenge, both for the group as a whole and for individuals within it and (b) to help learners to suspend disbelief and throw themselves into the imaginary situation. The following strategies can help:

- Use a video clip, or pictures to set the context and get learners thoroughly engaged with the topic before you start.
- Pair or group learners in a way that allows fluent but less accurate learners to demonstrate their strengths, and the less fluent to pick up useful language and conversational strategies. The more fluent speaker can play the more demanding role.
- Equally importantly, take account of learners' interests and experience when allocating roles. For example, the role of market trader should go to someone who has worked in a market or who enjoys acting, while the role of customer is one which everyone can manage. But make sure everybody gets their turn to play the role(s) they are most likely to take in real life (in this case, almost certainly, the customer's).
- If the role-play is a follow-up to dialogue practice using a handout, encourage learners not to refer to their handout while doing the role-play. Make sure they do not feel they have to remember the whole of the dialogue they have been practising. Prompts could be written on the board as 'scaffolding' for those learners who need it.

- An unpredictable element to the discourse can be introduced through role-cards, such as those below, designed to practise making complaints and apologies.

Role-play A

It is 2 pm and you are trying to sleep (you have to sleep in the daytime because you work at nights). Your neighbour's children are playing a noisy ball game just outside your ground-floor flat. You don't know your neighbour's name but you say hello to each other when you meet. You don't have his/her phone number so you get dressed and ring the doorbell to complain about the noise.

Role-play B

It is 2 pm during half-term week. Your children, aged 5 and 7, have been playing computer games all morning so ten minutes ago you sent them outside to play, near your ground-floor flat. You can hear them playing ball now. The doorbell rings and when you answer it you see your neighbour. You don't know her or his name and don't see her or him very often, but she or he is quite friendly and says hello when you do meet.

- If you use role-cards, keep them as simple as you can, and ensure that learners understand everything written on the cards before they start. Ask them not to refer to them during the role-play itself.
- Use classroom layout and props to help bring the role-play to life. If learners are practising buying material in a market, provide some material and arrange the furniture to look more like market stalls. If you can't provide material, use pictures of material. If the role-play is about a job interview, get each group of learners to arrange the 'stage' before starting. Where is the door, the desk and so on? How would the chairs be arranged?
- Consider asking learners to evaluate their own role-plays, or to give each other feedback, and establish criteria for doing this, but don't assume that they want to 'perform' their role-play for the whole group.
- Have a group-feedback session afterwards. Ask how similar it was to the real-life experience. Deal with any problems or gaps in knowledge that came up, for example in the market role-play, the word for a particular type of fabric; phrases for bargaining that you did not teach beforehand.

Using learners' own experience

One way to work on types of social interaction which learners continue to find difficult (in a group with well-established relationships and a sense of mutual trust) is to use learners' experience as a jumping-off point. Get a learner to describe an encounter (for example with a landlord) which he or she found difficult and to explain why. Identify aspects of the encounter that were problematic and any strategies, linguistic or otherwise, which would have helped. As a next step the group, or a sub-group, with the help of the teacher, might co-write a dialogue in which the learner (the tenant) manages the encounter more skilfully. Language that could help to bring about a more satisfactory outcome is identified and practised. Learners might then work in pairs to rehearse (and perhaps perform for each other, if they wish) role-plays based on the group 'reworking' of the problematic encounter.

The need for self-expression

Language is not just a negotiating tool for obtaining the goods, services and qualifications that we need to get by, or even to get on. It is our means of expressing who we are. One of the learners quoted in the first chapter of this book (studying at Level 1 of the *Adult ESOL Core Curriculum*) said: 'I am a polite person. If you speak simply, people think you are stupid or uneducated.' This man is frustrated by the limitation his language skills place on his social identity. The further he moves outside his 'comfort zone', the more keenly this hindrance is likely to be felt. Yet a proactive response to linguistic challenges presented by unfamiliar social situations and conversation topics will increase his opportunities to interact with other speakers and involve him in negotiation for meaning (the process by which the participants in a conversation work towards mutual understanding). Engaging in this process is likely to lead to further language development.

Many L1 speakers of English seem to lack the accommodation skills to communicate with L2 speakers whose use of English is inexpert. In consequence, the onus is on the L2 speaker to keep communication channels open. The ESOL class is an opportunity to develop essential listening and speaking sub-skills for this process. Some examples, taken from the ESOL core curriculum at Level 1, are listed below.

- be able to use a range of markers to indicate that they are listening ... (DfES 2001b: Lr/L1.1b)
- be able to use a range of ways of asking for clarification or repetition, appropriate for formal and informal interactions (2001b: Lr/L1.3a)
- be able to use a range of ways of giving feedback and confirming understanding, appropriate for formal or informal interactions (2001b: Lr/L1.4a)
- form questions to check that the listener has understood, and ask for confirmation (2001b: Sc/L1.3b)
- recognise when an explanation or instruction is required, and be able to respond with appropriate register (2001b: Sc/L1.3d)

A teacher might focus on one or more of these areas when giving feedback after a free-speaking activity and provide input as appropriate. In a subsequent lesson, he or she could set up an activity which lent itself to practising one of the strategies, providing learners with a series of utterances on cards which they attempt to use in the course of the activity.

For many language users, actual opportunities for contact with the target language community may be very limited, and when such learners come to an ESOL class it is important to provide a positive climate for them to engage with English and to express their feelings and views in that language, so that they begin to develop a social identity when using it. It is advisable, initially at least, to focus discussion on commonality of interest and experience rather than differences. Productive subjects for discussion can be facilities in the locality, work and leisure interests, life or study goals, strategies for study and learning styles and preferences.

As discussed earlier, the negotiation for meaning which goes on when people engage in discussion is inherently valuable in developing language skills. The more fully the learners engage in it, the more productive it is likely to be. So there needs to be a good stimulus for the discussion, such as a news item, a text, a picture or a recording. Grouping, too, is of vital importance: the groups need to be small enough to allow everyone to speak, and personalities and affiliations also need to be taken into account.

Even with the most careful planning, teachers often find that certain speakers dominate in classroom discussion, just as they do in the real world. So as well as expressing their feelings, views and opinions (DfES 2001b: Sd/L1.2a and 2b) learners should be encouraged, as appropriate, to offer turns to less forthcoming speakers (2001b: Sd/L1.3a) to use verbal and other strategies to obtain turns for themselves, and to deal with interruptions and use appropriate phrases for interruption (2001b: Sd/L1.4a). Watching videos can be a valuable aid in developing appropriate body language for offering and taking turns in discussion. Another idea to develop the skill of turn-taking is to provide each small group of learners with a ball of string. As each person speaks, the ball of string is passed to them, and they keep hold of the string when the ball is passed on to the next speaker. The pattern of the conversation soon emerges and everybody notices who is taking the turns and who is not. Quieter people are then offered turns and dominant people are abashed and hold back, at least for a while. Learners can also be asked to assess themselves (after the discussion) on some of the turn-taking skills listed above.

While discussions of abstract topics such as politics have their place, they should not be over-emphasized in speaking practice. The importance of using a range of different types of speaking 'task' is well documented in general ELT literature as well as in the literature on task-based learning. In *A Framework for Task-Based Learning*, Jane Willis (1996) defines 'tasks' as: 'activities where the target language is used by the learner for a communicative purpose (goal) in order to achieve an outcome'. She supports six main task types:

- Listing.
- Ordering and sorting.
- Comparing.
- Problem solving.
- Sharing personal experiences.
- Creative tasks (or projects).

The range of tasks activate different language and develop different conversational strategies. Also, through negotiating for meaning with people from different language and cultural backgrounds in class, learners develop the ability to adjust to different interlocutors and keep communication channels open when interacting with people outside the class. There are many creative and interesting ideas for different kinds of task-based speaking practice to be found in general ELT literature.

It is important to organize some kind of feedback on fluency-orientated tasks and for many teachers this often takes the form of an error-feedback session immediately afterwards. However, comment on the content of the activity is also in order, preferably from the learners. An important element of Willis's (1996) proposed framework for task-based learning is the report stage, in which learners feed back on some aspect of the task they have done. The 'public' nature of the report, as compared with the 'private' speech which goes on during the task itself, motivates learners to concentrate on clear and accurate language when planning it, which, Willis persuasively argues, is likely to: 'drive their language development forward and give them new insights into language use'(Willis 1996). Certain types of fluency activity lend themselves more readily than others to this kind of concluding phase. If you decide that a planned report is not an appropriate way to feed back on a particular activity, learners should still be invited to round the activity off by discussing what they did and how useful they found it.

Conclusion

> Learners are often more resourceful and knowing than either the teacher or the task allows for.
>
> (Roberts et al. 2004)

The quote above is taken from the NRDC (2006) *Embedded Case Studies*. In supporting the development of the speaking and listening skills which are so central to the process of language development, we should recognize and draw on learners' intelligence, personal qualities and experience. As importantly, teachers need to cultivate their own curiosity both about spoken language and about strategies for developing it, with a view to being *'resourceful and knowing'*, themselves. There is a wealth of published ELT material which can be recommended to ESOL teachers wanting to learn more about speaking and listening.

6 The written word

Helen Sunderland and Marina Spiegel

Being literate

TASK 6.1

Look at this advertisement and answer the questions below:

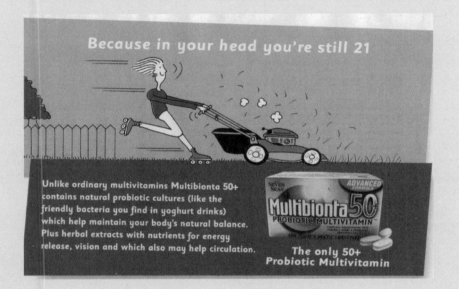

- What information does this advert give?
- How is the information presented?
- How much reading of actual words did you need to do to get the message?
- What gave you the best impression of what it was about – text or visual?
- What schematic knowledge (knowledge about the world) did you bring to the task?

In an increasingly multimodal society, literacy has become much more than giving or getting meaning from written symbols. If you compare newspapers today with those earlier in the last century, you will see that in today's papers visual images are much more central in imparting meaning. In work and in study, presentations and reports are expected to include graphics, photos and illustrations.

If you add the interpretation and use of visual images to the definition of 'literate', all learners we meet in ESOL will be literate in some ways, for example they will recognize the logo for Tesco; or the weather on TV, even with the sound off.

When teaching reading and writing, teachers need to keep in mind visual and multimodal literacy, build on learners' schematic knowledge (for example, that the weather on TV is usually accompanied by a map with weather icons) wherever possible, and enable learners to discuss this knowledge and compare their understanding with people from other cultures.

What learners want to read and write and why

TASK 6.2

Think about what might take place in the following literacy events – an appointment with a solicitor; and buying a mobile phone.

- Who is involved?
- What do people want to achieve?
- What literacy practices are involved and what oral interaction needs to happen?
- What are the relationships between the participants? Who holds the power and why?

COMMENT 6.2

These are some of the things you may have highlighted:

1. *Appointment with the solicitor.* Phoning and negotiating an appointment date and time, discussion with the solicitor, listening, asking for clarification, answering and asking questions, letters to read and respond to (the response could be by phone, email, letter, forms and possibly questionnaires), documents to read, reflect on, sign.
   The solicitor holds much of the power, in that he or she has the information and the understanding of legalese language. However, in some cases the client also has the power to take his or her custom elsewhere.
2. *Buying a mobile.* Reading of information (including looking at photos) in catalogues or on the Web, comparing prices and deals, asking

questions, asking for clarification and negotiating over contracts, forms to fill in, signing of contracts.

The power relationships here are not clear-cut either – in many cases the sales person holds much of the power, as he or she will have information of the bewilderingly large variety of possible contracts. However, again, the customer has the power to buy or not.

This analysis shows the complexity of literacy and how it is embedded in social contexts. It highlights issues of power: who initiates; who holds and discloses information; what is being withheld and how to ask for it; how carrying out supposedly simple skills (signing your name) can have far-reaching and costly consequences. Examination of these two literacy events also shows how literacy is often linked to speaking and listening, and the wide range and complexity of reading and writing practices that learners need to carry out in the real world. It shows the importance of using authentic materials in situations of interest to learners so that, as well as teaching discrete literacy 'skills', such as spelling, handwriting or punctuation, teachers are working to empower learners to carry out these practices as effectively as possible. Discussion of literacy events will lead to increased knowledge of the issues surrounding the event (this is known as schematic knowledge). In the case of the mobile phone, schematic knowledge may include knowing that consumers have rights, that they have a certain number of days to change their minds about a contract, that there are different types of payment for mobiles, that is contract or 'pay as you go'. All of this will lead to more effective reading and writing when the learner next needs to buy a phone or something similar.

TASK 6.3

Make a list of all the reading and writing you have done in the last one or two days and ask two or three people you know to do the same. Compare lists.

COMMENT 6.3

Here are the lists of what the authors did:

1   *Reading.*
   - Proofing a complex text.
   - Train timetable.
   - Address of meeting.
   - Road sign and street number of organization where meeting was held.
   - Agenda of meeting.
   - Emails.

- Papers for meeting and discussion of them with colleagues.
- Signs in supermarket.
- Ingredients on some products.
- Till for amount of bill.
- Magazine front pages in newsagents.
- Newspaper on way home.
- Numbers on TV remote.
- Novel.

2 *Writing.*

- Correcting a complex text.
- Emails.
- Notes during meeting.
- Soduko puzzle.
- Crossword.
- Outline of this chapter.
- Starting to write this chapter.

You will see that the list includes very simple reading and writing (address of meeting, TV remote) and some more complex (meeting papers and this chapter). On the list are reading for work and for pleasure; reading print and electronic texts; and writing on the computer and by hand. While most literacy practices in this list were carried out alone, at least two were done collaboratively. You may find it both useful and interesting to do a similar survey with your learners, to get a feel for the literacy practices they carry out, in English and other languages. However, you should not feel you need to restrict the learning only to the directly functional: just because we did not read any poetry or songs in the last couple of days does not mean we would not enjoy doing so in the future.

Transferable skills

TASK 6.4

Imagine you are learning to read and write in (a) Spanish, (b) Korean. What transferable skills would you bring with you to the process?

COMMENT 6.4

Transferable skills you will bring to learning to read and write

You may have thought of some of the following:

	Text level skills
Spanish	Know that print represents meaning.
Korean	Know that print represents meaning.
Spanish	Can recognize many contextual and generic clues. E.g. can recognize if something is an advert, or a bill, as the layout and visual design is very similar to English.
Korean	Can recognise some contextual and generic clues, for example the weather on TV, adverts in magazines.
Spanish	Reading strategies, for example the ability to predict, skim or scan.
Korean	Some strategies, for example the ability to predict, skim or scan, but this is likely to be hard to do until I acquire fluent word recognition skills.
Spanish	Writing strategies, for example consideration of audience and purpose, or of ways of learning spellings.
Korean	Much less able to utilize existing strategies, for example less familiarity with audience and purpose as cultural context quite different.
	Sentence level skills
Spanish and Korean	Knowledge of punctuation – though there are some differences in Spanish.
Spanish and Korean	Knowledge of sentence boundaries.
Spanish and Korean	Can use knowledge of similar syntax to inform both reading and writing.
	Word level skills
Spanish	Form letters in Roman script.
Korean	Some fine motor control – as you are used to forming letters, this may help when forming characters.
Spanish	Can recognize words where there are some lexical similarities – where words have common roots, e.g. estacion/station; medico/doctor.
Korean	Have some understanding that words with similar meanings or roots may have similar patterns, for example, Sunday, Monday, Tuesday. This may help in learning Korean which is a logographic system of writing.
Spanish	Can recognize some symbols (e.g. on door of ladies or stop sign).

Korean	Can recognize some key international symbols in some places (e.g. door of ladies' in airport).
Spanish	Can make out what words sound like by sounding out each letter, though there are a few differences in Spanish (for example 'll' is pronounced like a 'y' in English).
Korean	Can make a guess at spelling, using the same system.
Other	
Spanish	Can use a dictionary and organize words alphabetically.
Korean	Understand the concept of a dictionary.
Spanish	Study skills and strategies for learning.
Korean	Study skills and strategies for learning.

Just as you would be able to build on existing experience and expertise if you attempted to learn to read and write Spanish or Korean, so learners build on existing practices, skills and knowledge when they start to develop their reading and writing in English. The extent to which they can do this will depend on their level of literacy in other languages and also the similarities or differences (sometimes known as *language distance*) between their other languages and English.

The skills in the above list are sometimes called the sub-skills of reading or writing. A useful framework for analysing these sub-skills, used in the *Adult ESOL Core Curriculum* (DfES 2001b), is to organize them under the headings of text, sentence and word. Text level involves anything to do with the whole text, such as using contextual and generic clues to recognize the purpose and main message of a text. Sentence level skills cover English grammar, syntax and punctuation. Phonics and handwriting, knowledge of lexis, morphology and spelling make up the word level skills.

Challenges when learning to read and write in another language

In the previous section we discussed how all learners bring some transferable skills and knowledge to learning to read and write another language. In the same way, all learners face challenges in developing reading and writing, and some will face greater barriers than others.

Educational background

Learners with little formal schooling will probably have been exposed to a relatively restricted range of texts, and have had few opportunities to access reference sources or to compose a range of texts independently. They may have fewer study skills than other learners, and no experience of taking exams. On the plus side, they may come with fewer preconceptions and fixed expectations of how learning happens and may be highly motivated to make up for lost time.

Literacy in a different script

The task about learning to read and write in Korean shows that learners who are developing reading and writing skills in a language with an unfamiliar script will have considerably fewer transferable skills than those who can already read and write another language in the same script. Though these learners may be well-educated and used to language learning, they are likely to need more support.

The nature of English spelling

TASK 6.5

How many words can you find with the spelling 'ough'? How many different pronunciations are there in this list? What does this tell you about the nature of English spelling?

COMMENT 6.5

- Thorough
- Cough
- Through
- Thought
- Hiccough
- Dough
- Plough
- Rough
- Lough (Irish, loch)

You probably do not need to do this task to know that English spelling is not altogether 'transparent'; that is, it is not always possible to work out the sound of a word from the way it is spelled, or to spell a word from the way it sounds. This can prove difficult for all learners, but particularly for those who are used to a much more phonetically regular language such as Spanish or Arabic, as learners literate in these languages are not used to having to develop visual strategies for remembering words. Margaret Peter (1985), author of the very useful book *Spelling Caught or Taught* talks about 50 per cent or so of learners who can pick up the spelling from reading it as 'Catchers', the others need to use specific strategies to learn how to spell English words.

Discourse organization

Even learners who can write fluently and accurately in English may have challenges with accepted ways of organizing discourse in written English as discourse organization is culturally based. For example, we would feel a 'logical' and 'clear' piece of writing would state its purpose at the beginning, elaborate using examples and make a general statement at the end. However, in some other cultures, the general statement would be made at the beginning, often at length, and our discourse organization would be seen as blunt and possibly rude. Discourse organization can be a much more subtle and difficult aspect of writing to alter than, say, spelling or grammatical accuracy, and writers may not want to change a way of writing that they consider is part of their identity. Accordingly, this needs sensitive and explicit discussion between teachers and learners.

Schema

Readers of English at any level can be hampered by not having the required *schema* to understand a particular text. *Schema* is knowledge about the context of the text and the world around it and is often specific and cultural. For example, a recently arrived learner from Pakistan on an MA programme had difficulty understanding an essay question which asked her to compare the approach to bilingualism in the English and Welsh national curriculum documents. She did not realize that Wales had a policy of using two languages in official and everyday life, and so she could not understand what was required in the question. Oral interaction plays an important part in developing and activating schema before reading; this can be through video, role-play, discussion or research. Learners can work collaboratively to share strengths; those who have difficulties in decoding text and word recognition can work with learners who have these skills but less schematic knowledge.

Grammar

Written English has different rules to spoken English. McCarthy (2001) gives a helpful description of the typical (but not universal) differences between writing and speaking:

> The most useful way to conceive of the differences is to see them as scales along which individual texts can be plotted. For example, casual conversations tend to be highly involved interpersonally ... Public notices, on the other hand, tend to be detached, for example, stating regulations or giving warnings. But note we have to say tend; we cannot speak in absolutes, only about what is most typical. Speech is most typically created 'on-line' and

received in real time. Writing most typically is created 'off-line' i.e. composed at one time and read at another, and there is usually time for reflection and revision ... What is more, written discourses tend to display more obvious degrees of structure and organisation whereas talk can appear rather loose and fragmented.

(McCarthy 2001)

In addition, communicative fluency, or getting meaning across, is often a priority in 'meaning-driven' English classes. This means that many learners may be fluent in spoken English but still have difficulties reading or writing standard written English.

TASK 6.6

Imagine you are giving oral instructions about a process, for example using a new photocopier at work. What would you say?
Now write a set of instructions to be hung above the photocopier.
Compare the two.

COMMENT 6.6

This is what you might expect in the *spoken* instructions:

- Non-linguistic communicative features, e.g. gesturing; repeating and going back over what you said.
- Incomplete sentences.
- Vague language (for example, 'sort of', 'thingy').
- More use of pronouns than in writing.
- Use of 'headers' – e.g. 'you know that button, the one that ...'

And did you find these in the *written* instructions?

- Much more succinct language.
- Non-linguistic layout features, for example bullets or numbering.
- Laid out as a list as opposed to continuous text.
- More long noun phrases (for example, 'Select *Auto Paper Select (A.P.S) tray two*').
- The repeated use of a particular structure or grammatical feature, such as, in this example, the use of the imperative.

As you can see from this example, spoken English is much more immediate and capitalizes on the fact that, generally, the people communicating can see each other. This enables them to use gesture and facial expressions as well as tone of voice to help get across all their nuances of meaning. Thus, what is said does not need to be so exact, and the speaker may use what is known as 'vague language' – for example 'thingy', 'whatsit', 'kind of'. Spoken language is also time-bound – once said, it can be difficult to 'unsay' something, and time is short to plan and think before speaking. This results in much looser sentence structures, much rephrasing and repetition. Because it is not so immediate and the writer cannot rely on visual context to make meaning clear, written language needs to be more precise. This means language must be less 'vague' and standard linguistic forms tend to be used.

Enthusiastic speakers cut into each others' speech and interrupt each other. Written language, in contrast, has clear beginnings and endings, and gives the communicator time to think and plan. Written language can also be stored and referred to again, so that, for example, a quote for a job of work in writing holds more sway than a verbal promise.

However, Carter (2004) points out that the distinction between written and spoken language is more like a continuum than a clear line. Text messages, for example, do not require much planning, neither do they obey rules of standard grammar, while a speech may be composed over a long period of time and consist of very formal standard English.

Learning difficulties or disabilities

Composing text with a degree of accuracy can be a particular challenge for those learners who have not had a background in writing much in any language. It is particularly important for deaf learners from other countries who communicate in a sign language, including British sign language (BSL) as they too will be used to very different grammatical conventions, and just like hearing bilingual learners, will need to have the differences between spoken and written forms made explicit. Consider the following from *ESOL Access for All* (DfES 2006c: 499), 'BSL in relation to ESOL'):

> From an ESOL teacher's point of view, some of the most common significant grammatical differences between BSL and English are:
>
> - An English sentence is organised around the verb. Meaning depends on the word order of the other words in the sentence. BSL users begin with the topic and then comment on it
> - BSL does not use the auxiliary *to be*
> - BSL does not use the articles *a/an/the*
> - Word order can be markedly different
> - Verbs are inflected by changes of speed or placement
> - Modification of signs is also shown by changes of placement, speed or repetition and not by a 'word' ending

Barriers due to readability

TASK 6.7

1 What makes this text difficult to read?

Charges for Operator-connected calls are higher than direct dialled calls and are excluded from inclusive call packages.

(From the phone book)

Re-write it to make it more readable.

2 What additional factors can you think of that make texts difficult to read?

COMMENT 6.7

1 You may have found the following made reading this text difficult:
 - Type size.
 - Font.
 - Long noun phrases ('Charges for operator-connected calls').
 - Choice of lexis ('inclusive call packages').
 - Use of passive ('are excluded').

2 Additional factors that make texts difficult to read include:
 - Long sentences.
 - No graphics.
 - Complexity of grammatical structures.
 - Unknown or obscure lexis.
 - Density of text.
 - Colour and contrast between paper and print.
 - Lines of text too long (this is why text books and newspapers use columns).

Teachers need to be aware of issues of readability and choose or adapt texts with readability features appropriate to the reading level of their learners. Learners with little experience of reading in any language need to have texts in large print, with familiar lexis and simple grammatical features, wherever possible. This is not always easy to do with authentic texts and sometimes a compromise is necessary between authenticity and readability.

Developing reading

Good readers

When you talk to readers of different ages about how they were taught to read, a number of techniques emerge depending on which was fashionable in the year they were learning. Readers in their fifties from this country are likely to have learnt by a method known as 'analytic phonics' – that is going from letters to the sounds they can represent and using this knowledge to decode whole words. Slightly younger readers may well have learnt by 'look and say' – that is by learning what whole words look like and then putting them together to make very simple sentences. Reading books such as *Janet and John* or *Dick and Jane* were based on this principal. Readers in their twenties and thirties are likely to have learnt through a psycholinguistic or 'real books' approach. This approach relies on meaning-based techniques such as familiarity with the story, use of illustrations and interest in the topic to engage the reader and carry him or her along so that reading just 'happens'.

Theorists now believe that good readers combine all of these skills when they access meaning from text. They recognize a huge number of familiar words and instantly access their meaning. When they come to a word they do not recognize, they use phonic strategies to 'decode' it. And in order to really understand a text, readers need to have a schema for that subject. In other words, they need to have enough information and knowledge about the world that the text is reflecting to get meaning from it. When this does not happen, for instance if you read a technical text where the subject matter is unknown to you, no matter how many of the words you recognize, or how many of the sounds you can decode, you will find it very difficult to interact with the text in a meaningful way.

This has several implications for teaching learners to read in a new language. First of all, they need to know how to 'decode' phonically, and readers new to the Roman script will need to be taught this. Second, for fluent and rapid reading learners need to build up a visual lexicon of words they instantly recognize. This will affect all learners – however familiar they are with the Roman script, they are unlikely to have a large sight vocabulary of English words, and to 'decode' each word is much slower than to recognize it visually. Building up such a vocabulary takes time and practice, and has implications for the number of new words introduced in each text. Finally, in order to ensure learners can use schematic knowledge, it is really important to have texts that are relevant and interesting to the learners. Where there are cultural differences, it is important to ensure that the learner's schema is similar enough to the writer's for them to get enough meaning from the text. Again, this applies to learners at all levels in ESOL.

In addition, good readers do not read in a linear fashion. They may scan a text first to get an idea of what it is about, how it is constructed, and which parts are most important to read. They will regress and re-read if they are unsure of meaning or did not catch a particular word. They will use different reading techniques for different purposes, scanning for particular information, skimming quickly to get the gist of a document or reading carefully if they are trying to understand a difficult text. Good readers change speed when reading – faster over boring bits or if they want to find out what will happen next in a narrative, slower over bits they find difficult to understand or particularly want to enjoy and reflect on, as with poetry. While some learners will bring these skills with them, others will need to be explicitly taught how good readers read. For these readers, it may be helpful to discuss reading strategies, make them explicit and praise learners when they use them effectively.

What to read

If texts are to be stimulating for the reader, choosing them can also be one of the more enjoyable preparation tasks for the teacher. Which texts you choose will depend on a number of things:

- Your learners' interests and needs.
- What skills you are hoping to develop.
- Your learners' reading level.
- What is topical.

Because your learners have to read in their out-of-the-classroom lives, it is important to be able to prepare them to read authentic texts, even if these are not carefully controlled in terms of grammar and lexis. On the other hand, on occasion and particularly with lower levels, you may wish to use a reader written specifically for this level or to write your own text.

In many cases, learners will bring texts into the classroom that they need to read. This gives the teacher a ready-made lesson, real reasons for reading and motivated learners. Some readers want to learn to read with their children – in these cases it is best to ask them to bring in the books they want to read. In all other cases it is best to treat texts written for children with extreme caution as using them for teaching gives messages about how we see the learners.

As good readers read by rapid word recognition, practice is essential in building up a large lexicon. Learners need to be encouraged to read as much as possible, to buy magazines and newspapers, to borrow from the library and to take home texts to read as homework. They are much more likely to do this if the reading matter is interesting, clearly and well produced with illustrations and at the right level for them. Many publishers produce graded readers and the Quick Reads campaign has commissioned short books at Entry 3 and above from experienced authors such as Minette Walters. Homework reading can be incorporated into classroom learning through discussion or sharing the book with other learners either orally or by writing a book review for a class magazine.

Teaching reading: a staged process

Classroom reading activities are usually organized in a three-stage sequence:

- Pre-reading.
- Reading.
- Follow-up.

The main purpose of the *pre-reading* stage, is to activate the reader's schematic and generic knowledge, that is to make the reader conscious of any knowledge about the subject or the genre[1] that he or she may already have and that will help him or her make sense of the text. Pre-reading exercises may take the form of questioning, discussion, prediction, role-play, visual images or film – anything that will start the readers thinking about the subject. You may also wish to pre-teach specific vocabulary, if you feel that not knowing it will impair understanding of the text. Alternatively, you may prefer to support the learners in working out the meaning of unfamiliar vocabulary from the context of the text, or looking it up in dictionaries. All these approaches are valid and some will suit particular learners or texts better than others.

Reading can be done silently or aloud, alone or collaboratively, depending on the level and the purpose of the task. At a very beginner level, it can be supportive for the reader to read aloud in paired reading with the teacher or another learner, so that he or she can have immediate feedback and confirmation that he or she has read the word correctly. Learners should always be given a task to do while reading (such as considering the main point of the text, or looking out for the number of examples) as this helps the reader focus on the meaning of the text; the task should be given before the learner begins reading. There are a number of ways of checking understanding of the text:

- Oral or written questioning.
- Asking readers to re-tell.
- Transferring information to another form (such as from continuous prose to grid).
- Making a visual representation or map of the text.

Readers' reactions to the text can also be discussed at this stage (see below, *'critical reading'*).

All of the above are text-level activities (see above for an explanation of 'text', 'sentence' and 'word'). Sentence- and word-level activities are often done as a form of *follow-up*. Examples of these might be an examination of a particular grammatical structure or particular word families or derivations. These can be done orally or as written activities.

This three-staged process is a good basic way to approach teaching reading. Hedge (2000), Harmer (2001) and Scrivener (2005) have more on using this approach. Below, we outline some additional approaches which can be used in conjunction with the three-staged process.

A critical reading approach

TASK 6.8

Look at the pages from these three readers[2] (*Asmat Book 1, Housework, A Woman's Work*).

1   When do you think these were written and why?
2   What point of view is being expressed about women's roles?
3   What other ways of writing about the topic (daily routines) are there?

COMMENT 6.8

As can be seen from the task above, a critical reading approach encourages learners to consider the ways in which they, as readers, are positioned and their emotions and opinions manipulated by the images and language used in texts.

> The Critical Discourse Analysis perspective examines the embedded ideologies of texts. It is based on the view that texts are social constructs reflecting the beliefs and values of their time and culture, the point of view of the author and the underpinning ideology that informs that writer's attitudes and beliefs. Texts have multiple meanings, and readers are positioned by the language and images which are used, the connotations and inferences. As such, texts offer selected, partial versions of the world, producing, reproducing and maintaining unequal power arrangements.
>
> Spiegel and Sunderland (2006)

For learners with limited experience of reading in any language this approach can have a considerable impact on their view of the importance of literacy and their motivation to engage, even with quite complex texts.

Consider the following excerpt from an article in the *Daily Mail* Web edition, October 2006[3]:

Therapy on the NHS? What a crazy waste of £600 million!

By OLIVER JAMES (Oliver James is the author of They *F*** You Up – How To Survive Family Life*. His book *Affluenza – How To Be Successful And Stay Sane*, will be published in January.)

Depression and anxiety cost the economy £17 billion a year. Forty per cent of those claiming disability allowance do so as a result of mental illness. It's an expensive business, but the Government has found a quick-fix solution: cognitive behavioural therapy (CBT).

In June this year, Professor Richard Layard – labelled the government's 'happiness tsar' – proposed the training of 10,000 CBT therapists to be based in 250 centres across the country. A trial is planned.

Layard claims CBT 'can lift at least a half of those affected out of their depression'. Sounds great? If only life were so simple ...

What response do the words 'therapy' and 'crazy waste' elicit? What views about mental health do the words 'Depression and anxiety cost the economy' reveal? How are readers meant to respond to the claim that CBT is a 'quick fix'?

Critical reading activities can be used with learners of all levels, even those at Entry 1. For example, take a simple advertisement, like the one used in Task 6.1. Learners could be asked to consider how the image or words make them feel, what view of the world the text promotes, why they think those images or words were chosen. As has been said on many occasions, learners may be beginner readers but they are not beginner thinkers.

A genre[4] approach to reading

Take some utility bills you have received lately, for example gas, electricity, community charge, water, telephone. Spread them out in front of you and ask yourself, what do they have in common? Genre theorists say that texts which share the same communicative purpose, share a common structure and format. This includes sharing specific lexis, layout and grammatical features. Teachers adopting a genre approach can exploit the common features of genres to support their learners in making predictions about the texts they are reading. This in turn will help the reader to recognize audience and purpose as well as to find their way around the text. Genre theory (Cope and Kalantzis 1993) has its origins in the linguistic theories of Halliday (1975) which sees language as a social phenomenon with a purpose or function behind all communication. Language use is inextricably linked to context and it is Halliday's view that people use both linguistic and cultural knowledge when they make decisions about what to say or write.

So, using the example of the bills, even readers at an early beginner level can learn to recognize the conventional layout of a bill, the logos, how much to pay and when it has to be paid by. Teachers can laminate a range of real bills and ask learners to circle the amount to pay in red and the date it needs to be paid in blue. They can ask learners to add up the totals or sort the bills in date order. These activities can be collaborative and fun and can appeal to a range of learning styles. Using a variety of texts, teachers can ask learners to group texts by genre, or match key features.

The *Adult ESOL Core Curriculum* has further ideas for using a genre approach at all levels. Consider the following at Entry 1 (DfES 2001b: 81):

Writing (Wt/E1)

- Using a simple letter, an appointment card, a simple printed invitation, a very simple short narrative, a list, learners are asked to compare the differences and similarities in the layout and the language: Do they look the same? Do they all use sentences?
- As a pre-amble to form-filling conventions, learners look at examples of simple forms and discuss them, e.g. Are forms important in the UK? Are forms important in your country? Learners are then read a short text about a person and shown a simple form with his or her basic details filled in. They then discuss basic conventions of forms, eg, no sentences, use of capitals, black ink.

Cross-cultural comparisons of genres can lead to illuminating discoveries, for example Western concepts of written bus and train timetables do not apply in some Central American countries where there are no railways and buses run as and when there are sufficient passengers. At a more academic level, learners can look at a range of texts, for example biographical writing, thrillers, romantic fiction or factual writing, and analyse the difference in literary genres by exploring in more detail their generic linguistic and stylistic features.

PQ4R and DARTS – active reading approaches

These acronyms stand for approaches that are helpful for learners in making sense of longer or more difficult texts. They are particularly useful approaches for getting meaning and information from informational or academic texts.

PQ4R[5] is an approach for learners and stands for 'preview, question, read, reflect, recite and review'. At the *preview* stage, the reader scans the text, looks at headings, diagrams or illustrations, maybe reads the introduction and conclusion and gets an overview of what the text is about. The reader asks him- or herself *questions* about the text, things he or she wants to find out when he or she reads and considers these during the *read* stage, thus ensuring he or she is interacting with the text. After reading, the reader *reflects* on what he or she has read and considers whether or not his or her questions have been answered. If not, he or she goes back and *reads* again. These two stages may be repeated several times. He or she then *recites* everything he or she can remember about the text – it is at this stage that he or she may realize that there are parts of the text he or she cannot recall and will *read* them yet again. This is the stage to make notes of key points. Finally, at the *review* stage, the reader needs to consider all the main points and check he or she remembers important details. Reviewing can be done at regular intervals in order to hold onto the information from the text.

DARTS or 'directed activities related to texts' is an approach for teachers who want to support learners in gaining information from complex or difficult texts. There are different types of DARTS exercises, analysis and reconstruction activities. In the analysis stage, the learner works at getting the main information or key ideas of the text through a number of ways. These include, underlining key points, labelling paragraphs, segmenting the text into key ideas or themes, and grouping or ranking these ideas. Analysis can also include transferring information from one form to another, for example from the text into a list or table. Reconstruction activities can range from a simple cloze (gap-fill) exercise to more complex information-gap exercises (where information is shared out and learners need to read and pass on their information to their peers so that everyone has the whole picture) or sequencing activities (put the paragraphs in the correct order to form the text). They can include getting readers to set questions on the text for other learners to answer, or to summarize information in their own words.

DARTS activities are often carried out collaboratively in pairs or small groups and make reading an active and fun process. They are useful for all readers, but particularly those who lack confidence in accessing complex texts.

The above approaches are not mutually exclusive and you can draw on any of them when planning a lesson.

TASK 6.9

Read the description of a lesson on reading for Level 1 learners and comment on which approaches the teacher has used.

This lesson is based on reading a descriptive text. Two texts were used, one adapted from *Larkrise to Candleford* by Flora Thompson, and another about contemporary urban Cairo from a magazine article.

Pre-reading

Learners watched extracts from a short tv programme about life in rural China. In groups they then discussed the village, the houses, the countryside, the way of life. They compared rural life to life in London (where the class took place). They brought in their own experiences of living in urban and rural areas.

Learners were told they would read one of two texts about a place. After they had read one text, they would need to work with someone who had read a different text and tell them about it. They were given the texts, which both had images as well as text.

Learners previewed their text quickly, looking at the visual images, the title and then skimming the text. They then worked together to think of questions they could ask themselves while reading the text. They thought of questions such as 'where is the place?' 'when did the writer live?' and 'is it about urban or rural life?' They also asked questions that entailed more inference, such as 'does the writer like this place?' 'how do I know?'

The teacher reminded learners of strategies for reading, such as don't stop and look up too many words as you go along, try and keep reading and see if the meaning becomes obvious.

Reading

Learners worked in pairs to read one of the texts aloud together. They helped each other if they got stuck with either pronunciation or meaning. Some learners who shared a language worked together so they could discuss meaning in the shared language. They underlined words they did not understand as they went along. If they couldn't get the meaning they looked up words they still did not understand in the dictionary. They highlighted the parts of the text that gave them the answers to the questions they had asked themselves at the beginning.

Some pairs had a slightly simplified version of the text, but the structure, most vocabulary and meaning were the same.

After they had read the text, the pairs split up and learners worked with a partner who had read a different text. They told each other about the text they had read so that the listener was able to answer the same questions. Learners then went back to their texts to clarify anything they were still unsure of and to check that they had given an accurate picture to their partner.

Follow-up

Learners did a variety of exercises on their text – they matched words and phrases with definitions and synonyms. They looked at the use of adjectives and imagery in the descriptions and at the use of idiom in both the contemporary and older texts. They considered the meaning of some of the more complex sentence structures, by answering true false questions about the text and then they drafted similar sentences of their own, describing places they knew.

Learners who finished quickly read the second text.

The whole group then came together and learners discussed their reactions to the texts. They also looked at the viewpoint of the writers and at what linguistic and stylistic features gave this away to the reader. For example, the phrase that the writer of the magazine article 'was the guest of X tours' as well as more subtle indicators that the text was trying to promote a particular view.

Finally, the learners worked on analysis of the text type and considered what features the texts had in common, even though they had such different subject matter. For example, they identified features such as an introduction which situated the place being described, how the text moved round the place as if the writers themselves were moving, the use of the simple past tense, the number of adjectives and evocative images.

In the following lesson, the learners would start to plan and write their own description.

COMMENT 6.9

This is a *top–down* approach, in that it starts with text-level work and then progresses to sentence and word-level.

The TV programme and following discussion activated learners' *schematic knowledge* about places, both rural and urban, and prepared them for the reading.

In skimming the text first and then thinking up questions to answer while they read, learners were starting to use the *PQ4R approach*. Telling someone else what they had read (or even reciting to themselves) is also part of this approach.

Paired reading has been shown by research (Brooks et al. 2007) to be an effective strategy in making progress in reading.

Underlining and highlighting key words and phrases is a *DARTS* strategy, as are the grammar and lexical activities that the learners did after they had read the texts.

In looking at writer viewpoint, and discussing why the writers might use particular words and phrases rather than others with a similar meaning, learners were beginning to take a *critical reading* approach.

The final task was based on a *genre approach*.

Developing writing

A process approach to writing

Writing is a complex and multistaged process involving different cognitive and motor skills. Good writers need to be able to organize and express their thoughts in a way that will be understood by their intended audience and then present these thoughts on paper or electronically using both written language and other graphic illustrations. The first parts of the process, thinking what to say and how to say it, are the most difficult and complex to teach. Possibly this is why teachers sometimes concentrate on the other parts of the process, such as handwriting, punctuation and spelling. The process approach to teaching writing addresses all stages of the writing process and these are outlined below. Whether you are working with learners on writing a postcard, a short story, an assignment for an academic or vocational course or a formal letter, you need to consider the following stages of the process.

1   *Consideration of audience and purpose of text*:
   - Discussion about who is going to read this and why, how will you handle the topic, what is your intention?
2   *Ideas generation and decisions about content*:
   - Discussion and brainstorming of ideas and of sources of information and ideas.
   - Find, compare and critique examples of similar writing.
   - Come to decisions about content, what and how much – link back to discussion on audience and purpose.
3   *Planning*:
   - Come to decisions about structure/order, layout, detailed content.
   - Note down plan using a range of formats, as appropriate to the learners – spidergrams, tree diagrams, list.
4   *Drafting (first draft)*:
   - Compose, illustrate where appropriate.
   - Revise plan if need be.
5   *Editing/proofreading/re-drafting*:
   - Check that meaning is clear, also grammar, lexis, punctuation, layout, quotations, etc.
   - Re-write where necessary.
6   *Producing the final version*.

These stages are not linear; writers may edit and decide that the ideas are not clear and so plan again. The editing and proofreading may be done by someone other than the writer and may be done several times. Neither is it neat in that it involves learners going through different stages, some of which occur more than once or simultaneously. It is therefore not a fixed sequence, rather 'a dynamic and unpredictable process' (Tribble 1996).

Learners can be encouraged to work individually or collaboratively, using computers to research the topic and to word-process plans and drafts. Peer work can enhance both communicative interaction and aid differentiation, for example learners can be grouped so that those:

- with good lexical skills but less accuracy work together with someone who has good accuracy but a more limited range of vocabulary and idiom;
- with shared experience or shared knowledge of certain languages work together;
- who have less advanced reading skills work with someone who can support them in paired reading.

Teachers can '*scaffold*' the writing process. This term, coined by Lev Vigotsky[6] means that teachers support the writer and then gradually withdraw the support so that the writer becomes increasingly able to produce writing independently. One good example of scaffolding for less confident writers is to give models or writing frames for the first texts they write. As learners become more practised and confident, they will no longer need these scaffolds.

A genre approach to writing

We have already looked at how a genre approach can be used to teach reading by familiarizing readers with generic features so that they are better able to predict and use these features to make meaning from texts. The same theory underpins a genre approach to writing, one which has had considerable impact on the teaching of writing in schools in the UK, and has also been influential in the teaching of literacy to adults. As with reading, the approach essentially involves analysing particular types of texts to identify key generic features and then reconstructing the genre to produce new texts. The genre approach is not distinct from the process approach but makes more explicit the generic features of particular texts and offers writers models and structures for producing specific genres.

However, it is important for teachers to be aware that genres should not be taught as a set of fixed rules. Genres change over time, just as society's values, expectations, attitudes and ways of behaving change. Take this textbook as an example of a genre. How different would it have looked if it had been written 30 or 40 years ago? What pedagogical values and precepts would it have exemplified? Clearly textbook writers in the early twenty-first century have reinterpreted the tradition and its conventions, challenging the premises and practices of earlier days, and the genre itself has changed. Such genre changes happen all the time and this knowledge needs to be embedded in the approach teachers take, so that learners too are aware that genre conventions are not set in stone.

The following is an example of an activity that takes a genre approach to writing. This activity will be most effective when:

- Learners work collaboratively, sometimes in small groups, sometimes in pairs, and are encouraged to interact among themselves as well as with the teacher during discussion and feedback.
- You consider a range of modalities (visual, auditory, tactile, kinaesthetic) – for example, questions can be written on cards that have to be handled, feedback is asked for on flipcharts that go up on walls or which stay on tables and learners circulate around to read.

Example activity

1   Take two authentic examples of a particular genre, for example a short report, a folk tale, a CV or an email asking for information. Read them and discuss content, checking comprehension.
2   Engage learners in text analysis – set a number of questions, including what the genre is, its purpose and audience. Discuss how this genre may have changed over time by looking at an older version of a similar genre and possible reasons for the change.
3   Discuss the key features (then and now): organizational structure, register, textual features, key lexis and structures.
4   Discuss the similarities and differences between spoken and written language use in relation to the particular genre and why it is important to note these. Work on aspects of the spoken genre as appropriate.

5   Discuss whether a similar genre exists in other cultures and whether there are similarities and differences, and whether they too have changed over time.

6   Set up a range of practice activities of key features at sentence and word level: for example tense and aspect, spelling of key vocabulary, use of key lexical chunks, paragraphing, etc.

7   Set up a differentiated discussion with learners with more advanced language skills – how far would they want to stick to the model, what changes might they make, would the text still be fit for purpose, suitable for the audience?

8   Set up reconstruction of text – in groups, with or without support of model, writing frame, etc., then as an individual activity.

9   Organize peer editing and proofreading activities, followed by re-drafting.

The genre approach is not without its critics who point to instances where too narrow an interpretation of genre has led to a restriction of creativity and a 'writing-by-numbers' approach. Nevertheless, many ESOL teachers find it a helpful approach in literacy teaching because it gives new writers a starting point. Once learners are familiar with some of the current conventions and features of the genre, they can choose to use them or not, change them or even defy them. Just as with reading, genre also gives teachers a framework for comparing the English conventions of particular types of writing with those in learners' other languages.

A reason to write

Learners can be encouraged in their writing if there is a real product of some kind for their texts. This might be writing and sending a letter to a local councillor, a reading event which is organized as a small celebration, a class magazine or a website. In Bolton (Slayen and Osmaston 2000) learners in the college made '*keypals*' with learners in Blackburn and arranged reciprocal visits. Learners' texts may be used as reading texts for future classes or as the basis for work on general proofreading, or specific grammar or spelling points. The end point may be electronic rather than print; learners' writing might be put on a website for other learners to access, or put onto the computer and used as a basis for a range of drag-and-drop, matching and other self-correction activities.

Working with learners with basic literacy

What is different about working with these learners?

Learners who have never formally learnt to read and write in their own language, let alone in a foreign language, will have fewer transferable skills to bring to the process of learning to read and write English. However, everyone has some knowledge about literacy and no-one starts with an absolutely clean slate.

Nevertheless, teachers of basic literacy in ESOL need to have a specific and fairly specialized body of knowledge, which they draw on and apply when assessing and teaching beginner literacy learners.

These are some of the specific things that teachers will need to work on with learners who have never formally learnt to read and write in any language:

- Some initial concepts, such as that print carries meaning or the concept of a sentence.
- Developing initial word and letter recognition.
- Principles of phonics, that is the way that letters and letter combinations represent different sounds.
- How to form letters and the best way to sit when writing.
- How to spell key words such as name and address.
- Very initial punctuation (full stop and capital letters).

See the *Adult ESOL Core Curriculum* (DfES 2001b) 'Reading and Writing' sections for much more detail and some ideas of suitable activities at this level.

Have you ever tried to read or write a different script? Even as an experienced reader and writer, you probably found it took a long time to learn. Children learning to read and write in school can take years of frequent and regular instruction. Learners who have never formally learnt to read and write in any language need to be given enough time to learn and the learning needs to be broken down into very small steps. So, teaching something that appears to come naturally to the teacher, such as how to form all the letters, or learn the sounds that letters represent, has to be done in small steps too. That is one of the reasons that we favour teaching these skills in the context of meaningful texts, otherwise too long is spent on somewhat boring and meaningless tasks. One of the best ways of getting meaningful texts is to use those that have been produced by learners.

See activities in *Friends, Families and Folk Tales* (Spiegel and Sunderland 1997) which practice word recognition (word level) and punctuation (sentence level) in the context of a text written by a learner and Spiegel and Sunderland (2006) for many more ideas of how to teach basic literacy to ESOL learners.

Language experience[7] – where to begin with learners with basic literacy

Language experience is a technique that stems back to the ideas and writing of Paulo Freire (Moss 1999), and is the most effective starting point for learners with very limited literacy both in their first language and in English. The reasons for this are numerous:

- The approach gives a voice to the learner; value and status to the learner's experience and opinions; and to the learner's use of language. For this reason the content will be meaningful and relevant.

- For learners with very limited experience of reading and writing in any language, it demonstrates that literacy is within their reach, creative and personally empowering.
- It ensures that the reading text contains language and vocabulary at the right level for the learner.
- It uses a top–down approach which can go on to provide relevant texts for further skills work on, for example, punctuation, grammar, phonics or handwriting, as necessary for the learner in question.

A suggested procedure: working one-to-one

1   *Introduce the topic*:
    - Begin with *oral work* to engage the learner's interest in a particular topic, choosing one that you think might be suitable for a particular learner. Use visuals and a lot of discussion drawing on the learner's experience, ideas and opinions.
2   *Joint production of text*:
    - Following the oral work, tell the learner that you are going to write down some of his or her ideas. As the learner speaks, write what he or she says on a large piece of card. Write the text down in a fairly large, consistent hand as continuous prose and do not have line breaks after each sentence.
3   *Correcting learner error when writing down their words*:
    - There are different views on whether learners' errors should be corrected before writing down what they say, and there is probably no right or wrong answer. Much will depend on the source of the error and the learner involved and you will need to make discreet and individual judgements. Sometimes a learner may make a mistake while speaking, and in this case it is probably important to model and write down the correct structure, so that the learner has an opportunity to 'internalize' the accurate form.
4   *Reading back the text*:
    - Ask the learner to read back his or her text. Read it with him or her at first if necessary. After he or she has finished reading it may be a good opportunity to talk to the learner about the number of sentences in his or her text, capital letters, full stops, etc. Teach the metalanguage, words such as sentence, full stop, etc., as you go. Discuss the similarities and differences with his or her first language if he or she is literate in it. The important thing is to get the learner to notice.
5   *Text reconstruction*:
    - Make two copies of the text, so you have two masters of the original. Then, cut up the original into separate sentences and ask the learner

to re-order the whole text, matching with the original if necessary at first, and reading as he or she goes.

6 *Sentence reconstruction*:

- Next, take the first sentence and cut it up so that each word is on a separate piece of card. Cut up the full stop separately too. Ask the learner to re-order the sentence, reading as he or she goes. Repeat the process for each of the sentences, eventually reconstructing the whole text.

- Give the learner the cut up text and ask him or her to practice at home with one of the master copies of the original.

7 *Copying the text*:

- Ask the learner to copy his or her text from the other master. As the learner copies, watch and support him or her as necessary with different aspects of the copying/writing process.

- Ask the learner to keep his or her copy in his or her class file for future reference. At a later stage you may ask him or her to word-process the text and illustrate it.

Assessing and marking writing

As teachers it is important that we respond to the content, ideas and structure of our learners' writing. They need to know whether their texts work at discourse level, if they are interesting, moving or amusing, whether there is sufficient detail and if they are well organized and formatted within accepted conventions.

We also need to give learners tools to help make them more independent writers. To do this they need to develop self-assessment skills so that they can become more proficient editors and proofreaders. To this end, we can encourage learners to self-correct, training them to use a marking scheme and asking for re-drafted texts. For example, by putting 'sp' (spelling) or 'w.o.' (word order) in the margin, rather than writing the correct word above the error, we are preparing the writer to search out and correct his or her own errors. Research among Chinese learners of English (Chen 1997) has shown the considerable difference that this kind of approach can make to learners' progress in writing.

In some cases, for example at a very early stage of writing, you may wish to identify mistakes, suggesting alternative forms, and correcting errors. However, this needs to be done with sensitivity, taking account of the background of the learners, prioritizing the areas of written language that individual learners need to work on.

TASK 6.10

Look at this example of writing done by a learner at E2:

1. **Write a paragraph about yourself:**

Here are some ideas about what to write:

- Where are you from? How is it different from England?
- What do you like to do?
- Why are you coming to English classes?
- Why do you want to learn English?

My name is K   my husband
name Sooriyapalan. I am married.
I'm come From Sri Lanka. I live
Colliers wood I speak Tamil and
English. Sri Lanka Country. wary
nagish country. I have Twe
Children One doughter name is
Sowmiya one son name is Ramyan
I live English class start 10.00 - 1.00
I live lisning, Rajitting, speaking

Total   12

Consider how you would feed back to the learner.

COMMENT 6.10

K has done what the task asked of her and, even where she makes mistakes, the meaning is clear. Much of her grammar is accurate. Her handwriting is readable and mainly on the line. She has spelt key words such as 'name', 'country', 'married', 'husband', 'speak', 'Colliers Wood' and 'children' correctly but some words wrongly, probably because of the way she hears the sounds. She has not managed to write the more complex sentence about her children and their names, or the one about the English classes accurately. She has not written the possessive 's' ('husband name'). She generally uses capitals for the beginnings of sentences and for names, but also sometimes uses them incorrectly in the middle of sentences ('Twe Children'). She uses full stops correctly.

It's always nice to start the feedback by saying what she has done well. You could praise her for getting her meaning across, for her accuracy in simple sentences (including sentence punctuation) and for her spelling and handwriting.

Then you could ask her to self-correct for some of the spellings and for use of capitals by putting 'sp' or 'c' in the margin. The grammar would probably need some discussion; at this stage you may suggest that she break the complex sentences up into shorter simple ones. You would probably need to demonstrate the possessive 's' and could ask her to re-write the sentences which would use it.

Conclusion

Reading and writing are taught processes rather than naturally acquired ones. Successful reading and writing in an additional language depends on many factors: whether or not the learner is literate in any other languages; whether or not the script is the same; and, if not, how different it is. There are a myriad sub-skills in both reading and writing and it can be easy to get bogged down in the detail and not see the whole. We believe that, while it is important not to neglect the sub-skills, reading and writing should be taught as holistic processes. We recognize that this takes time, especially with learners who are used to a different script or who do not read and write fluently in any language. However, we believe that all learners have some experience and expertise they can bring to the process and that, given time and active tuition, all learners can make real progress.

Notes

1   See below for discussion on genre.
2   With thanks to Catherine Wallace who has a similar activity in *Reading* (*1992*).
3   www.dailymail.co.uk/pages/live/articles/health/healthmain.html?in_article_id=412252&in_page_id=1774&in_a_source
4   Genre: a type or kind of text, defined in terms of its social purpose (Cope and Kalantzis 2000).
5   Thanks to Cynthia Klein
6   www.dfes.gov.uk/curriculum_literacy/tree/speaklisten/listenrespond/accessguidance/3/
7   Adapted from Spiegel and Sunderland (2006).

7 Developing accuracy

Meryl Wilkins and Anne Paton

Accuracy and fluency

What do we mean when we say a person speaks English well? What do ESOL learners mean when they say they want to improve their English? Does it mean using English without error? Or being able to communicate effectively? Or both?

These questions raise the issue of fluency and accuracy as goals for our learners. Accuracy is normally seen as meaning the ability to use the language correctly, without error. Fluency is less easy to define, but could be said to involve using the language easily, without much mental effort; the ability to express a wide range of ideas, at some length if required; and to communicate appropriately in a range of situations.

TASK 7.1

Look at the piece of text written by a learner of English. We will consider the strengths in the text at a later stage, for now what errors of accuracy do you notice and how would you categorize them?

1   When I was a child, my parents left us to my grandfather because they haven't got
2   any time to look after childrens.
3   My granddad lived in old town, he was a teacher and headmaster. We lived
4   upstair of school. Every morning I can see the pupils enter into their classroom
5   and I listened what they reading.
6   A new modern school was built, many parents would send their childrens there.
7   We know that problem would coming true someday but Granddad kept silence as
8   usual we can't found any saddness in his face, we were worried about how to
9   alive. I know that problem was so cruel even I just a child.
10 Once I got up on midnight and can't slept again. Then I went into my Granddad's
11 room, he was still working on his desk. He looked like weakly and alonely. I felt

---

12 my eyes were full of tears because he shall lose his job soon. Granddad turned

13 round and said, "everything could be happening. My knowledge was still old

14 fashionable, we must went from here" That's why I always remember Granddad

15 he was a brave man to facing problem.

16 Granddad was died when he was seventy-three. I never forgotten it was a cold

17 season. Granddad was illness since autumn, he was weak and pain. We were full

18 of saddness. He was died one day morning, peaceful as usual. My granddad died

19 few years but I always remember him because he like a light can bright up my life

20 forever and ever.

COMMENT 7.1

You probably noted the following:

Spelling error	E.g. 'Saddness' (line 8 and line 18).
Punctuation errors	E.g. line 8; line 14.
Errors in use of words	
• Wrong word	E.g. 'alive' for 'live' (line 9); 'alonely', confusing 'alone' and 'lonely' (line 11); 'old fashionable' for 'old fashioned' (line 13–14).
• Wrong phrase	E.g. 'few years' for 'a few years ago' (line 19).
Other errors related to single words	
• Pluralization	E.g. 'childrens' (line 2 and line 6).
• Wrong preposition	E.g. 'left us to my grandfather' (line 1); 'on midnight' (line 10).
• Omission of indefinite article 'an'	Line 3.
Errors in verb grammar	
• Wrong tense	E.g. 'they haven't got' (line 2–3).
• Inaccurate formation of verb	E.g. 'can't slept' (line 10).
• Confusion of active and passive	E.g. 'he was died' (line 18).
Problems with sentence construction	E.g. 'even I just a child' (line 9); 'a light can bright up my life' (line 19).

Some of the errors, for example in spelling and punctuation, could have been made by a first-language speaker of English. However, many of the errors are typical of learners whose first language is not English, usually errors of lexis and grammar. In this chapter, we will concentrate on accuracy in these two areas as these are central concerns of the language classroom.

Now, leaving aside the question of accuracy for the moment, consider your personal reaction to what you have read. Did you understand the writer's message? Did you feel any emotional response to the content?

TASK 7.2

Consider the checklist below and re-assess the piece of text in Task 7.1

Ability to communicate message
and feeling:

Clarity of meaning:

Organization of ideas:

Range of lexis:

Accuracy of lexis:

Accuracy of grammar:

Accuracy of spelling and
punctuation:

COMMENT 7.2

When you first assessed the piece of work, you were asked to consider only accuracy. On the second occasion, you have obtained a more complete picture of the learner's ability. You have 'put accuracy in its place', considering it in the context of overall communicative ability and general fluency. It follows that feedback to learners should comment on communicative ability and fluency as well as on accuracy, presenting a balanced picture of the language skills demonstrated. This applies to feedback on oral activities as much as on written texts.

Practice activities are often categorized as being designed to develop either accuracy or fluency. Unfortunately, this can give the mistaken impression that the two are in some way in opposition to each other; this is not the case. If we describe fluency as the ability to communicate easily and effectively, successful communication must involve quite a high degree of accuracy. So fluency and accuracy are closely linked as goals for the language learner.

Accuracy and fluency in language learning

Historically, approaches to language teaching have differed in the relative emphasis placed on fluency and accuracy. A prominent approach used in the past was *'grammar-translation'*, in which languages are taught through the medium of the first language. Approaches developed at a later date, such as *'the direct method'* and *'the audio-lingual approach'*, used the target language as the medium of instruction, prioritizing the development of speaking skills and presenting examples of specific grammatical structures rather than talking about grammar. They both involve a great deal of repetition of often uncontextualized language. However, notwithstanding important methodological differences between the older grammar-translation approach and these two later approaches, all three were based on a view of language learning which emphasized grammatical structure and prioritized accuracy, with the belief that fluency would follow.

It was noted, however, that fluency did not necessarily develop, and alternative approaches were sought. A *'functional approach'* prevalent in English language teaching in the 1970s and 1980s aimed to foster the ability to use language communicatively, focusing on the way it was used in real life. Because of its obvious relevance to learners needing to use the language immediately, the functional approach was enthusiastically taken up in UK ESOL classes. A widely used version involved noting the situations in which learners needed to use English, deciding which language functions they would need to express in those situations, for example making requests and teaching to those needs. With the *'functional approach'* emphasis the focus shifted from accuracy to fluency, and any work on grammatical accuracy was confined to the language needed in specific situations. This may have resulted in some cases in a 'pendulum swing' from an underemphasis on fluency to an underemphasis on accuracy.

Most ELT course books now claim to follow a communicative or a task-based approach, and take a more integrated view of the relationship between fluency and accuracy.

Accuracy in lexis?

Denotation

Perhaps the most important aspect of lexical accuracy is using the right name for the object or concept we are referring to or, to put it more technically, using a word or phrase with the right denotational meaning. When a learner says 'the chicken' in her flat is too small, meaning 'the kitchen', she has chosen a word with the wrong denotation. The same applies when somebody tells you they are 'constipated', meaning that they 'have a cold'. The first error probably arose because of the similarity in pronunciation between the words 'kitchen' and 'chicken', and the second because there is a similar word constipado in the first language (Spanish) which has a different meaning. This type of word is often referred to as a 'false friend'.

Connotation

'Connotation' is the term used to refer to the association, emotional or otherwise, which the word or phrase evokes in addition to its central, denotational meaning. Errors of lexis often occur because the word or phrase chosen has emotional or attitudinal associations other than those the speaker intends to convey. In other words, the word or phrase does not have the right connotative meaning. The words 'compact', 'little', 'small' and 'poky' could all be used to describe the same flat, but would convey very different impressions.

Collocation

The writer of the passage in Task 7.1 expressed her meaning and feelings very clearly and made few spelling mistakes. However, there are some problems (as well as strengths) in the way she puts words together. Some of these difficulties are grammatical and will be dealt with under the next main heading. Others concern a different aspect of word combination known as collocation. Collocations are, 'those combinations of words which occur naturally with greater than random frequency' (Lewis 1997).

TASK 7.3

Write a list of 6–10 nouns which typically follow the adjective 'sour'. If you can, compare lists with one or more colleagues.

COMMENT 7.3

There is likely to be considerable overlap between your lists, which probably included some of the following:

- Milk.
- Cream.
- Taste.
- Expression.
- Look.
- Face.
- Mmemory.
- Aftertaste.
- Grapes.
- Note.

This demonstrates the strong associations between the word pairs. Related to collocations are what Lewis calls fixed or semi-fixed expressions (normally of between two and seven words). The collocation 'sour note', for example, often forms part of a longer expression 'ended on a sour note'. Fixed expressions, which do not vary at all, are less common than semi-fixed expressions, which have a certain amount of flexibility): 'while some lexical phrases such as "by the way" or "on the other hand" are set phrases allowing no variability, the majority are more like skeletal frames that have slots for various fillers' (Nattinger and De Carrico 1992).

Functional phrases such as 'would you like a/some ...' fit into this second category, and there are many other types of semi-fixed expression, and many more categories of fixed expression. Learning such prefabricated 'slabs' of language is an aid to developing fluency but all the elements must be there, and in the correct order. In other words, accuracy is necessary if the effect created is not going to be odd or even comic.

The writer of the text in Task 7.1 says 'we know that problem would be coming true someday'. This sounds odd, because we do not usually speak of a 'problem' coming true, although we might well say that a 'wish' or a 'dream' came true. In other words, the expression 'come true' collocates with 'wish' and 'dream', but not with 'problem'. On the other hand, the writer correctly uses the high frequency collocation 'few years'. That said, it would express her meaning better and more accurately if extended into the semi-fixed expression 'a few years ago'. If the writer learned this expression as a whole she would not have to consider, each time she used it, whether 'few' needs to be preceded by an indefinite article. The learning of fixed and semi-fixed expressions, as well as improving fluency by supplying ready-made chunks of language, can help with accuracy in areas of grammar such as the use of articles.

Pronunciation

Words and phrases (and indeed, fixed or semi-fixed phrases which might form whole utterances) need to be pronounced in such a way that they are recognizable. One of the most important factors here is correct stress, as we discussed in Chapter 4. Stress needs to be treated as a property of a word or phrase and to be noted in learners' vocabulary records.

Spelling

Learners need to record lexis in writing if they want to develop accurate spelling. They also need to cultivate strategies for memorizing the spellings they have written down.

Accuracy in grammar

In Chapter 2 we noted that the study of grammar involves attention to syntax and morphology and the linked area of word class. We referred to David Crystal's (1997) definition of syntax as 'the study of sentence structure' and of morphology as 'the study of the structure of words'. We noted also that word class involves categorizing words as nouns, verbs, etc., according to their function within a sentence.

This section addresses some relevant points connected with the analysis of grammar, but does not attempt to be comprehensive. You are advised to read it in conjunction with more detailed texts.

Word class

In the sentence '... granddad was illness since autumn' from the text in Task 7.1, the writer uses a noun 'illness' instead of an adjective 'ill'. This is an example of a problem with word class. Word class can be viewed either as an aspect of lexis or as an aspect of grammar. It is useful for teachers to be able to categorize words in this way, whether or not they decide to use the terminology with their learners.

TASK 7.4

Read the text below, which was written by another ESOL learner.

> My granddad lived in an old town. He was a teacher and headmaster. We lived above the school. A new modern school was built and many parents wanted to send their children there. We knew that we would have problems one day, but Granddad kept silent as usual. We couldn't find any sadness in his face.

Find examples of a noun, verb, adjective, adverb (or adverb phrase), preposition, pronoun, determiner.

COMMENT 7.4

You might have noted some of the following:

Noun:	Granddad, town, school, problems, sadness, face.
Verb:	Lived, was, was built, knew, kept, couldn't find.
Adjective:	Old, new, modern, silent.
Adverb or adverb phrase:	There, one day, as usual.
Preposition:	In, above.
Pronoun:	He, we.
Determiner:	A, an, the (these are articles, which are one type of determiner).
	Many, any (these are not articles, but are another type of determiner).

It is important to note that words can often only be assigned to a word class in a particular context. In another context, they may perform another function, e.g. in the text above 'face' is a noun, but in another sentence it could be a verb, e.g. 'he was a brave man who could face problems'.

Morphology

Morphology is concerned with the way the base form of a word changes in certain circumstances. For example, in the phrase 'the shortest distance', the ending 'est' has been added to the base form of the adjective to form the superlative.

TASK 7.5

Look again at the text in Task 7.4 and note cases where the base form of a word has been modified in this way.

COMMENT 7.5

You probably noted changes in forms of verb and noun, e.g.:

- 'Lived' and 'wanted' add 'd' or 'ed' to form past tense.
- 'Problem' adds 's' to form the plural.
- 'Child' adds 'ren' to form the plural.
- 'Teach' adds 'er' to make a noun.

Syntax

Syntax is concerned with the relationship between words within sentences and between the different elements within sentences. A common sentence type in English has three elements – subject, verb and direct object. In the following sentence, each of these elements is represented by a single word:

Grandfather teaches history

- Subject: Grandfather.
- Verb: Teaches.
- Direct object: History.

The elements of a sentence can be represented by either a single word or a phrase. Thus, we can expand this sentence to make it more informative:

> My best friend's grandfather is planning to teach the history of Europe in the 19th Century.

The sentence is longer and contains more information, but it has not become more complex structurally. In fact, the structure is exactly the same as before:

- Subject: My best friend's grandfather.
- Verb: Is planning to teach.
- Direct object: The history of Europe in the 19th Century.

TASK 7.6

Find the elements *subject/verb/direct object* in the following sentences:

> A number of British supermarkets have started to sell inexpensive clothes for men, women and children.

All the students in my class have lots of experience of catering work.
  My son is hoping to study politics and sociology.

COMMENT 7.6

Did you write?

Subject	Verb	Direct object
A number of British supermarkets	have started to sell	inexpensive clothes for men, women and children.
All the students in my class	have	lots of experience of catering work.
My son	Is hoping to study	politics and sociology.

All the sentences have the same three elements.[1] One reason for concentrating on three elements is that the typical word order of any language is usually described in terms of the normal order for subject, verb and direct object in a declarative sentence. English is a subject–verb–object (SVO) language. Another pattern is subject-object–verb (SOV), which is the usual order in Turkish, Urdu and Farsi, among other languages. For example, the sentence 'grandfather teaches history' would translate into Turkish as 'grandfather history teaches'.

It is worth noting that the issue of word order in different languages extends beyond the subject–verb–object example. Some languages place the adjective after the noun, whereas it comes before the noun in English. Also, where in English we say 'on the table' with a preposition before the noun, in Urdu it is normal to say 'table on'.

Another important element of sentence structure is the adverbial element. Single words or phrases can be added to a basic sentence to give more information, for example about time, frequency, place or manner. We could add to the basic sentence 'grandfather teaches history' in one of the following ways:

- Grandfather usually teaches history.
- Grandfather teaches history for the local adult education institute.
- Grandfather teaches history on Tuesday mornings.
- Grandfather teaches history very well.
- Grandfather teaches history with great enthusiasm.

Each of the above example sentences includes one adverb, consisting of either a single word (e.g. 'usually') or a phrase. In fact, it is possible for a sentence to contain more than one adverb (e.g. Grandfather usually teaches history on Tuesday mornings at the local adult education institute).

Analysing the phrase

1   *The verb phrase.* In any sentence there will be a verb phrase. This may consist of a single word, e.g. 'teaches' or several words, e.g. 'is planning to teach'. It is common practice to use the term 'verb phrase' regardless of how many words are involved.

    When teaching the verb phrase, there is often a focus on verb forms such as present simple, e.g. 'teaches' or present progressive (sometimes called continuous), e.g. 'is planning'. Strictly speaking, not all these verb forms are *tenses*, but for teaching purposes they are often referred to as such.

    Learners need to know how to form these 'tenses' and what meanings they convey. For example, with the verb 'teach, the *base form* or *infinitive* is 'teach', sometimes referred to as 'to teach'. There are two *participles*: 'teaching' and 'taught'. Different forms of the verb can be created by combining either the infinitive or a participle with an *auxiliary verb*, i.e. 'to be', 'to have' or 'to do', e.g.:

    - He was teaching (past progressive).
    - He has taught (present perfect).
    - He doesn't teach (present simple – negative).

There is also another common type of auxiliary, known as a *modal auxiliary*, e.g. 'can', 'should', 'must'.

    This normally combines with the infinitive, e.g. 'he can teach'.

    For learners it is as important to know what *concept* these verb phrases express – e.g. When would you say 'He teaches' and when 'He is teaching'? When would you say 'He was teaching' and when 'he has taught'? – as it is to know how to form them. Meaning should never be secondary to form in the language classroom.

    In addition to the range of forms touched on above, verbs can be used in the *active* or *passive voice*, e.g.:

- He teaches Spanish (active voice).
- Spanish is not taught in my children's school (passive voice).
- At school I was taught to read Spanish (passive voice).

2   *The noun phrase.* In any sentence, the subject and direct object are likely to be expressed by noun phrases, which will include a noun or a pronoun. Like a verb phrase, a noun phrase may consist of a single word or several words. The following are all noun phrases:

- Grandfather.
- My best friend's grandfather.
- He.
- History.
- The history of Europe in the 19th Century.

In a longer noun phrase, there are likely to be words before the head noun, such as articles, other determiners and adjectives. Sometimes there are words after the head noun. In the last example above, there are two prepositional phrases, 'of Europe' and 'in the 19th Century', but these phrases belong with the noun 'history' and are therefore part of the same noun phrase. This shows the importance of dealing with both verb phrases and noun phrases as whole units, showing learners how a phrase fits together, rather than overemphasizing the single words within the phrase.

Analysing clauses

The sentences we have looked at so far are simple sentences. That is, they are simple in structure, despite being long. This simplicity can be accounted for by the fact that there is only one verb phrase. In complex sentences, there will be two or more *clauses*, each with a verb phrase and most often other elements such as subject and direct object. For example: 'He teaches history, even though he has a geography degree'.

If we look again at the text written by an ESOL learner, we can see that there are some problems with sentence structure:

- 'I know that problem was so cruel even I just a child'. The phrase 'even I just a child' needs to be expressed as a clause with its own verb: 'even though I was just a child'.
- 'My granddad died few years but I always remember him because he like a light can bright up my life forever and ever'. In this example, the structure of the beginning of the sentence is good: 'my granddad died a few years [ago] but I always remember him because ...' However, there is a need to follow the word 'because' with a subordinate clause containing a verb: 'he was like a light'. This clause is in turn followed by another subordinate clause: 'that can brighten up my life forever'. The reformulated sentence then reads: 'I always remember him because he was like a light that can brighten up my life for ever and ever'.

As ESOL learners progress to higher levels, issues connected with clause struc-ture of this kind become more and more relevant, especially where accuracy in writing is concerned.

Concept and form

Syntax and morphology help us to describe the way the language is structured. However, the selection of the correct form can only occur if learners are clear about the meanings that each form can carry in particular contexts. So, for example, when selecting which form of a verb to use, speakers and writers need to be aware not only of the way the verb phrase is constructed, but also of the concept it expresses. For example, in the sentence, 'I live in London', the present simple is used, to express the idea that the this is a permanent state. By selecting the progressive aspect in the phrase 'I'm living in London'. The speaker can suggest that this is a temporary state.

Written and spoken grammar

It is important to note that all the examples above refer to *written* grammar. Syntax in particular can vary considerably between written and spoken language, as the following example shows:
    'Just love it, don't they? Kids.
    It is important, when teaching speaking skills, not to automatically impose the rules of written syntax, as the grammar of the spoken language is different in some important respects. Examples of this kind demonstrate the high frequency, in spoken English, of incomplete sentences and repetition or rephrasing. Ellipsis (leaving out words which can be 'assumed' by both listener and speaker), is also very common in speech. The query – 'ready?' – might mean – 'are you ready?' – or – 'is everybody ready?' The listener is normally able to infer from the context what is meant. If not, he or she is free to seek clarification from the speaker.

A typology of grammatical errors

An understanding of morphology and syntax allows us to analyse the type of grammatical errors that ESOL learners might make. In doing so, it is important always to be aware of whether we are referring to spoken or to written English.

1   Errors relating to morphology might include:
    • Using the wrong form of a word (e.g. 'he is tallest than me').
    • Errors in subject–verb agreement (e.g. 'he like, or they doesn't like').
    These would definitely be seen as errors in writing, but although they are technically errors in speech too, the ephemeral nature of spoken language makes them less noticeable.
2   Errors relating to concept and form (using the wrong form to express a particular meaning) e.g. 'every day I am starting work at 8 o'clock' where

the learner has used the progressive aspect, in this context suggesting a temporary situation, which seems to conflict with the adverbial 'every day'. These would be noticeable errors in both writing and speech, as they can compromise meaning.

3   Errors relating to syntax might include:
    - Getting elements of the sentence in the wrong order, e.g. in questions.
    - Repeating an element, such as the subject, e.g. 'my father he likes'.
    - Getting words in the phrase in the wrong order e.g. 'a car blue' rather than 'a blue car'.
    - Leaving out words from the phrase e.g. 'I going' or 'all people in the world'.
    - Confusion in trying to combine sentences or use subordinate clauses.

There can be a big difference between the syntax of formal writing and the syntax of speech. In addition, some genres involving informal writing, such as an email to a friend, will have more in common with the syntax of speech than the syntax of writing. The errors described in the above paragraph would clearly be errors in formal written English. However, they may not be classifiable as errors if used in speech or even in informal writing, e.g.:

    - Word order in questions, e.g. 'Do you like it?, is the standard written form. 'You like it, do you?' or 'you like it?' (said with rising intonation) are very common in speech.
    - Repeating an element, e.g. 'my father he likes', happens a lot in informal speech.
    - Leaving out words (ellipsis) is a common feature of spoken grammar (although it is far from arbitrary which words can be left out).
    - Speech allows much more flexibility in the area of sentence construction and sentence combination than does writing.

TASK 7.7

What features of spoken, as distinct from written, language can you find in the dialogue below.

<Speaker 1>   I'll just take that off.

<Speaker 2>   All looks great.

<Speaker 3>   [laughs]

<Speaker 2>   Mm.

<Speaker 3>   Mm.

<Speaker 2>   I think your dad was amazed wasn't he at the damage.

<Speaker 4>   Mm.

< Speaker 2> It's not so much the parts. It's the labour charges for

<Speaker 4> Oh that. For a car.

<Speaker 2> Have you got hold of it?

<Speaker 2> Yeah.

<Speaker 2> It was a bit erm.

<Speaker 1> Mm.

<Speaker 3> Mm.

<Speaker 2> A bit.

<Speaker 3> That's right.

<Speaker 2> I mean they said they'd have to take his car in for two days. And he says All it is is s=straightening a panel. And they're like, Oh no. It's all new panel. You can't do this.

<Speaker 3> As soon as they hear insurance claim. Oh. Let's get it right.[2]

COMMENT 7.7

You probably noticed the following:

- Ellipsis in Speaker 2's first turn (ellipsis of subject pronouns is common in spoken English).
- Flexibility in word order in Speaker 2's third turn. In written English, the question tag 'wasn't he' would be at the end, if at all.
- What Carter describes as 'phrasal utterances, communicatively complete in themselves but not sentences' ('Oh that'; 'For a car'...).
- Speaker 3 uses a subordinate clause not connected to a main clause: 'As soon as they hear insurance claim'.
- The second 'take that off' in the first line of the dialogue could be, as Carter points out, an ellipted form of 'I'll just take that off' (repeated) or could be an imperative.
- There are no examples of unusual word order in questions in the data. This may be because there are not many questions in it.

You probably noticed other interesting features of spoken language which are exemplified by the dialogue and these are commented on by Carter in the article from which it is taken (see Carter and Nunan 2001).

In summary, there are certain aspects of accuracy, such as use of correct verb tenses and of appropriate collocations, which are common to both writing and speaking. There are other aspects of written grammar, particularly those relating to syntax, which are not the same in spoken grammar. In view of this, teachers should beware of imposing the rules of written grammar on speech. There seems no justification for such traditional classroom practices as requiring learners to speak in complete sentences, particularly in response to questions.

Approaches to accuracy work

Here we will outline some of the decisions ESOL teachers need to make about suitable approaches for their learners.

Top–down and bottom–up approach to language focus

One decision ESOL teachers need to make concerns the place of accuracy work within an overall approach. Do we itemize the grammatical points that need to be worked on and plan our syllabus around covering them all, or do we follow a topic-based or skills-based scheme of work (informed by the interests and needs of the learners) and allow this to lead the work on accuracy in grammar and lexis? And when it comes to planning individual lessons, do we start from a grammatical point we want to deal with or do we begin with a topic and the lexis associated with it, and go from that to the accuracy work?[3] The first approach might be described as *bottom–up*, because it starts with a discrete language item and works up to its use within a stretch of discourse. The second can be described as *top–down* because it begins with the global and works down to the discrete.

Both top–down and bottom–up approaches to accuracy work can be useful in individual lessons. For many ESOL learners there are distinct advantages in a top–down approach. Spoken or written texts chosen for their inherent interest or relevance to learners' lives and interests are likely to be engaging and memorable. Furthermore, the real-world application of the language to be focused on should be easily apparent. A top–down approach also offers opportunities for other language exposure, skills focus and input.

A drawback, however, can be that the content of the recording or written text used sometimes turns out to be so interesting to the learners that it proves difficult to get around to the language focus work, without it being perceived as an anticlimax. When this happens it may be best to postpone the language work, until the learners have explored the content to their satisfaction.

Another potential problem with top–down approaches, particularly when authentic texts are used, is that they may not contain sufficient examples of the language you want to focus on, with the result that learners cannot generalize patterns or rules. Most narrative texts, for example, have a high proportion of irregular past tense verbs, and may not lend themselves to a focus on regular verbs. In response to this problem, materials writers have produced texts and dialogues which exemplify a language point but still come over as reasonably realistic. Although these have been written for the express purpose of focusing on a discrete language point, a top–down approach can still be applied to them in the classroom. Alternatively, you may decide to adopt a bottom–up approach.

A bottom–up approach can give a teacher more control over the language input, allowing him or her to deal with specific points to which he or she wants to draw learners' attention without being distracted by other features in the surrounding text. Bottom–up approaches are particularly useful for clearing up areas of confusion, for example pointing out differences (in both form and meaning) between the present-simple and the present-progressive tenses. They can also be quick and effective when a language point 'comes up' unplanned, either in response to a question from a learner or when a teacher is giving feedback on errors. Also, certain learners respond very positively to a discrete language focus approach, either because they have learned in that way in the past or because of their own learning style and preferences.

On the negative side, overusing this kind of approach can lead to learners perceiving accuracy as divorced from their own language use. Alternatively, particularly in the case of grammar, they may be led into overemphasizing its role in achieving their language goals. On a practical level, thinking up or finding material which covers all the aspects of a language point that a teacher feels should be covered, whilst keeping a realistic feel to these materials, is a challenge that can be hard to meet.

TASK 7.8

Categorize each of the three approaches below as top–down or bottom–up:

- *Lesson 1*: You talk about learners' experience of DIY stores and the staff there. You activate any key lexis and then play a recording of somebody asking for information in a store, first establishing the global meaning of the conversation, i.e. the information being sought and given. You then play the tape again, pausing before and after each request for information, and ask learners to listen intensively and notice the way the requests for information are formed (they could also study the tapescript). After a feedback session involving clarification of the grammatical patterns involved, learners do various practice activities, including a role-play, attempting to use the forms correctly.
- *Lesson 2*: You take as the lesson topic 'finding things out'. You begin by telling the learners something you yourself want to find out and which they may be able to help you with, such as how to use a particular feature on your mobile phone. You elicit examples of things learners want to find out, perhaps retaining the context of mobile phones, or technology in general. You write these on the board, as direct questions. You then discuss contexts in which they might want to make the question more indirect. You elicit phrases they could use to introduce a less direct question, such as 'do you know' or 'I'm

trying to find out'. You ask the learners to re-phrase the questions using these expressions, and either elicit the correct forms from the learners or demonstrate them yourself if they don't know them. The learners then practise using the phrases with the correct word order, asking questions to which they genuinely want to know the answers (and getting some of the answers). Later in the lesson, you might play a recording in which some indirect questions are located within a natural-sounding stretch of discourse building on the type of exchanges the learners have just been practising. Learners then do a freer speaking activity such as a quiz, or some kind of role-play.

- *Lesson 3*: The lesson begins in the same way as Lesson 1, discussing the topic of DIY and activating key lexis. Learners (paired) then do a role-play in which they ask for information about products in a DIY store. After this, each pair prepares to report back on what they learned about the products and how successful they were in obtaining the information they wanted. When the pairs have reported back to the class, you play a recording of expert speakers of English asking for information in the DIY store. After the general meaning of the conversation has been established, learners are asked to listen specifically to the way the questions are asked, noting the phrases used and the word order, and establishing similarities and differences between the recording and their own role-plays.

COMMENT 7.8

Lesson 1: This is a *top–down* approach, starting at discourse level, drawing on learners' knowledge and experience of DIY stores and going on to look at the kind of conversations that might take place there. Only when the meanings expressed in the example conversations have been established does the lesson focus in on a particular bit of language which the learners need to notice.

Lesson 2: This is a *bottom–up* approach, because it isolates a language item which needs to be learned and practised, before placing it within a stretch of discourse once its salient features have been noted and practised.

Lesson 3: Again, this is a *top–down* approach, working from discourse level to noticing discrete bits of language. This approach follows a *task-based* model, similar to that proposed by Jane Willis (1996) in her book, *A Framework for Task-Based Learning*. The rationale for this sequence is that, having struggled to express their meanings with the language available to them, the learners clearly see the purpose of the language being focused on and feel the need for it more keenly, making its acquisition more likely. In many versions of this approach, including that proposed by Willis, it is not thought necessary to practise the new language, but only to notice it and attempt to remember it for future use. This takes account of the fact that practising language does not always lead to its acquisition.

Focusing openly on grammar

Once a model for the lesson has been selected and the place of language focus within it decided, the next question concerns our strategy for dealing with the grammar. If a teacher has decided to have an overt focus on grammar in a particular lesson, there are further decisions to be made. One of these is whether to explain a rule to their learners (known as the deductive approach) or to provide them with examples, from which they can work out the rule for themselves (known as the inductive approach).

Working out the rule

TASK 7.9

Look at the following words in Kiswahili, with their English translations. Can you express in your own words the rule for pluralization, as you understand it from this data?

mtoto	child
watoto	children
mnyama	animal
wanyama	animals
mtu	person
watu	people

Write the plural forms of the next four words:

mvuvi	fisherman
....	fishermen
mke	wife
....	wives
msichana	girl
....	girls
mti	tree
....	trees

COMMENT 7.9

In completing this task you looked at the data and tried to work out the rule for yourself. Most people will have got the first three correct, but the last one wrong. These are the correct answers:

wavuvi	fishermen
wake	wives
wasichana	girls
miti	trees

You probably formed a hypothesis that you express the plural by replacing the prefix 'm' with 'wa' and you tried out your hypothesis. However, when you weren't given enough data to realize that the rule you had worked out does not always apply and that you had overgeneralized. If you had been given more examples, you would have been able to work out that the 'wa' prefix applies with animate beings, but not with inanimate objects.

This example gives you an opportunity to try the process of working out a rule for yourself (an inductive approach) and to decide how it compares with being given the rule by a tutor (a deductive approach). It also demonstrates the importance of giving sufficient examples to facilitate hypothesis formation.

One model of language learning which includes the idea of hypothesis formation is known as the input–interaction–output (IIO) model (Gass 1997). According to this, people first need 'comprehensible input', in other words they need exposure to the language either through listening or reading, and they need to be able to understand what they hear or read. Ideally this 'input' should be at a slightly higher level than the language they can currently use themselves, and it is made comprehensible both through context and through interaction. When learners are interacting directly with a speaker of the target language (as opposed to listening to the radio, for example) they can indicate whether they need the other speaker to modify the way he or she is speaking, for example by asking for explanation or simply by failing to understand. This should result in the other person adapting their way of speaking, so providing 'input' which is at a suitable level to assist language acquisition.

However, being able to understand the language one hears or reads is only part of the story. To be able to use the language fluently and accurately themselves, learners need to be aware of some of the ways the language is structured. Once they have understood the message of what is said or written, they begin to 'notice' features of the language, for example how words are ordered or how similar language patterns can re-appear. This 'noticing' may be done consciously, but it may also be done without the learner being particularly aware of doing it. Linked with 'noticing' is 'hypothesis formation', whereby the learner works out a rule based on recurring patterns they may have 'noticed'. This rule may be accurate, but it may occasionally lead to overgeneralization, as was probably the case with most people doing the Swahili exercise above.

The IIO model recognizes the need for 'output', i.e. for the learner to attempt to speak or write the language themselves, not just at the end of the process of acquisition, but throughout. When learners attempt to use new language to express their own thoughts they need to go beyond simply understanding the message and to pay attention to the form of the language. It is in their own language use that they get the opportunity to try out the hypotheses they have formed and discover whether they are correct, noting the reaction of the people they speak to or being given direct feedback.

When ESOL teachers use an inductive approach, they are working with the understanding that 'noticing' and 'hypothesis formation' are important for language acquisition and, in class, learners can be encouraged to do this consciously.

Some examples of activities which encourage 'noticing' are:

- Learners read a horoscope and pick out all the different ways of referring to future time.
- Learners listen to a taped discussion about football and pick out examples of comparative and superlative.
- Learners read a set of instructions and underline examples of the passive voice, discussing why it is used.

An example of an activity which encourages 'hypothesis formation' is:

- Learners read a text which uses different narrative tenses, then are asked to underline simple past verbs in one colour and past-perfect verbs in another. After checking that this has been done correctly, the teacher asks them to speculate about the rule. Can they put in their own words the rule that informs the choice between these two verb forms?

The point about developing the skills of 'noticing' and 'hypothesis formation' in class is that these are not meant to be confined to the classroom – learners should be encouraged to practise 'noticing' outside the class, when reading, when watching TV and even when overhearing people speaking. They should also be given opportunities in class to ask questions about language they have heard or read – in other words opportunities to test the hypotheses they have formed.

Bilingual approaches

Another point about Task 7.8 is that it uses *another* language, in this case English, to facilitate the hypothesis formation. It is, in fact, an example of a bilingual approach. The justification for using bilingual approaches in ESOL has been discussed in Chapter 2, and links closely with ideas of language identity and language use within the bilingual community. As with other aspects of ESOL teaching, work on grammatical accuracy can be assisted by the use of bilingual approaches.

Clearly, a bilingual teacher who speaks his or her learners' languages can choose either to explain rules or to assist learners in working out rules, through the use of the first language. At the same time, any teacher, whether he or she speaks his or her learners' languages or not, can encourage language comparison among his or her learners. One very simple example, which can be used even in Entry 1 classes, is given here:

The teacher writes 2 phrases, one in English and one in French:

- 'A blue pullover'.
- 'Un pull-over bleu'.

explaining that both have the same meaning. Learners then say whether their first language has a similar structure to English or to French.

The advantage of this, in circumstances where learners appear to be wrongly applying a grammatical rule from the language system of their L1 to English, is that learners begin to make a conscious comparison, noting differences and avoiding direct translation.

Use of metalanguage

One moral decision for the teacher who decides to focus overtly on grammar is whether to use grammatical terminology or metalanguage with learners. For example, with the French and English phrases above, is it appropriate to use the terms 'noun' and 'adjective'? Some learners may have learned previously through an approach which involves the use of linguistic metalanguage and may expect this and benefit from it. However, with others, it may only confuse the issue.

Do I take a grammar-led or a lexis-led approach?

In a grammar-led approach, language appears to be a collection of structures into which we slot the lexis we need to express our meanings. On reflection, however, this does not seem to correspond to the way people actually use language. We begin with words and expressions, using grammar as the organizing principle to express our meanings. The primacy of grammar in language learning and teaching has been challenged in recent years by proposals for a lexical approach. Central to this approach is the idea that, in Michael Lewis's words, 'language consists of grammaticalised lexis, not lexicalised grammar' (Lewis 1993). It is lexis that 'leads' grammar and not vice versa. So in a lexical approach, grammar is approached through lexis.

By lexis, Lewis means not just individual words but the various kinds of lexical chunk which he and other researchers have identified through their use of language corpora, and which expert speakers of English use as wholes (examples of these were given earlier in this chapter when we were discussing collocation).

As few lexical phrases are fully fixed, it is sometimes difficult to decide where a lexical phrase begins and ends. 'Would you like a cup of tea' might be seen as a (semi-fixed) lexical phrase on the basis of its high frequency. It is useful for learners to see that other items can be substituted for the noun phrase 'cup of tea'. The longer phrase can therefore be 'unpacked' into a language frame 'would you like', used for offering things, with a slot at the end for noun phrases, such as 'a banana', 'a lift home' or 'a cup of tea'. Learners' attention can be drawn to the fact that a noun phrase is needed here.

Even the frame 'would you like' is not entirely fixed, although it is more fixed than 'Would you like a cup of tea'. Suggesting a snack for a visiting friend's toddler, for example, you might say: 'Would he like a banana?' A different pronoun has been substituted, subtly changing the function of the phrase. We seem to have taken a step in the direction of a grammatical pattern, and from this we can see that the distinction between semi-fixed phrases and grammatical patterns is not absolute.

A significant change occurs, however, if you change lexical rather than grammatical elements in the phrase. Other verb phrases can be substituted for 'like' (we can say 'would you go on *Big Brother*?' or 'would you *pass the butter*'). When we do this we express very different meanings. We have moved even further towards the grammatical patterns end of the lexis–grammar continuum. These patterns are the organizing principles of language that we use to express more original thoughts and ideas, as opposed to those which we summon automatically.

Lexical phrases need to be learned with the grammatical patterns that can follow them. As we have just seen, the phrases 'would you like …' and 'would he like …' can be followed by a noun phrase of one or more words. But they can also be followed by other grammatical patterns. Imagine your friend is now attempting to get her toddler onto her knee and into his bib whilst keeping him away from the cup of tea you kindly made for her. You might say helpfully: 'would you like me to chop up that banana?'

You are using the same lexical phrase, 'would you like' but in this case you are offering not just a thing (cup of tea or banana) but to carry out an action. The phrase leads in to a different (and more complex) grammatical pattern.

In a lexical approach a learner or teacher does not avoid grammar but looks at it from a different perspective. He or she takes lexical phrases as a starting point and the word grammar of those phrases decides the type of constructions that can follow. Learners are encouraged to pay attention to the language surrounding lexical phrases as well as the phrases themselves.

Developing accuracy with fluent but inaccurate learners

As discussed earlier, speakers of a language may be more accurate than they are fluent; they may have roughly equal accuracy and fluency; or they may be more fluent than accurate. Most books about teaching English and most teaching materials have been written with the first two of these groups in mind, so it is less challenging for an ESOL teacher to find the right approach and materials for them. There is already a great deal of interesting and useful ELT literature which addresses their needs.

Less has been said about the third group, the relatively fluent but inaccurate speakers who are found in many ESOL classes. These learners may have acquired English in a naturalistic setting, concentrating out of necessity on getting their message across, rather than on accuracy. Some may have attended classes where they were not sufficiently encouraged to become accurate or they may have been introduced to accuracy work without being able to relate it to communication in the outside world. They may not be able to relate to techniques requiring thinking skills that have no real-world equivalent. Examples of these are cloze procedures (where, as we discussed earlier, learners have to guess missing words and insert them in a gapped text) and exercises requiring learners to write the questions that would elicit certain answers (e.g. in response to the cue 'I live in Bradford' the learner has to write 'Where do you live?'). Other learners can deal with and even enjoy these classroom activities, but their own way of speaking is so established that the accuracy work done in class has little or no apparent effect on it.

Some pedagogical approaches recommended for developing accuracy cannot meet the needs of these learners, as they draw on experience and knowledge gained from teaching a different kind of learner. The ideas in the next section are designed with the needs of fluent but inaccurate learners in mind.

Contexts for grammar work

Sometimes learners can do grammar exercises in class and get the answers right, but they do not transfer what they have learned to their use of English outside the classroom. It is therefore essential to situate grammar teaching within contexts which relate to the learners' normal use of English. A 'top–down' approach, as described above, allows the learner to be fully aware of the communicative context in which the grammar is used. So, for example, a group of learners who are in work or seeking work might learn about the passive in relation to reading written instructions displayed in the workplace. Or a group of learners with children might practise comparative and superlative forms while discussing play facilities or schools in the area where they live. In these cases, the teacher has predicted which grammatical forms are likely to be well represented in a particular context. Now the learners need to be encouraged to notice these forms.

Inductive approaches and 'noticing'

We have seen above that an inductive approach involves learners working out a rule for themselves and that this is closely linked with the skill of 'noticing'. With learners who have developed fluency without accuracy, it is possible that their process of acquisition has involved too little of this 'noticing'. At an earlier stage of their language learning, they may have been too focused on meaning to pay attention to form. Helping them to become more aware of form can be extremely useful, but in order to be effective, it will almost certainly have to be done with reference to the type of language they encounter already in their daily lives. For example, a teacher of a group of parents might play a tape of a mother talking about what she did with her children at the weekend, and ask learners to notice how she talks about the past. Or a teacher of a group of job-seekers might take a person specification and ask learners to find words like 'must' and 'should' and notice the form of the verb which follows. The advantage of this process for learners who already have a degree of fluency is that they can already understand what they hear and read, and they can use this understanding as a basis for starting to pay attention to form.

Bilingual approaches

Noticing language forms involves to some extent adopting an analytical approach to language, thinking and talking *about* it, rather than just using it. For some learners, particularly those who have learned English fairly easily in a naturalistic setting, this is a new experience. There is, therefore, a strong case for encouraging them to do this with reference to their first language, that is the one with which they are most familiar.

For example, if a group of learners are not using definite and indefinite articles in their formal speech and in their writing, teachers can start a discussion about whether their first language uses articles and in what way. Learners could be asked to translate sentences such as 'I am a teacher', 'there's a bank on the corner', or 'the sun is shining' as a preliminary to discussing use of the articles or lack of articles in their first language and in English. By discussing and comparing features such as use of articles or word order, learners increase their general language awareness and should understand more about the particular features of English they need to focus on.

Monitoring and proofreading

No matter what work is done on grammatical accuracy, there will be mistakes in learners' speech or writing. 'Monitoring' involves learners examining their own use of English and self-correcting. Clearly, this is easier to do in writing than in speech, and is linked with the skill of proofreading. All competent writers proofread their own work and ESOL learners also need to learn to do this. An approach which can help develop this ability is 'scaffolding'. Scaffolding involves giving support at the beginning of a process, then gradually withdrawing support until a learner can work independently. A common way of doing this is to introduce a marking scheme which moves gradually from teacher correction to learner correction. Many marking schemes categorize mistakes by means of an agreed 'code' where, for example, 'T' in the margin indicates a problem with verb tense; 'WW' (wrong word), a lexical mistake; and 'WO' (word order), a mistake with syntax. Such codes can be useful in helping the learner develop awareness of the areas where they are most likely to make mistakes which they can rectify themselves, allowing them to proofread more effectively.

The situation is different with spoken English. Some learners can and do monitor, as we can see from the following extract from the video, *I Came to England*:

> I am sure I write very good in the grammar, I write very good *and I didn't, I don't speak good*, yes because I am shy little bit or maybe think little bit.

In this example, the speaker is talking about her present ability in English, but she initially uses the past tense, immediately correcting herself. This is an example of effective monitoring. However, there are some learners who have a tendency to overmonitor, which can have an adverse effect on their confidence and fluency, many ESOL learners who have developed a degree of fluency seem to undermonitor or not to monitor at all.

Teachers can encourage self-monitoring. However, it may be unrealistic to expect the learner to focus on more than one feature at a time. Teacher and learner(s) together can identify a feature – the choice of past or present tenses, in the case of the learner quoted above – and monitor that feature carefully, ignoring other errors.

Rehearsing

Accuracy in the spoken language is most important in formal situations, and, as people often do when speaking their first language, learners may be well advised to spend time rehearsing what they will say. This rehearsal might involve listening to a recording, noticing the forms used, practising those forms, possibly writing down key phrases; then rehearsing in as realistic a way as possible, monitoring their own speech and the speech of other learners; then discussing the degree of accuracy achieved. In the course of such activities, the teacher can 'feed in' ways for learners to communicate their own meanings more clearly and accurately, giving them the necessary support to move to the next level of 'comfort' in language use.

The relevance of learning styles

Some learners cannot relate well to a visually orientated and analytical approach to language work. In this case, it is important to consider kinaesthetic activities (involving physical movement) and tactile activities (using the sense of touch) which can achieve the same purpose as the more traditional kind.

Two examples are given here:

Type of approach	Aim	Procedure
Kinaesthetic	For learners to be aware of when to use the gerund and when to use the infinitive.	• Write sentences on card, e.g. 'I want to work in an office'; 'I am interested in learning Arabic'. • Cut the sentences into 2 parts, just before the gerund or infinitive. • Give learners half a card and ask them to circulate until they find someone with a suitable other half.
Tactile	For learners to be aware of word order within sentences.	• Write a number of sentences on card and cut each one up into words. • Ask learners to re-assemble each sentence.

Working from strengths

As we have noted earlier, published material for developing accuracy in English language may be aimed at learners who do not yet have a high degree of fluency. However, if we use this material uncritically with learners who have been using English in day-to-day situations for a long time, we are not making use of the lexical knowledge and communicative ability they have developed over time.

As an example, consider a learner who speaks like this:

Every day I going to work ...
Two weeks ago I going to work ...
I going to work day after tomorrow ...

This learner certainly needs accuracy work. At the same time, he has his own way of making meaning clear, through the use of adverbial phrases (e.g. 'every day', 'two weeks ago'). A lot of teaching material for introducing new verb forms would look first at the verb form, then move on to looking at the adverbials which can be used with that verb form. Yet unlike some learners of English, this learner probably has an extensive knowledge of adverbial phrases. So instead of learning adverbs that can go with certain verb forms, this learner needs to learn the verb forms that go with certain adverbs, and would benefit from an approach which starts with what he knows already.

It is important, when using published material which was written with a different type of learner in mind, to consider working from a different starting point, as a way of recognizing the strengths of a learner such as the one above. There are many people who have lived in the UK for a long time whose accuracy is on a par with the examples given here, but what they lack in accuracy they make up for in lexical range, receptive understanding and general communicative ability. It is important to give credit for what they can do, and not be tempted to regard them as beginners on the basis of accuracy alone.

Task-based and lexical approaches

Task-based approaches and a lexical view of language, are particularly suitable for encouraging fluent but inaccurate learners to pay attention to features of language which have so far escaped their notice, or which they have not felt to be important. Learners respond positively to the realistic (preferably authentic) discourse which is central to both approaches. They can use their well-developed receptive skills to access global meaning with relative ease, leaving energy to concentrate on the detailed language focus that will help them to develop accuracy.

In her proposed framework for a task-based approach, Jane Willis (1996) distinguishes between public and private use of language. While learners are doing a task, they are free to concentrate on communicating. When they prepare to report back on it, publicly, to the whole class, they are supposed to pay more attention to accuracy. This may be helpful in activating language features not yet fully automatic but on the point of becoming so. Taking account of the distinction between public and private use should help learners to prepare for demanding situations such as telephone calls, interviews or confrontations, where inaccuracies might undermine their credibility and effectiveness.

An approach involving the recognition and memorization of lexical chunks is also likely to suit fluent but less accurate learners for several reasons. First, the primacy of meaning in a lexical approach is likely to make sense to such learners. Second, a lexical approach can be a new way of looking at difficult areas of grammar. The way articles and prepositions combine with other words may be easier to remember than strings of rules about their general uses. Finally, if a learner's speech contains a high proportion of lexical chunks, accurately reproduced, speech will be both more fluent and more accurate.

Correction

TASK 7.10

Think about how far you agree with the statements below, representing teachers' views about correction, then discuss your answers with a colleague.

- Teacher 1: 'I do correct my learners, because they want me to, but I'm not sure that it does any good'.
- Teacher 2: 'There are things that some of my learners just can't seem to get right. If I keep on correcting them they just lose confidence'.
- Teacher 3: 'I'm selective about what I correct, both in spoken and in written work'.
- Teacher 4: 'My learners have asked me to correct all their mistakes, but if I corrected every mistake we'd all lose track of the conversation'.
- Teacher 5: 'I correct "on the spot" when we are focusing on accuracy. During free speaking activities I write down the mistakes I hear, and we correct them together when we've finished the activity'.

COMMENT 7.10

Those who find, as does Teacher 1, that their corrections do not seem to be having any noticeable effect, particularly on grammatical accuracy, may wonder whether there is really any point in correcting at all. Often the learners manage to speak more accurately when they are consciously attending to form, but as soon as they express themselves spontaneously, the mistakes are back. As Teacher 2 points out, this can also be disheartening for the learners themselves, if they are aware of it.

One theory is that learners acquire structures in a particular order and formal instruction, including correction, does not result in a structure being acquired unless a particular learner is 'ready' to acquire it. A well-known and documented example of this is the third person 's' on the present simple tense, which is taught at Entry level 1 of the curriculum but rarely fully acquired until much later. People who learn a language in a naturalistic context can and do acquire certain grammatical features without studying them. The ones they acquire are probably those most important for successful communication, such as English word order. However, there are other features, such as the use of auxiliary verbs in questions, which seem to be very difficult to acquire without formal study. Many teachers, and learners, have continued to believe in the usefulness of focusing on grammar and correcting it, and some researchers share their view.

The fact that a person may make the same mistake a day, an hour or even a few minutes after it was corrected does not necessarily mean that the correction is having no effect. One possibility is that consciously focusing on that piece of language will help the learner to acquire it when they are ready to do so. The approach favoured by Teacher 5 would be useful in raising awareness, which should eventually lead to acquisition.

What correction strategies should we adopt?

There is sometimes a tension between the correction strategies favoured by teachers and those favoured by learners. The latter may expect a great deal of correction, feeling that a teacher who (in their view) undercorrects is falling down on the job. Teachers may take the view that learners' requests for more correction stem from conventional (and misguided) ideas about the role of the teacher and the nature of language learning. Teacher 4 makes a practical point: correcting all mistakes would involve such frequent interruptions that neither the learners nor the teacher would be able to follow or respond to the content of the conversation. During pre-service training, teachers are often recommended to minimize 'on-the-spot' correction during fluency activities. Immediate correction during such activities, it is argued, would be counterproductive as it would (a) risk inhibiting learners so that their fluency development is impeded; (b) interrupt the conversation; and (c) shift the focus of the activity to accuracy. So teachers are advised to note down errors and deal with them at the end of the activity, in a separate phase of the lesson. Teacher 5 has taken this advice to heart, and indeed it is sound advice when a teacher is dealing with people whose fluency lags behind their accuracy, particularly if the learners are inclined to overmonitor their own accuracy. Learners who are afraid of making mistakes or embarrassed when they hear themselves doing so are unlikely to benefit from teacher interventions while they are speaking, and the best strategy is to intervene (helpfully and tactfully) only if communication breaks down. During the correction phase, nobody is 'singled out', as there is no need to identify who made which of the errors.

Learners who are fluent but inaccurate are a different case: they need to monitor their language closely, particularly if inaccuracies are impeding their ability to communicate successfully. Such learners may not realize how inaccurate their speech is (as we have already discussed, it is common for people to have studied and even 'know' a piece of grammar but underuse it in free speech, and some people do not realize that they underuse it).

It can be helpful to intervene when fluent but inaccurate learners are speaking freely. Of course, as Teacher 3 is aware, it is not practical (or desirable) to correct all the mistakes 'on the spot'. Neither is it advisable to interrupt a free-speaking activity to give a lengthy explanation of a piece of grammar or lexis. But in instances where learners have the theoretical knowledge to correct themselves, free-speaking activities can be an opportunity to facilitate the acquisition of 'learnt' language. You and the learner(s) can agree on a focus for correction which is both helpful to them and appropriate for the activity. For example (to return to an example given earlier when we talked about self-monitoring), a group of learners may be able to write a narrative using the past-simple tense but revert to using the present simple either all or part of the time when they talk about past events. When setting up an activity requiring the use of the past simple you can agree that, when monitoring that group, you will prompt them to pause and self- or peer-correct when they forget to use it (so much the better if they also decide to prompt each other when you are not monitoring the group). Another learner, or group of learners, may know the rule for pronunciation of '-ed' endings, but have got into a habit of enunciating the vowel in every case. They could be corrected on that point during the same activity. As an appropriate focus for correction has been selected, and agreed, recognition that learned rules have not yet been fully acquired should not result in any loss in confidence (as feared by Teacher 2) on the part of the learners. This is especially true if the teacher explicitly acknowledges that mistakes are to be expected and part of the process of acquisition, and that feedback may have a significant role in helping learners to become more consistent in their use of language features which they understand but use variably.

The practice of peer correction (when proofreading written English as well as when monitoring spoken English) is likely to assist in this process, but, as with teacher correction, it is important that the person who made the mistake recognizes the difference between his or her original utterance and the reformulated version. For this reason, when the teacher is monitoring it is best to prompt self-correction before inviting peer correction (such prompting may be done by means of a gesture, or perhaps by repeating the incorrect form with a questioning intonation). If the learner cannot self-correct, he or she can be asked to repeat the correct version after one of his or her peers has corrected it for him or her. Learners who are used to peer monitoring and correcting when the teacher is present are more likely to do so when he or she is busy monitoring a different group.

A technique which is particularly suitable for use with fluent but inaccurate learners is recording a conversation and analysing the errors afterwards: a variant and refinement of the approach favoured by Teacher 5. Pairs can record themselves doing a role-play, for example, then play back and evaluate their performance using suitable criteria (including the effectiveness of the communication as well as accuracy and range of grammar, pronunciation, lexis and so on, as appropriate).

TASK 7.11

After you have finished reading this section, you may want to review the questions in Task 7.8 and see if you have modified any of your views.

Notes

1 There are further elements to sentence structure than those exemplified here, e.g. we have not chosen examples of sentences with an indirect object or complement – see the recommendations for further reading.

2 The excerpt below is reproduced from data used in Ronald Carter's (2002) article, 'The grammar of talk: spoken English, Grammar and the Classroom'.

3 Planning is discussed in more detail in Chapter 10.

8 Developing and adapting resources[1]

Clare Fletcher and Vivien Barr

Introduction

Good learning resources are a major component of an excellent ESOL lesson. They keep learners and the teacher interested and focused, and they deliver the key learning points in context in a way that is memorable and interesting. There is an increasing amount of material available which is directed at ESOL learners; much of it is now online and, so, easy to find. This chapter will also look further afield at other sources of material with examples of how these can be customized for ESOL learners: ELT coursebooks, originally designed for EFL learners; adult literacy resources; vocational resources; authentic material; and self-created own resources. The use of ILT will feature in each section.

First a look at resources in general

Resources are powerful learning tools and it is important to choose them wisely. They need to be motivating for the learner, sufficiently challenging but not daunting. Material that is of poor quality or unreliable or out of date must be avoided and the type of material needs to vary over a series of lessons so that learners encounter different genres.

Good teachers can put themselves in the learners' position. They recognize that a lively mind is easily frustrated by having only basic English as the form of expression. They know that learners want to know about UK life and culture, that what learners gain from the ESOL class is more than just English, and that they are learning outside as well as inside the classroom. Good ESOL teachers are aware of cultural assumptions, and are especially mindful that the way we do things in the UK is neither the only nor necessarily the best way. In their work they are sensitive to the learners' first languages and culture and to what their learners may have experienced before and after arriving in the UK. All these considerations come into play when choosing resources.

Starting points and lesson priorities

Your starting point is what your learners need in order to progress. You will have key learning priorities for each lesson, derived from learner need, the curriculum and/or assessment requirements. You will be looking for resources with your priorities in mind. In this chapter, we will give examples of different starting points – some grammatical, some to do with pronunciation and some which are functional or context-based. Varying starting points in this way is motivating for learners.

Evaluating resources

Below are some questions to consider when selecting resources for use in the classroom.

1   *Language focus*:
    - Does the material fit in with your course aims, and your lesson objectives? Is it suitable for teaching what you want the learners to learn?
    - Which language skills are involved? Does the material focus on developing a particular skill or does it integrate skills?
2   *Content*:
    - Is the context relevant to the current lives of your learners or their likely future lives, in the most ambitious sense?
    - Is there anything which might cause distress or offence?
    - Are there cultural assumptions underlying the material, and if so do they suit the group of learners? What knowledge is assumed, about language or the context? (This chapter includes some examples of dealing with assumed knowledge.)
    - Is the content up-to-date?
3   *Appearance and use*:
    - Are the resources attractively presented and likely to engage learners?
    - Can it be exploited in various ways?
    - Over a period of time, are you using a variety of resources? Recognize your own preferences and inclinations and avoid overusing the same kind of material at the expense of other kinds.

Exploiting material

You will need to think about how to present the material to your learners in such a way that they gain maximum benefit. Plan how to introduce the material or the topic, what learners need to get started. It may be the context, some key lexis, the function or a mixture of all these and more. How will they relate the new material to what they know already? This may mean getting them to think about their own experience, in the UK and in their country of origin. Are there cultural sensitivities which need to be explored?

Plan what your learners will be doing while they hear or read the material. Will they tackle the material in stages or all of it at once? How many times will they do this? Will they have a chance to let you know when they have had enough exposure to the material? Will you share with them why they are learning in this way?

Once learners have engaged with the material, you and they have a variety of possibilities for follow-up activities. You can move between the various language skills and use written material to stimulate speaking and listening and vice versa, and you can also use your material to build learner independence by encouraging research and work outside the classroom.

Finally, exploit the material in as many different ways as you can. Learning is cyclical not linear – so re-use resources, for example a text used for skimming and scanning could be used for reading comprehension another time.

ILT

Every section in this chapter will make reference to information learning technology (ILT). ILT refers to technology being used to enhance and support teaching and learning. It includes both computers and telecommunications. It can involve a computer or other device connected to a network and the Internet, giving the user access to forms of communication such as email, fax, chat, online forums as well as computer software. Digital technology is creating new ways of linking, for example, mobile phones, cameras and music players. Tools such as multimedia projectors and interactive whiteboards are also included.

Teachers can find many resources directly relevant to ESOL learners in electronic form. The *Adult ESOL Core Curriculum*, and Skills for Life ESOL material are available on CD-ROM and online; they can be searched and adapted. Teacher-made resources can be shared within colleges and through collaborative websites (such as www.talent.ac.uk). There are also a large number of language-teaching websites with downloadable materials and teaching tips.

Learners can also use ILT as a tool for learning, and teachers may help learners develop the necessary skills (and vice versa!) As an ESOL teacher, you are doing several things at once. First, you are teaching English and unlocking the host culture for learners who want to build new lives in the UK. When you use ILT you are also promoting computer literacy, making sure that the learners have the English and the skills to function effectively in an increasingly IT-based society. You are teaching the language of confident computer users, often rapidly changing, and also the relevant grammar and lexis.

For example, to use the expression: 'Did you Google it?' requires the ability to use the past tense and also an understanding of search engines and contemporary ways of talking about them.

You should ask your learners how they use computers and the Internet. There may be a wide range of experience within a class. If your class can have access to computers, you can assess their level of familiarity and supplement it as necessary. If you have access to an interactive whiteboard, use it little and often, and ensure that it is interactive and not just a presentation tool.

ELT books

English language teaching (ELT) coursebooks are aimed at learners of English as a foreign language (EFL) worldwide. Their many strengths make them a popular resource for ESOL classes, but teachers need to be aware of possible drawbacks.

Advantages of using an ELT coursebook

ELT books are usually attractively presented, and learners may take pride in having a 'proper book' as do learners of other subjects. They also gain independence from having their own copies; can see where the course is going; and can catch up if they have been away. Moving through the units in the book gives a sense of progress.

For teachers, coursebooks with the accompanying teachers' books provide a clear linguistic framework with systematic coverage of language skills and systems. The writers are experienced teachers and the books are piloted before publication, so they are a source of tried-and-tested activities. Indeed, coursebooks are a means by which new methodology and new ideas from linguistics are spread among teachers. There is often a package of supporting material, such as audio and video recordings, and supplementary exercises in workbooks or online. For hard-pressed teachers, having a ready-made source of material for use in class and homework removes the pressure of constantly generating teaching resources.

Possible drawbacks

- The books assume good literacy and a fairly consistent level across all four language skills. Learners in ESOL classes may need a good deal of supplementary work. This is particularly true at early levels, beginner and elementary.
- ELT coursebooks do not usually teach literacy skills. Due to this learners may never finish the book, which can counteract the sense of progress which the book offers.
- The typical ELT coursebook is aimed at a wide international market. This can result in rather bland content with little about the skills and knowledge which enable learners to participate in British society.
- The content often assumes an affluent lifestyle and cosmopolitan outlook and ESOL learners may not identify with the people depicted.
- For some learners, the books are expensive, especially if they never get to the end.
- A sophisticated visual layout may be hard to follow, and the amount of text on a page may be daunting to learners with early literacy skills.
- The material will not be local or topical. The teacher may be tempted to use the easily photocopiable TV listings or maps of a town contained in a book rather than getting up-to-date and local material.

If the teacher selects specific pages from a book, this avoids some of the drawbacks but not all. Content may still be inappropriate and the assumed level of study skills and literacy may be too high.

How to use ELT books

Published material should be evaluated in the light of the learners who will be using it. With ELT coursebooks it is particularly important to screen for distressing or offensive content. Teachers also need to consider what contexts are used:

- Do these show diversity and cultural sensitivity?
- What assumptions are made about learners' education, literacy level, lifestyle, age?
- What knowledge of English is required to tackle the material?
- What work on skills is included?
- How could spiky profiles, where learners are stronger in some skills than others, be catered for?

In selecting material – and this of course is true with any type of material – be clear what you want to achieve. How does the material fit the objectives and learners' needs? Is it effective learning material for the language you want to teach?

A good maxim for using published material is '*select, adapt, supplement*'. The following two examples apply this to a complete coursebook, and to an exercise.

Selecting from a coursebook

The contents list or course outline at the beginning of the book is a useful tool for selecting for particular classes.

COURSE OVERVIEW				
Unit	Language focus	Vocabulary	Topics	Review
1 FINDING OUT	*To be* *There is, there are.* Articles: *a, an, any.* Adjectives; sentences structures.	Names, addresses, jobs. Buildings and facilities.	Meeting people. Giving directions inside a building. Important things in life. Learning languages.	Instruction words. Expressions of location.

2	WHAT HAVE YOU GOT?	*Has got / have got.* *Some (some/any).* Subject pronouns and possessive adjectives. Contractions.	Families and countries. Personal possessions. Homes and furniture.	Asking about family. Asking about homes and possessions.	Dates, months, years. Unit 1.
3	WHAT WOULD YOU LIKE TO EAT?	Present simple question forms. The verb *to have.* *Would like* and *I'd like.* Countable and uncountable nouns.	Food and meals. Prices.	Breakfast food. Room service. Ways of memorizing names. Prices in different cultures.	Unit 1. Unit 2.
4	A SENSE OF COLOUR	Question forms with present simple verbs. Present simple verbs in positive sentences: 1st/3rd person.	Clothing, colour. Time expressions: *never, once a year, twice a year.*	Uniforms. Buying clothes. Cultural meaning of colours. Producing a blue rose.	Unit 2. Unit 3.
5	GOOD HABITS, NEW ROUTINES?	Present simple verbs: positive, negative, questions.	Daily routines. Habits and customs.	Morning people. Language learning habits. National customs. Queues.	Unit 3. Unit 4.

Figure 8.1 A course overview

There are various starting points; three examples are given below.

Source: From Collie and Slater (1995).

1   *Learners' situation*: You might start by considering what is relevant and useful for the learners in that situation. For example, you are teaching a class of care assistants and you are looking for contextualized language practice with some connection to their work setting:
   - *True to Life Elementary* is available, and is at about the right level, Entry 2.
   - Unit 3 covers possible topics: food and meals. 'Room service' could be adapted to taking meal orders from patients. Present simple question forms are useful. 'I'd like' could enable the learners to be assertive about their shift pattern. So this unit might form the basis for a lesson (or lessons). It would be worth looking at the unit in detail.

2   *Curriculum component skill*: For example, you are looking for material to teach this particular component skill from the ESOL curriculum (DfES 2001b: Sc/E2.2a); ask for directions and instructions:

- *True to Life Elementary* Unit 1 includes giving directions inside a building. So it would be worth looking at this to see if there is useful material – perhaps a recording of someone giving directions.
3 *Grammar*: For example, your learners need contextualized work on the Entry 2 grammar point, countable and uncountable nouns:
  - *True to Life Elementary* Unit 3 has a language focus on countable and uncountable nouns which might provide relevant material for learners to consolidate their understanding.

TASK 8.1

Look at the *Adult ESOL Core Curriculum* for Entry 2. Find a component skill for speaking and a grammatical point which are included in the course overview from *True to Life* on the previous page.

Adapting Coursebook Material – Listening And Speaking

Entertaining friends

1 Have you ever been a guest in someone's house in a foreign country? When? Why? What happened?
2 T.29 You will hear three people describe how they entertain guests in their countries. Sumie is from Japan, Rosa is from Spain, and Leslie is from the United States.

Listen and take notes under the following headings:
  - the kind of invitation, formal or informal
  - the time of day
  - the preparations that the host or hostess makes
  - the presents that people take
  - the food and drink served

3 Work in small groups. Compare information. What similarities and differences are there?
4 What happens in your country? Is it usual to invite people to your home for a meal? What are such occasions like in your home?

Figure 8.2 From *New Headway English Course – intermediate* (L and J Soars, OUP p 43)
Source: From Soars and Soars 2009: 43.

This is useful recorded material for developing listening skills at E3/L1 level. The speakers sound fairly natural, and have different voices and accents. There is scope for note-taking practice, and the material can be further exploited for speaking and writing practice. However, the task requires learners to listen and take notes and this assumes that learners' listening comprehension and writing skills are at a similar level. This might not be the case.

There are opportunities for cross-cultural comparisons. But for refugees and asylum seekers, the follow-up question What happens in your country? might be a painful question.

Having evaluated the material in this way, the teacher can plan how to 'select, adapt and supplement' it for a particular class.

This material has three speakers in succession, which might be too much listening to do at once. You could select one or two.

You could adapt the introduction, by starting with your own experience as a guest or host. What happened when you went to someone's house, or had people round to your place? If learners are going to be invited to talk about their experiences, it is only fair that the teacher is willing to share his or hers.

The recorded material is given, but you could use it in different ways and supplement it to cater for different strengths and weaknesses:

- Learners who are good at listening comprehension but slow readers could read the transcript while listening. For those people, the objective is to increase reading speed.
- Learners who need to concentrate on listening actively, could be given a short summary of the information containing two incorrect statements. Learners read this first, then listen and spot the mistakes. (The summary could later serve as a model for learners to write their own summary after they listen to the second speaker.)
- Learners who need to improve study skills might work on note-taking with an outline of the notes which they complete as they listen.

You could adapt the order of activities. Learners could work together after hearing the first speaker, to check what they understood, discuss what they heard, contribute ideas about what happens elsewhere or ask questions. However, before this is done, you might choose to play back the second speaker, so that learners can compare what the two speakers say about their customs. This would give learners something objective to talk about, if they do not want to talk about their personal experiences.

You could adapt the follow-up activities. Invite people to say what happens in their ethnic communities in this country. Or learners could share information about what is supposed to happen and what actually happens. How much do they know about conventions among English families?

TASK 8.2

How could you supplement the listening and speaking with some work to develop writing skills?

> **COMENT 8.2**
>
> Expanding notes – learners could turn the notes they made while listening into a paragraph on each speaker; they could write a description of customs in their community or record what they have found about from other learners.

ILT in ELT

Many ELT books have an accompanying CD-ROM and ELT publishers often have websites with resources for teachers and learners:

- *For teachers*: lesson ideas and activities, free worksheets, short articles by experienced teachers and writers on teaching tips and methodology.
- *For learners*: exercises, games, interactive activities.

Useful websites:
   www.OUP.com/ELT
   www.onestopEnglish.com (MacMillan)
   www.longman.com
   www.cambridge.org/elt

Computer software is available on CD-ROM or licensed for use on a network; packages often offer learners immediate feedback. ELT bookshops stock multimedia and computer software, and their catalogues show what is available. Sometimes websites show sample material (for example, www.skysoftwarehouse.com and www.clarity.com.hk).

Electronic dictionaries provide swift access, and users can hear pronunciation of new words. The major ELT dictionaries have versions on a CD-ROM. Bilingual dictionaries on a hand-held device can be useful but need to be treated with the same caution as with any small bilingual dictionary.

Literacy and vocational material

Resources for both vocational teaching and adult literacy are primarily aimed at native speakers. However, many vocational and adult literacy classes have a mix of native speakers and speakers of other languages. In addition, policies aimed at getting ESOL learners into mainstream education or job training as soon as possible mean that ESOL teachers may work alongside subject teachers on vocational courses.

Advantages and possible drawbacks of using adult literacy resources

Literacy resources often focus on learners' real-life purposes for literacy, and where these coincide with ESOL learners' purposes they can be very useful. Short books for adult literacy learners, sometimes written by learners themselves, often have adult contexts and interesting content and can provide ESOL learners with good reading material. Literacy teaching material focuses on relevant component skills at word, sentence and text level.

However, adult literacy resources often assume a knowledge of culture and everyday life which ESOL learners may not have and texts written by adult literacy learners may be highly personalized and full of colloquialisms.

Using adult literacy resources

It is important to evaluate the assumptions made within adult literacy resources to see whether there are aspects of everyday life or culture of which knowledge is taken for granted. The teacher needs also to evaluate linguistic content; in adult literacy work, the basic assumption is that learners are learning to read and write a language which they already know. But ESOL learners are learning the language as well as how to read and write it. Their needs are different.

Consider the following extract from a worksheet (illustrations have been omitted):

> Silent 'b'
>
> The **plumber** hit his thumb.
>
> **Comb** the **crumbs** from the **lamb**'s coat.
>
> Remember: plum**b**er thum**b** com**b** crumb**s** lam**b**
>
> all have a silent '**b**'

> (*Essential Communication n.d.*)

Literacy learners know how to say the words; they need to remember to write the letter 'b'. Whereas ESOL learners would need to learn to write the letter 'b' *and* not pronounce it.

Some questions to ask when evaluating literacy teaching material:

- Are there features of 'everyday life' which learners are assumed to know about, or beliefs or customs which they are assumed to share?
- Is pronunciation taken into account?
- Are lexical items presented in a context?
- Are instructions clear, avoiding the use of language which is more difficult than the task itself?

TASK 8.3

Here follow three extracts from adult literacy material. Evaluate each extract in the light of the questions above:

1   *Instruction following a short text**

'Put circles around the capital letters and full stops.'

2   *An inductive exercise to work out the rule for hard and soft 'c' gave the examples**

'cyst, cigarette, ceiling'

3   *Advice following a reading text**

'Are there any words you do not know?

Look at the word and break it into letters:

bank = b–a–n–k

Try another way. Find words inside words.

You can find the word "her" or "here" in "there".'

* *Note*   From DfEE 20061a: *Literacy E1, Unit 1, 2.*

COMMENT 8.3

1   The instructions to the learner are more difficult than the task.
2   Lexical items are not presented in a context.
3   Pronunciation has not been taken into account: 'her', 'here', 'there' all have different vowel sounds.

Using vocational resources

Relevant vocational resources are motivating. Language systems and skills are embedded in a natural context and learners enjoy learning about the subject as well as the language. However, it can be difficult for the ESOL teacher to use vocational learning resources if they feel unfamiliar with the area. Technical concepts and procedures may be explained in contexts which are unfamiliar to the ESOL learner and, instead of making it easier, they make it harder to grasp the concepts. What's more, there will be cultural differences for ESOL learners already trained in the vocational area in their country of origin.

ESOL learners often want to gain vocational qualifications as soon as possible. On vocational courses, they may find themselves in a class with native speakers of English, taught by subject teachers with varying degrees of understanding of the particular needs of ESOL learners. Alternatively, they may be in a class for ESOL learners, but using materials specific to the vocational field. Some learners will know the vocational area well but lack the requisite English, while others will be learning both simultaneously. The former will have had training in their country of origin and this may have had a different emphasis from the training on offer in the UK and the assessment methods may differ greatly. Cultural factors are likely to have an impact, for example accepted ways of interacting with customers may be different.

ESOL teachers may be involved in various ways:

- Working alongside subject teachers.
- Supporting learners outside the vocational classroom, for example in a workshop setting.
- Using vocational material in the classroom to improve cultural awareness and to sharpen the learners' strategies for dealing effectively with this kind of material.

It is important to clarify what it is that the learners need. In some situations, they may be familiar with the vocational area and possibly highly qualified in it in their country of origin. They need to learn how to operate in this field, in English and in the British setting. Other ESOL learners may be new to the vocational area. They need to learn the subject and also the necessary language. Confronted with a piece of specialist equipment, the first group would ask 'What's it called?', the second group would ask 'What's it for?' For both groups, of course, learning specialist vocabulary requires also knowing how it is used grammatically, the constructions in which it habitually appears and other words which often occur with it.

Below are two approaches to vocational material, applied to two different vocational areas. The first shows how the teacher can aid understanding by identifying underlying assumptions and colloquial language. The second looks at some ways of adapting a text to make it more accessible.

Identifying underlying assumptions

Extract 1: From an interview with a motor vehicle trainee[2]

[Interviewer:] What do you think the future holds for you and the industry?
[Interviewee:] Some of the backstreet garages might have problems keeping up with the pace of technological change in the industry – so much of it is tied up with computerization and diagnostics already and that trend is only going to increase. However the prospects for hardworking, well-trained individuals are good because there is actually a shortage of decent people and there will always be room for more. So I'd advise anyone to get a proper training and go for it.

Suggested approach

Introduce some of the assumed knowledge and colloquial language before learners read the extract and use discussion and comprehension questions to make sure learners understand the rest.

Assumed knowledge

- Small, local garages have tight profit margins – the idea of economic survival and what aids it and what damages it.

- Computer technology makes cars more and more technologically sophisticated and so harder to fix.
- 'Diagnostics' to mean sophisticated ways of determining what is wrong with the car.
- The implied contrast between small garages and large ones.

Colloquial language

- 'Backstreet', to indicate small and local garages.
- The use of 'decent' to refer to those who are 'hardworking, well-trained individuals' who are useful to the industry.
- 'Go for it', meaning work hard to get into the motor industry.

Possible follow-up activities

1   *Discussion:*
     - Consider short-term and medium-term issues for the motor industry. Base your thinking around small garages, large garages, dealerships. How have cars changed over the past ten years? What differences has computer technology made? Why is it getting harder to put things right when they go wrong?
2   Using the internet and your local area:
     - Research garages in your local area and the range of services they offer.
     - Consider how these services are advertised. Note specialist lexis.
     - Research one large garage and compare prices for various services with one of the smaller ones, e.g. for a 30,000 mile service.
     - Research training pathways in the motor industry and local vacancies in the jobcentre and employment agencies.

Adapting vocational texts

A vocational text can be adapted to suit the ESOL learner in a number of ways. It can be shortened or rewritten in simpler English. Key words in a text can be omitted as part of a gap-fill exercise or merely underlined. The teacher can present vocabulary and collocations in a diagrammatic form, showing the relationship between words. This is often called a word web. It could be either a complete web or partial web for learners to complete, perhaps by matching words to definitions. A diagram or picture could be the first stimulus with text to follow, or the text could be used to label a diagram. Learners need to become familiar with the conventions of instructional language, with its semi-formal register, imperatives and sequencing word. Learners can convert it to a DO's and DON'Ts list in a more informal register.

Predictive reading techniques are useful for opening up concepts before learners meet the text itself. If learners are given the title, or a summary of part of the text in oral form, and discuss what they predict the text is likely to contain, their first skim reading and subsequent intensive reading may be used to see how accurate or otherwise their predictions were. Alternatively, if the learners work on one section of a text, they can discuss what they anticipate will be the content of other sections.

Extract 2: From Food Handling and Health & Safety NVQ level 2: (online material)

What is Food Hygiene ?

Food hygiene is following good practices which lead to the safe production of food in clean workplaces. Keeping workplaces, staff and equipment clean is an important part of food hygiene.

Working in a clean area:
- reduces the risk of producing harmful food;
- prevents infestation by pests;
- is more attractive to customers.

The Food Safety Act 1990 was introduced because of public concern about risks during food preparation.

Observations

Understanding of the food handling text involves a number of features:

1   Linguistic:
    - Past tense passive: *'the Act was introduced'*.
    - Noun phrase subjects: *'Keeping workplaces clean is . . .'*
2   Format:
    - Convention of having statements first followed by more detail in bullet points.
3   Assessment method:
    - Assumption that this kind of information needs to be learned because it is likely to be tested by multiple choice.

Suggested introduction to extract

All vocational areas involve health and safety rules. Discuss why that is and the way the law is involved. Why do we need rules about food hygiene? What happens if we don't have these rules? You can use visuals here of what shouldn't happen, mice or beetles in food containers, etc., to elicit responses.

After learners have read the text, provide some activities to aid understanding, for example,

1   *Collocations for learners to complete, using the text*:
    - It is important to ... with safety ... [keep the rules!]
    - The Food Safety Act was ... in 1990 [the first time we had this Act of Parliament].

- There was ... concern about risks during food ... [people were worried]

2 *Word web to complete*:

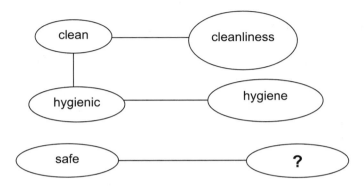

Suggestions for follow-up work

- Learners produce a list of DO's and DON'Ts using less formal English.
- Groups of learners could focus on one part of the text only and make up comprehension questions for another group.
- Learners could draft health and safety notices to go up in kitchens, using graphics and cartoons to make them memorable.
- Learners could summarize the main points or return to the text as a gap-fill exercise.
- One group could produce a word web of key lexis and collocations.

ILT

Adult literacy

Interactive versions of the Adult Literacy and Numeracy Core Curricula, searchable and cross-referenced to the guidance manual *Access for All* are now available at: www.dfes.gov.uk/curriculum_literacy

Skills for Life literacy materials are available on CD or online at:

www.dfes.gov.uk/readwriteplus/LearningMaterialsLiteracy

Vocational

Use a search engine to get an overview of a vocational area. You can find summaries and course outlines on awarding body websites such as BTEC/Edexcel or from sources of careers advice such as Connexions. Once you identify the vocational area you can use your search engine to find sample material at various national curriculum levels.

There are also vocational resources in a range of subjects, with work on literacy and numeracy embedded within them at: www.dfes.gov.uk/readwriteplus/ embeddedlearning

Authentic material

'Authentic' implies material that was not produced for the purpose of language learning, such as newspapers, soap operas, advertisements, information leaflets, instructions on medicine bottles, rail timetables, etc. They are aimed at an intended audience with a purpose in mind – to inform, persuade, entertain – just the kind of thing learners might want to or need to read, listen to or watch. The ability to tackle some of this material is necessary for survival and participation in the host community; this makes authentic material a rich resource for the ESOL teacher.

Advantages of using authentic material

Authentic material can support learners in understanding the host culture. Using authentic material in lessons is a good way for learners to become familiar with various genres, from payslips to poetry, from news broadcasts to chat shows. A wide range of material can be brought into the classroom establishing a direct connection with the world outside the classroom. Learners can be encouraged to bring material that interests them and thus have an opportunity to influence the content of the lesson.

Possible drawbacks of using authentic material

- Authentic is not always best.
- The reliability of the information is variable, as is the quality of the English.
- The language is ungraded with the risk that the text may be confusing or discouraging or boring.
- Topical material dates quickly.
- What is real and relevant for some people may be less so for others.

How to use authentic material

Authentic material needs to be chosen wisely, with the learners' level, needs and interests in mind – you need to consider whether it is topical, local, newsworthy, funny. The teacher is always juggling, trying to ensure that over a series of lessons everybody encounters something real and relevant to them.
Authentic material can be used in various ways:

- To introduce a genre.
- As part of a topic-based curriculum.

- To promote survival English, extracting from it the key language which the learner might need to use.

At higher levels it can be used:

- To practise research skills as part of a project promoting independent learning.
- To compare and contrast how different media present information.
- To develop critical reading skills (which will be a new idea for some learners).

It is sometimes argued that authenticity lies not only in the material but also in its use, and that studying it in a classroom is not authentic use. Many teachers think the advantages outweigh this objection. Still, it is often good advice to make the classroom use reflect 'real-life' use; activities can reflect the way people use the material while also reflecting the purpose of an English class. For example, use TV listings to practise skimming and scanning rather than intensive reading. Learners can scan for a time they will be at home; read to find a programme they like; discuss with other learners which programmes they all like; negotiate which one they would watch if some programmes clash; and tell the rest of the class what they have chosen. And if the material is sufficiently compelling or relevant, they can watch the programme and then talk about it in the next lesson or write a review.

Learners do need to be able to deal with practical matters, and some useful lessons focus on things such as timetables and information leaflets. Often these meet pressing needs and help to develop transactional language skills. But language is also an expressive medium. Learners can be introduced to material where English is used to express and evoke feelings. The short poem below appeared on a placard inside a London underground train as part of the Poems on the Underground scheme. It could be enjoyed by most learners beyond Entry 1.

MY CHILDREN

I hear them talking, my children,

in fluent English and broken Kurdish.

And when I disagree with them,

they will comfort each other by saying

'Don't worry about mum, she's Kurdish'.

Will I be the foreigner in my own home?

(Choman Hardi b. 1974, *Poems on the Underground* 2005)

As always, think about the learners in the class. The subject matter of this poem might be too sensitive for some. Consider how much to talk about the genre; speakers of some languages may expect a poem to be more formal, longer and governed by very different conventions. You need to decide how much needs to be done beforehand, and what learning activities will follow from this poem.

Before

You could ask what languages people speak outside class and to whom. What languages are they fluent in (explain the word 'fluent' if necessary)?

- Young learners – what language do they and their parents speak? What about their friends? Is it important to keep their *first* language?
- Parents – what do they and their children speak? Do some of them have children whose English is better than theirs? Do they want their children to use their language? Why?
- Do they feel different when they speak English from when they speak another language? Are some subjects easier to discuss in English than others?

At lower levels, check or teach some vocabulary e.g. foreigner, fluent.

During

Read the poem aloud to the class a couple of times. For some learners, you might have copies available for them to read as they listen.

After

Give learners time to read the poem. Invite them to respond. Learners who are moved by the poem may want to express their feelings to other learners in their first language. Perhaps the poem puts into words their own experiences, or makes them aware of someone else's point of view. Give the class the opportunity to discuss in groups or as a whole class. Be prepared for anything to come up: identity; racism (do people seek to be 'English' to avoid discrimination?); relationships between genera-tions (do children grow away from their parents more quickly in another country? How does English affect the relationship between the young and older members of the community?).

For learners with limited English, you could ask comprehension questions which would guide them in ways to express their response, for example:

- Do the children speak good Kurdish? How do you know? ('Broken' things are not good).
- What about their English? (Good – 'fluent').
- What do you think the mother's Kurdish is like – good or broken?
- The children say, 'Mum … is Kurdish'. Do they think that *they* are Kurdish? So do they think she is the same as them or different?
- How does that make her feel? Which word shows that?
- Is a language important for people to feel they belong?

- Do you know anybody who feels like that? (This is a good question in that it doesn't push people into revealing their own feelings but enables them to do so if they wish.)

ILT

The Internet is a source of authentic material. Teachers can select material from the Web to work on in class. Learners can find information from online encyclopaedias, news sites and online guidebooks. Learners can use ICT for real communication.

To make the best use of the internet, learners need to:

- Use reading strategies to find what they are looking for as it is easy to be overwhelmed especially when it is not your first language.
- Realize that the quality of websites varies and that they need to assess the reliability of what they read.

Teachers can help by:

- Developing learners' skimming and scanning skills.
- Encouraging critical reading.
- Training learners in research skills. Initial tasks may involve finding answers to specific questions.

Look online for ready-made web quests and web searches with questions to be answered from specified websites/pages (some are listed on www.wmc.ac.uk/learning_resources/esol.htm).

Creating your own resources

As the teacher of a class, you sometimes know what material would best suit your learners but cannot find resources ready-made to do the job. The obvious solution is to create your own material. Some teachers like the idea of making their own material, while others have mixed feelings or are wary of taking on the task. They may lack confidence in their ability to develop good material or worry that it could be too time-consuming. Those who enjoy it soon discover that it gets easier and see it as the best way to produce resources in the most relevant context which fit the learners' needs.

Advantages

One advantage of using resources you have produced is that you already know them. There is no need to try to absorb someone else's ideas. We have seen that all material embodies certain assumptions about learners and what they know. Your material can be really focused on *your* learners, using your knowledge about their previous experience, recent language learning, level of skills, and learning styles and preferences. You can deal with a specific learning point, in a specific context varying the approach to provide for multi-skill and multi-sensory learning, and to support different learning styles: inductive or deductive; learning alone or with others.

Another advantage is that you can use the resources at different levels and in different ways so that you gain maximum benefit from the time you have invested. Moreover, there is no danger that the learners have used this material before. Finally, using published resources can become boring, whereas when you make your own, there is the creative spark to keep you interested, and you can add visuals and interesting layouts, include local references, and vary the tone with a little humour or unpredictability.

Possible drawbacks

Poorly conceived material is unlikely to achieve the teacher's aims. Creating material requires skill and linguistic sensitivity and the process can be time-consuming. However, to counter these drawbacks, teachers can improve with practice, and writing your own material may be quicker than trawling through books, trying to find material on the point you want to teach.

How to create your own material

It is important to be clear what you want to achieve. Below are examples of two approaches. The first example is aimed at a higher level class and the second at a lower level, but both approaches can be used at any level.

One approach is to think about what a competent native speaker would do in the context to achieve a positive result.

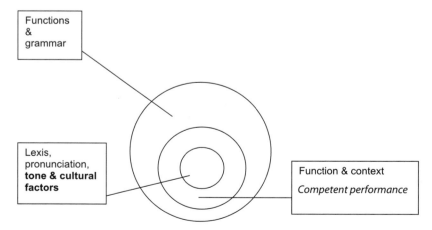

Figure 8.3 Competent performance model

Figure 8.3 summarizes the process. The innermost circle is where you start. You decide on the relevant context and what the speaker wants to achieve. You consider the function(s) involved. You imagine a native speaker operating successfully within the context and this gives you a dialogue. From there you move to the middle circle and consider the grammar a speaker would need to know. Finally you consider lexis, pronunciation and also tone and implicit cultural factors.

Example 1

Many ESOL learners have low paid jobs and need to know how to ask for changes in pay and working conditions and responsibilities. A recent news item on hotel cleaners being paid less than the minimum wage and lobbying for fairer wages provides a useful context for practising negotiating skills. The example is intended for learners working towards Level 1, but the model can be applied at any level.

1   *Focus on a competent performace*. Devise a dialogue showing somebody performing competently in the hotel context, negotiating with the employer.

Prompt	Employee	Employer
Opening	Mrs — **would it be possible** to talk to you for a moment?	I'm rather busy but I've got a few minutes. What is it?
Begin to outline the issue	**It's about** cleaning the rooms in the annex.	Yes, what seems to be the problem?
Explain the issue, give reasons and say what you want to happen.	They are bigger rooms than in the main hotel and they take longer to clean. **I'd like to be paid** by the hour instead of by the room.	That's not company practice. We pay £2.25 per room and you should be able to clean two rooms in an hour.
Continue to make your point and refer to doing the job well.	The rooms in the annexe **are often taken** by younger people who leave them in a mess. It takes **longer** to clean them and they are **bigger**. You want the rooms done properly and it can take up to an hour to do a good job. That means that I am working for very little money, **much less than** the minimum wage.	I see. Well I will have to look into it.

Offer to provide evidence of the problem.	**Would it be possible for you to come over** and see what I mean? I will be in the annexe this afternoon from 2pm.	Yes, I think that would be useful. I'll see you there and we can look into the problem.
Thank the other person.	Thank you.	

2 *Analyse the material.* Once you have written your dialogue, then you can analyse the language features and cultural aspects involved.
  - *Functions*: asking for something; negotiating.
  - *Grammar*: comparatives; modal verbs in phrases using a formal register; passives.
  - *Pronunciation*: sentence stress; assertive tone.
  - *Lexis*: 'annexe'; phrasal verb e.g. 'look into'.
  - *Cultural*: finding the right person; finding the best available time and place; recognizing when the other person wants to end the conversation; saying thank you.

3 *Use the material.* A natural way to present a dialogue is as a listening text. The content needs to be clear but it is also important for the speakers to sound natural.

The analysis provides you with various starting points in using the dialogue to improve learners' performance. You may choose to start with:
  - Cultural aspects – You could ask learners how someone would go about this task in their country of origin, and stimulate discussion of similarities and differences.
  - Key phrase – 'What's the problem?'; 'They are bigger rooms and they take longer to clean'. Work on sentence stress, emphasizing the comparatives, slowing down as appropriate to add emphasis – 'That means I am working for very little money, much less than the minimum wage'.

You can provide material for the learners to practise the pronunciation:

Mark the stressed syllables. Underline the most important words.

Practise saying the sentences, so that the important words are very clear.

```
        O                    O      O   O    O     O   O
e.g. That means I am working for very little money, much less than the
        O        O
minimum wage.
```

Some of the guests are very untidy; it often takes an hour to clean the room.

I want to do the job properly but that takes much longer in the annexe rooms.

Bigger rooms take longer to clean but the pay is the same.
- A grammatical structure such as the passive – 'I'd like to be paid by the hour'. Structure for polite request, use of the passive infinitive. 'The rooms are often taken by young people who make more of a mess'. Passive puts the work first. Adverb position, use of plural.

You can cue practice of the same patterns:

Music/play/ at 2am   Drink /spill/ floor

- The dialogue as a model – Let learners listen to the whole dialogue as often as they wish. Then get them to practise it giving them the chance to play both parts. They can then reconstruct the dialogue from prompts only.
4 *Follow up and involve other language skills.* Progress from speaking and listening into reading and writing:
    - Research the minimum wage and employee rights.
    - Write a letter to your employer on the same issue.

TASK 8.4

Choose your context and level, and use the competent performance model to create material focusing on one of the following functions:

- Asking to work in a different location.
- Asking to change working times.
- Asking to take on more tasks / more responsibility.

Starting from a specific language point

Another approach to devising material starts with a specific language point which the learners need to master. This might be new language, something which learners have asked about or something which the teacher has noticed that learners have difficulty with.

Example 2

For example, imagine that you have noticed learners making mistakes with sub-ject–verb agreement. ('I like, she likes, they like'). In particular, they may miss out the final third person singular '–s', or may mispronounce it 'she likiz'. Learning is cyclical, and third person singular '–s' is a late-acquired structure, so learners will have encountered this before. You do not expect immediate accuracy, but want to encourage correct use in writing.

1   *Focus on the target language.* Note points involved in using the structure correctly. Research the grammar point if necessary. In this case, points would include:
    - Adding '-s' ending in third person ('I like', 's/he likes').
    - Spelling of ending: adding '-s' ('sits', 'comes'); adding '-es' ('watches', 'misses'); changing 'y' to '-i' ('tries', 'carries').
    - Pronunciation of ending: 's/z' ('sits', 'likes'/'stands', 'loves'); 'iz' ('watches', 'misses').

2   *Contextualize the language.* Choose a context which is of interest to your learners. For example, interview someone in the class about his or her job or make use of a job which a former member of the class is now doing. Write a short text:

> Jay is a security guard at Firewall, and works at night. He starts at 11 pm, so he gets up at half past nine. He has breakfast and leaves home at half past ten. He catches a bus to the factory and clocks on at eleven. He sits at a security desk. There are cameras around the building with screens above the desk. Jay watches the screens. Every hour, he walks round the building ...

3   *Develop the material.* The text can be presented in various ways using different language skills, to cater for spiky profiles and a range of learning styles. For example:
    - Orally, followed by comprehension questions (listening and speaking)

        —   What time does he start work?

        —   How does he get to work?

        —   What does he do? (Note use of open questions to encourage use of target structure.)
    - Project the text onto screen for class to read. Produce flash cards of key phrases for learners to identify. Prepare a gapped version of text, learners put the flash cards in the correct gaps (Reading.)

Focus on the target language point: '-s'. You could point it out in context on the screen. On the screen or worksheet, highlight the construction:

he work**s** he watch**es**

Elicit or teach the spelling patterns; you could include a section on a worksheet with examples and practice. You might illustrate the verbs to appeal to learners with a visual learning style. To make the worksheet more personal, use learners' names instead of she/he.

work leave use	+ s	catch miss wash	+ es	try carry	y > i +es

Write the correct verbs:
I *write* letters ... She _____.
I *watch* TV ... He _____.
I *shut* the window ... She _____.
I fly on easyJet ... He _____.
etc., etc.

Point out the pronunciation of '-es' endings. Again, this could make a worksheet exercise.

REMEMBER
Say IZ if the verb ends with the *sounds*
s   misses
z   uses
sh   washes
ch   watches
dge   judges
SAY THESE VERBS
He *likes* coffee
She *kisses* babies
He *catches* a bus
She *hides* her money
etc., etc.

Provide further practice activities, which can be at different levels:

- cards for learners to sequence
    - he watches the screens
    - he gets up at half past nine
    - he has breakfast
    - he clocks on
    - he cycles to work (reading).
- True/false statements (reading):
    - Jay gets up late – T
    - He gets a train to work – F.
- Worksheet with the text and questions. Learners write answers to the questions (which they may have previously answered orally; reading and writing).
- Conversion of first person to third person narrative. Provide a first-person narrative e.g. Maria talks about her job – 'I work in a bakery. We make fresh bread in the morning. The bread shop opens at 9 am. I start work at 5 am ...' Learners read this and write a paragraph about Maria – 'She works ...' or for

weaker writers, you can give a gap-fill – 'Maria _____ in a bakery. She _____ work at 5 am …' (reading and writing).

Remember that making material is not the sole prerogative of the teacher. Learners can make true/false sentences, comprehension questions, or a quiz, for others to answer. Learners could word process a text about someone they know, using the text from the lesson as a model, and then base exercises on it.

4   Follow up and involve other language skills. A questionnaire is a useful format. It integrates speaking, listening and writing, and the results lend themselves to further exploitation. Adjust the question cues to reflect the lifestyles of the class – are they working or full-time learners? Are they parents of school-aged children? Etc.

	Marek			
Where … work?	Restaurant			
get up?	10 am			
How … get to work?	Walks			
Finish work?	Midnight			

The questionnaire can be completed in different ways:
- Mingle and ask as many people as possible, 'Where do you work?' 'What time …?'
- Work with a partner and complete the questionnaire for them. Then change partners and ask about the previous partner, 'Where does Marek work? What time does he …?' This practises third person questions – if necessary drill these first.
  Exploit the completed questionnaire for further practice of the target language but also going beyond it, especially for stronger learners:
- Learners report to a group or the class what they have discovered (speaking/listening).
- Write about one person: stronger writers write about more than one (writing).
- Compare two people: Marek works in a restaurant, but Maria works in a bakery. Maria gets up early, but Marek gets up late. Marek finishes work late.
- Compare yourself with somebody: I get up earlier than Jay. Marek gets up the latest (speaking and/or writing).
  Discussion:
- Whose schedule would you prefer – working at night, getting up early …?
- What other jobs involve working at night (e.g. nurses, call centres) ? What does a person in a call centre do?
  Collect in the questionnaires and use them, perhaps next lesson, for a quiz.
- What time does X start work?

- Or describe someone using information gathered in the questionnaire and learners guess who it is.

Homework: learners find out about the schedule of someone they know.
They can write about it, or record themselves speaking.

TASK 8.5

Choose a language point for a class of learners. Contextualize it in a short text
which is interesting and relevant to the class. Plan how to use it involving a
range of language skills.

ILT

Word-processing and publishing software means that teacher-made printed material
can have a high standard of design and production. Graphics and pictures can be
incorporated. Different versions of the same worksheet can be produced to cater for
different levels.

Teaching and learning material can also be devised and used via electronic
media. Authoring tools make it easier to create exercises in particular formats, in print
or on screen. Three well-known sources are Wida (whose Storyboard was one of the
first tools), Clarity and Educational Software.

Notes

1 The terms 'resources' and 'material(s)' are widely used in ESOL teaching to
  refer to the same thing. *Material* designed to enhance learning provides a
  resource for teachers and learners. In this chapter, 'resources' generally has a
  broader use, and specific items may be referred to as, e.g., reading or
  listening 'material'.
2 Source: '*The Motor Industry*' by Mike Hobbs: '*A Real Life Guide to the Motor
  Industry*'.

9 Planning and assessment: reflection, evaluation and the learning cycle

John Sutter

Introduction – Two Perspectives On Planning

Perspective 1: Through the learners' eyes

TASK 9.1

What makes a good lesson? Think of a lesson you have experienced as a learner that you remember as particularly helpful or effective. Make a list of reasons why you felt it was a 'good' lesson.

COMMENT 9.1

There are, of course, an infinite number of reasons why a lesson might be considered 'good' by learners. But it is quite likely that it had some or other of the features below:

- It was enjoyable (in the broadest sense – perhaps you laughed a lot, or perhaps you enjoyed the 'hard-working' or 'studious' atmosphere).
- It built on knowledge or skills you already had and extended them (perhaps it clarified your thinking about something, or enabled you to do something better).
- The teaching style helped you learn.
- It motivated you to learn.
- The processes of the lesson were clear to you.
- The teacher's expectations were clear and achievable.
- You weren't bored and you didn't feel rushed. The pace seemed right.
- It engaged you and got you thinking.
- It broadened your horizons in some way.
- It helped you clear some sort of hurdle in your learning.

Perspective 2: The teacher and the 'technologies' of teaching

---

TASK 9.2

Imagine you are starting a new English teaching job. Your manager says to you: 'There are some learners in classroom X waiting for you – they'd like to learn some English'. What would you want to know before you started teaching them?

COMMENT 9.2

As well as general details such as their names, nationalities, approximates ages, etc., you would probably want at the very minimum to know:

- Their existing levels of English in each of the four skills.
- Their reasons for wanting to learn English.
- How, where, or in what contexts they use English or wish to use English in the future.
- What languages they already speak.
- How long they will attend classes for.
- Their past experiences of attending classes.
- Whether any of the group have special needs or disabilities that may impact on their learning.

In most institutions, some or all of this information will be available to teachers before they begin teaching their classes: there will have been some *initial assessment* of learners in order to place them in the most suitable class and to provide teachers with information to help them plan. *How* this assessment can be done is discussed below, along with other forms of assessment.

Aside from knowledge about *these* learners in *this* class, teachers' preparation and planning is also informed by their own knowledge and beliefs about 'good' teaching. They bring their pedagogic and subject knowledge to the process of designing or planning their lessons. They may also be constrained by institutional requirements or policies in that they may, for instance, be required to produce a written lesson plan in a particular format. They will certainly consider the planned lesson from a more 'technical' point of view than learners do:

Aims and objectives	• Are they realistic?
	• Do they fit the needs of the group and the stage and level of the learning programme?
	• Are they process or product objectives? (And why?)

Timing and pace	• Is it realistic, based on what you know of the group and the subject-matter?
	• What will you do if timing goes seriously over or under your expectations?
	• If you get very behind, will you still meet aims/objectives?
	• How will you match timing/pace to learners: for instance, if timing gets behind, will you chivvy them along, or follow their lead?
Staging	• Is there a stage you could drop, if necessary; or an extra activity if you have time left over?
	• How will you link stages together?
	• Are some stages particularly 'tricky'? Do you have some strategies for coping if things go wrong?
Methodology	• Will you use a variety of methods/activities?
	• Will your methodology fit the group in terms of learning styles?
	• Will your approach be inductive or deductive?
Materials	• Are they user-friendly (e.g. is font large enough)?
	• Are they accurate in terms of content?
	• Are they attractive and engaging?
	• Do they conform to copyright law?
Content	• Is your knowledge of the content sound and up-to-date?
	• Will you make links between this content and other lessons?
	• What are the key points/issues you want learners take in?
Interaction	• How will you arrange the room and furniture?
	• How will you arrange group/pairings?
	• What roles will you occupy?
Differentiation	• How will you address individual learners' needs, as well as those of 'the group'?
Equal opportunities	• How will equal opportunities issues impact on this lesson?
Technology	• What technology, if any, are you going to use?
	• Do you have a backup plan in case it fails?

For experienced teachers, many of these 'technical' aspects of the planning or design process may eventually become unconscious, or implicit in their practice. Beginner and newer teachers, however, will need to consciously address each of these areas. And, of course, it is vitally important that learners' knowledge informs the teacher's planning in relation to each category above; in may ways the most difficult aspect of planning is the drawing together of the two perspectives we have discussed. As we saw in Chapter 3, learners and teachers alike are highly affected and influenced by their past experiences of schooling, and their beliefs about what 'good teaching' actually is. And 'learning' itself seems to be a social activity: bringing all these experiences and beliefs together – along with institutional requirements – into a workable and effective 'community of practice' is not always easy!

In Task 9.2 you were asked to consider what information a teacher might want to have before teaching. It's equally important to think about what information you would want to have after teaching? In this our answers here would probably fall into two overarching categories:

- Did learning take place, and if so, what was learnt by whom?
- What did learners think and feel about the lesson?

This information, if obtainable, would be extremely useful in planning future lessons.

Although we have so far been primarily discussing individual lessons, it should be apparent that similar *before* and *after* considerations will also apply to the planning of *courses*; there is great similarity between lesson and course planning in terms of the information teachers will wish to be able to make use of in relation to both. In fact, both lesson and course planning are ongoing activities that can be best thought of as *cycles*.

The learning/teaching cycle

David Kolb's theory of 'experiential' learning (Kolb and Fry 1975; Kolb 1984) is one source for the concept of a learning or teaching 'cycle'. 'Experiential' here means learning directly from the experiences of life. However, it is worth noting that *experiential learning* has also been used by educational theorists and practitioners to mean direct (but classroom) encounters with the thing being studied rather than just 'thinking about it' – as occurs in a perhaps more 'traditional' classroom. This, of course, has great relevance for language teaching and learning; much of ESOL teaching is experientially based, for good reasons. Learners need opportunities to *use* the language they are learning in the classroom: merely studying the grammar would not get them far. In the ESOL classroom 'talk is work' (Roberts et al. 2004).

Kolb saw learning as a continuing cycle involving four elements (see Figure 9.1).

A real-life example might be the process Luis, aged 10, undergoes in learning how to make a cup of tea:

1   *Concrete experience*: Luis makes his first cup of tea by pouring hot water in a cup and briefly adding a teabag. He adds some milk, and four teaspoons of sugar.
2   *Observation and reflection*: Luis finds the tea undrinkable – it's too sweet and tastes only of milk.
3   *Abstract conceptualization*: Luis considers that maybe he should add less sugar, and leave the teabag in longer.
4   *Active experimentation*: Luis goes off to make another cup of tea, using the new method.

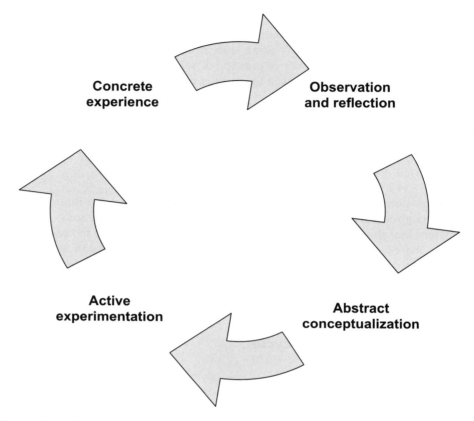

Figure 9.1 Kolb's continuous learning cycle

Of course, the above example is only one possible interpretation of Luis's experience – it could be mapped in other ways. And it will probably take many runs around the cycle until Luis learns to make a decent cup of tea. In fact, the process should really be represented as a spiral; learners do not repeat the cycle at the same 'level' endlessly. If learning has taken place then a new context for experience is set (using what has been learnt) so that the next round of the cycle takes place at a 'higher' level. Further, learning can begin at any of the four stages, though Kolb (1984) suggests that it will often begin with the consideration of some sort of concrete experience: a person takes an action of some sort and then sees (or experiences) the changes that the action causes.

TASK 9.3

Think of a learning experience of your own; could it fit Kolb's cycle? How would you 'map' your experience to the cycle?

Variations of this 'cyclical' approach have been applied to many aspects of learning and teaching, especially the cycle involved in planning and teaching lessons, or planning and delivering a course or curriculum (see Figure 9.2).

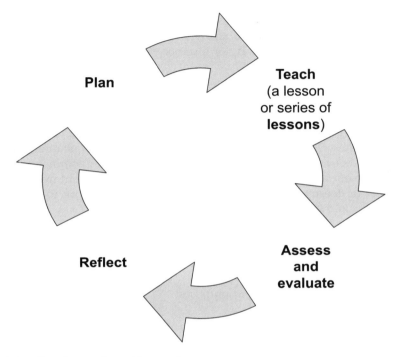

Figure 9.2 Planning and teaching cycle

Kolb's cycle is a useful conceptual tool teachers can use to address the particularly acute difficulty mentioned above, that of bringing together learners', teachers' and institutions' perspectives on planning for learning. Therefore, we will now go on to examine each of the stages of the cycle in more detail.

Assessment and evaluation

We have seen above the importance of obtaining initial information about learners before any teaching can take place, so it makes sense to start our analysis of the cycle at this stage. *Assessment* and *evaluation* are grouped together as one stage because both are concerned with gathering 'information' (this word is used here in the broadest sense and will include more than just factual data). However, assessment and evaluation are distinct in their concerns. Assessment is to do with measurement, levelling and grading in order to answer such questions as:

- What does this learner know already?
- What level is this learner?

- What *can't* this learner do?
- What was learnt in this lesson/on this course?
- How good or effective is this learner's writing?

Evaluation, as the word itself suggests, is to do with placing *value*. So although assessment procedures may provide answers to 'what was learnt in this lesson?', evaluation is still needed to find out, for instance, whether:

- what was learnt was of value to the learners;
- how it was learnt was perceived as effective or enjoyable.

Answers to both of these may well be a matter of opinion rather than dry fact.

In many ways the distinction between assessment and evaluation is a bit like the distinction between price and value, as in Oscar Wilde's comment: 'the cynic knows the price of everything and the value of nothing'. Assessment may tell us what a learner does or doesn't know, evaluation will help us decide with the learner what he or she values knowing, and therefore needs to learn.

Assessment

Assessments can have many different purposes:

- *Initial assessment* – to decide what level or class to place a new learner in.
- *Diagnostic assessment* – to find out in more detail what strengths and weaknesses learners have in their knowledge and skills.
- *Formative assessment* – to find out what has been learnt from a course (or part of it) so far, and to inform future planning and teaching on the course.
- *Summative assessment* – a 'final' assessment, usually at the end of a course, perhaps an external exam.

Assessments often take the form of tests or exams, but given that the aim of much assessment is to give both teacher and learner a much clearer idea of where individual learners are in their language learning, it need not, and probably should not, merely be a matter of *testing* learners in the strictest sense of the word. Remember, the purpose of (especially *diagnostic*) assessment is to find out what the learner *can* do, as much as what they *can't*.

Tests themselves can be flawed in a number of ways, and when this is the case they will give biased results. Some factors we need to consider are:

- *Test content* – can we make valid inferences from learners' performance in a test? For instance, if the purpose of a test is to discover how well learners can understand academic text, does it matter which academic discipline the text is drawn from? In other words, does the *context* of the materials used matter? It probably does.

- *Test method and test construct* – The *test construct* is the underlying ability that the test is trying to assess; the question here is how well the *test method*, the task or tasks required by the test, relate to this. For instance, if answering test questions designed to test *listening* skills involves a lot of *writing*, the test method will very likely be interfering with, and possibly invalidating, the test construct.
- *Learner familiarity* – how familiar are learners with the test format, and how aware of the purpose of the test are they? Clearly, if the format is entirely new to them, and if they are not sure what the test is for, this will have an impact on their performance.

Tests also don't allow much leeway for factors such as confidence, past educational experiences and 'on-the-day' variation in performance. So when teachers *do* use tests they should try to involve and familiarize learners with the assessment process and format as much as possible.

Assessment tests and teaching

Another potential problem area around testing is to do with 'how testable' different aspects of language are. Some are certainly easier to test than others: a set of spellings, for instance, is easier to test for than, say, broader fluency or negotiation skills. Tests, and assessment in general, tend to favour such items because they are more *measurable*.

The upshot of this can be that only, or mainly, *measurable* items and skills get assessed to the detriment of other less test-amenable items and skills; and this will only give a partial picture of a learner's true abilities. This possible effect of tests, where the objects and methods of the assessment process *over*determine what elements of the curriculum get selected for teaching, is called *backwash* or *washback*. Essentially, something gets taught because it is *testable*, not because it is necessarily needed.

The other key problem is *timing*. Just because something has been taught does not mean it has been learnt. In the case of language teaching this problem is particularly acute when we differentiate between what learners *know* about language (e.g. grammar rules) and what they can *do* with language. For instance, a learner may know quite early in their English-learning career that you add '*s*' to third person verbs, but be unable to *do* this in fluent communication until a very long time later; it is a mistake even advanced learners often still make. So, tests may show that a learner knows something, but fail to recognize that they can't do it, or alternatively indicate that someone *can't* do something without recognizing that they *know* it, or at least that at some level learning is nonetheless taking place. This means that testing, if not monitored carefully, can lead to teaching which is, at best, misguided, at worst, both needless and futile.

Sometimes the *Test–Teach–Test* paradigm is very useful: the teacher finds out by testing what learners are not able to do or don't know, then teaches towards that ability or knowledge, then tests again to see how far they have progressed. 'Test' here can mean the most informal sort of testing, for instance doing a practice activity, to find out what learners can or can't already do *before* an input phase. This can be of great assistance to teachers and learners in terms of pinpointing and then working to alleviate areas of learner difficulty. It is also reflective of the cyclical nature of language learning and teaching, items need to be reviewed and revisited before they are fully understood or integrated into the learners' repertoires.

So, overall, teachers need to use tests and assessment sensitively. They need to be aware of their limitations and possible biases, and be clear about what they will and won't reveal. They need to involve learners in the process and to ensure that when testing and assessment is done, it enables learners to perform at their best. And, of course, formal testing should work alongside other more informal means of assessment, tutorials, or one-to-one interviews in relaxed and friendly settings, class discussions, ongoing coursework and, *particularly*, a focus on what the learners themselves say they want or need to learn. Opportunities for learners to self-assess or at least reflect on their own language, needs, abilities and skills should also play a role.

TASK 9.4

Find an assessment or test that you have used with learners, or one regularly used at your place of work. How far do you think it satisfies the criteria for assessments mentioned in the section above?

Evaluation

Although learners should sometimes have the opportunity to self-assess, most assessment is carried out by teachers and institutions. Evaluation, however, allows far more freedom in terms of *who* evaluates. Indeed, it will often be evaluations carried out by learners that provide the teacher with the most useful information about his or her teaching.

Evaluation often addresses such general questions as:

- Did I (the teacher) achieve my aims and objectives?
- How effective did *learners* feel this lesson to be?
- What did learners like or not like about this lesson?
- What did learners feel was learnt from this lesson?
- What wasn't learnt (that could have been)?

TASK 9.5

Evaluation in an ESOL lesson can also address more specific issues. Make a list.

COMMENT 9.5

Evaluating the effectiveness of different aspects of classroom life can be hugely helpful to teachers and should be carried out regularly. Depending on individual context, a very large number of potential issues can be addressed, for instance, how:

- Effective was my methodology?
- Effective was the classroom layout?
- Clear was my boardwork?
- Appropriate was the staging and timing?
- Clear were my instructions?
- Useful was this lesson for learner X?
- Useful and effective was the technology I used?
- Effective were the materials themselves?

In fact, the more focus and precision evaluation has, the more useful the information it provides. It should also be apparent that evaluation of these kinds of features of classroom life will be greatly enhanced by direct involvement of the learners themselves and by the elicitation of their views and opinions. A teacher will probably have their own estimation of the clarity of their boardwork or instructions, but it is *learners* who have to understand these and who will be able to give a truer picture of just how comprehensible they were.

The question remains: *how* does one evaluate? This will certainly be dependent upon what it is that you are trying to evaluate, but two central concerns stand out. First, *establishing a record of what actually happened*. It is notoriously difficult for an individual teacher to remember all the detail of a single lesson, let alone an entire course. Some possible solutions to this are:

- Tape or video-record teaching part of a lesson, an entire lesson or even a series of lessons.
- Ask a colleague to come and observe a lesson in order to record 'dry' factual, quantitative, data (e.g. which learners participated, and for how long).
- Ask learners to keep an 'events log' – a record of classroom activities or key moments.
- Keep some sort of teaching notebook to hand in which you can record aspects of your teaching in action (e.g. ticking off the number of times you nominate individual learners).
- Keep a teaching diary in which you note down key elements or events directly after teaching a class.

The second central concern is to find ways to elicit learners' (or colleagues') evaluations of your teaching: again, here are some simple ways in which you can do this.

- Formal questionnaires which directly address aspects of a lesson or course you wish to evaluate (e.g. 'Did you have enough speaking practice today?' 'Do you feel this course improved your pronunciation?').
- Formal or informal interviews with learners to probe their opinions on aspects of a course or lesson. Be aware, though, that many learners may find it difficult to say anything negative about your teaching to you directly.
- Leave Post-it notes out for learners to note down thoughts/opinions as they occur during lessons; collect these in at the end.
- Get to know your learners, chat to them before and after lessons to elicit opinions. As with interviews, this may elicit mainly positive comments.
- Ask learners to work together, perhaps in small groups or as an entire class, to write a 'report' on a lesson or course.
- Ask learners to email you comments on teaching whenever they want to.

TASK 9.6

How could you evaluate the appropriateness of *timing* in lesson? Consider who you would involve and what your procedure would be.

COMMENT 9.6

To do this effectively, it would be important to:

- Have a record of the *planned* timings.
- Have a record of the *actual* timings (perhaps a colleague could record this).
- Obtain *learners'* opinions about the appropriateness of the *actual* timings.

This last point would itself need planning. If a teacher simply asked learners at the end of the lesson, 'What did you think about the timings of the stages', learners, as we saw above, would probably be unable to:

- Identify what each stage was.
- Remember what exactly happened in each stage.
- Identify the rationale for each stage.

In this case learners would probably be more able to give useful feedback if they were given some sort of lesson plan to refer to during the class, and if the teacher clearly signals the staging as it happens during the lesson. It would probably also be sensible to obtain learners' feedback after each individual stage of the lesson.

Of course, this is not to say that learners are always right, or that their evaluations are always going to have more primacy than the teacher's own.

> They may have blinkered views of what a lesson should be like, or they may simply be unable to make judgements about their own learning. However, it hardly needs to be said that learners are the key stakeholders and it is nearly always a good idea to obtain learner feedback with respect to evaluation.

Of course, a further issue is *when* to evaluate or ask learners to evaluate. For instance, whilst with some issues – for example, classroom layout – it would clearly be useful to ask learners for feedback directly after the class, it may not be so easy with other questions, particularly those related to learning. To ask whether a particular lesson on, say, the present perfect, was effective seems legitimate; however, one would not expect learners to have 'learnt' the present perfect in the space of that lesson. 'Effective' here probably means something like: the teacher managed to provide opportunities for learners to practice the present perfect; provided a useful contrast with the past simple; or highlighted typical contexts relevant to the learners where this tense might occur. In fact, it may be a few months down the line before the learners themselves can make truly useful judgements about the learning of larger linguistic items or skills. (Of course, they can certainly make judgements about how useful a particular lesson appeared to be to them.)

TASK 9.7

Choose a particular aspect of a lesson that you are about to teach and then design and carry out an evaluation process which involves obtaining learner feedback.

Reflection

Much has been written about *reflective practice* in teaching (for some excellent further reading on this, see Hillier 2002; and Moore 2005). Reflection is fundamentally an opportunity to ask *why* and *how* questions, informed by the evaluative data and feedback you have collected. Reflection can range from narrow questions like:

- How can I get Omar to participate more?
- Why didn't that pairwork task work very well?

But, it can also include much wider ones such as:

- What is my own attitude to pronunciation?
- Why don't I enjoy teaching writing?

In most cases, reflection generates further questions; it is itself a tool for enquiry and learning. For instance, the question, 'How can I get Omar to participate more?' may lead on to a whole series of further questions:

- Why doesn't Omar participate much? (And is this true?)
- Does he want to participate?
- Is he equally quiet in his L1?
- Will it benefit him to participate more?
- How will it benefit him?
- What exactly do I mean by 'participate'?
- Is there some alternative to participating in this particular way?
- Why does this issue trouble me so much?
- Does it trouble Omar?

Assessment, evaluation and reflection only become truly meaningful when they are carried forward into *planning*. Therefore, reflection, as well as looking back, needs to contain an element of *theorizing forwards*. In other words, taking the outcomes of assessment and evaluation, and the questions (and possibly answers) suggested by reflection, and then finding ways to incorporate these into future teaching.

Planning

As we have seen above, planning involves making use of a lot of information that will have emerged or been elicited during other stages of the cycle. Whether planning for a single lesson or an entire course, the teacher will be trying to gather, collate and *interpret* an awful lot of individual pieces of information, and somehow assemble or synthesize these into a coherent whole. And as the word 'interpret' suggests, this is not a mechanical activity, the learners' and teachers' reflections have an important role to play too; it is not simply a matter of gathering factual data. Some writers, for this reason among others, prefer to talk about 'designing' lessons (and courses) as opposed to merely 'planning' them; for more on this, see Cope and Kalantzis (2000).

'Online planning' and 'reflection in action'

In Chapter 3 we saw that the creation of 'learning opportunities' is central to good practice in teaching. Research has found that effective and experienced teachers make good use of what has been called 'online planning' (Baynham et al. 2007; Cooke and Roberts 2007), in order to seize or create such opportunities. This is similar to Donald Schön's idea of 'reflection in action' – teachers' ability to 'think what they are doing while they are doing it' (Schön 1983). In other words, they constantly respond to learners' changing needs and interests, thinking on their feet to adapt or change lesson plans as they teach. The ability to do this effectively and appropriately comes with experience; it requires excellent subject knowledge, excellent 'procedural' knowledge (i.e. how to respond to different situations and changing contexts, and a repertoire of appropriate routines to draw on), and excellent knowledge of the learners. This, of course, means that lesson plans, whether written down or in your head, should not be set in stone; lesson planning is not a process that ends at the classroom door.

Applying the learning cycle to course planning

TASK 9.8

Here is the checklist of lesson planning questions we saw earlier. Which questions do you think would also be relevant for *course* planning?

Aims and objectives	• Are they realistic?
	• Do they fit the needs of the group and the stage and level of the learning programme?
	• Are they process or product objectives? (and why?)
Timing and pace	• Is it realistic, based on what you know of the group and the subject-matter?
	• What will you do if timing goes seriously over or under your expectations?
	• If you get very behind, will you still meet aims/objectives?
	• How will you match timing/pace to learners: for instance, if timing gets behind, will you chivvy them along or follow their lead?
Staging	• Is there a stage you could drop, if necessary, or an extra activity for if you have time left over?
	• How will you link stages together?
	• Are some stages particularly 'tricky'? Do you have some strategies for coping if things go wrong?
Methodol-ogy	• Will you use a variety of methods/activities?
	• Will your methodology fit the group in terms of learning styles?
	• Will your approach be inductive or deductive?
Materials	• Are they user-friendly (e.g. is the font large enough)?
	• Are they accurate in terms of content?
	• Are they attractive and engaging?
	• Do they conform to copyright law?
Content	• Is your knowledge of the content sound and up-to-date?
	• Will you make links between this content and other lessons?
	• What are the key points/issues you want learners take in?
Interaction	• How will you arrange the room and furniture?
	• How will you arrange group/pairings?
	• What roles will you occupy?

Differentia-tion	• How will you address individual learners' needs, as well as those of 'the group'?
Equal oppor-tunities	• How will equal opportunities issues impact on this lesson?
Technology	• What technology, if any, are you going to use? • Do you have a backup plan in case it fails?

COMMENT 9.8

Compare your ideas with a similar table addressing course planning:

Course aims and outcomes	• Are they realistic in relation to the duration of the course? • Do they fit the needs of the group? • Is the course externally accredited? Is there an exam?
Content	• Is it appropriate to the needs of the group? • Is it appropriate/relevant to the course aims and outcomes? • Is there an appropriate balance between work on the four skills? • Is there an appropriate balance between work on accuracy and fluency? • Is content linked to the national curriculum?
Mode of delivery	• Is the course intensive or part-time? How will this affect learners' attendance/attention-spans? • Is content sufficiently flexible to be adjusted to learners' changing needs and abilities? • How will you make links between different parts of the course? (e.g. revision) • How many teachers will work on the course? How will they liaise/share admin?
Methodol-ogy	• What methods and learning activities will you use? • Will your methodology be appropriate to group/individual needs and past learning experiences? • Will methodology be familiar to learners?
Materials	• Will you use published materials (e.g. a coursebook) or self-produced material, or a mixture of the two? • Are they appropriate to the needs and contexts of the group?

	• Are they attractive and engaging?
	• Will they be easily accessible to learners?
Assessment	• How will learners be finally assessed on the course?
	• What progress assessments will there be?
	• How will assessment outcomes be communicated to and discussed with learners?
	• What opportunities will learners have to discuss their progress with tutors?
Evaluation	• How will the course be progressively and finally evaluated?
	• What opportunities will there be for learners to evaluate the course?
	• What opportunities will there be for course review meetings?
	• How will evaluations feed into future planning?
Differentia-tion	• How will you address individual learners' needs, as well as those of 'the group'?
	• How will ILPs feed into course planning and review?
Equal opportunities	• Do course methods and materials conform to/promote equal opportunities?
	• Do any learners have disabilities/learning difficulties? How will these be addressed during the course?
Technology	• What technology is available?
	• Is technology/IT integrated into course delivery?
	• Will technology used present learners with any extra difficulties? If so, how will these be surmounted?

'Groups of learners' are generally classes formed as an outcome of some assessment process of placement testing. This is usually an extremely broad and often inaccurate process, which only gives a general sense of the 'level' a learner is at. We are not going to consider placement testing in any detail here.

Course planning, after initial placement testing, can involve the following elements:

- Diagnostic assessment.
- Individual/group tutorials.
- Individual Learning Plans.
- Identification of group needs and goals.
- Identification of individual needs and goals.
- Course/syllabus writing.
- Production of a scheme of work.

However, the order in which these are done may vary greatly.

TASK 9.9

Consider the three case studies below. What order do the stages above appear to occur in? Are all present? What would you say are the pros and cons of each approach?

1   *Teacher A* works in a big college with a large ESOL department. Her manager gives her a syllabus, consisting of a list of items to cover and a set of group goals to work to. She has to write a scheme of work based on the group goals. She then has to give her learners a diagnostic assessment, which is based on the group goals, and from it she will work out specific priorities for each learner. She meets each learner in tutorial in order to discuss the diagnostic assessment with them, and also to find out what their personal priorities are. (She will have ten minutes per learner for this.) She has to draw up individual goals for each learner.

2   *Teacher B* works off-site, with a mixed ability class. She has a small group but it is 'open to all-comers'. At the beginning of the year, she talks to her learners a lot, finding out their level and what they particularly want to work on. Then, if they are not complete beginners, she gives them a diagnostic assessment related to what they have said are their priorities. She then uses all the information she has to decide what each person should try to achieve in the time available. Having done this she makes a list of items they could all work on together; writes some goals for the group as a whole; and a rough scheme of work, which is open-ended enough to add things as they come up. She fills in her scheme of work as she goes.

3   *Teacher C* works in a college, with graded classes. He starts the year by looking in the curriculum for the level he is teaching and sets a very general diagnostic assessment, based on the appropriate level of the curriculum. As a result of this, he notes those areas of need which seem to apply to a number of learners. He makes a list of these and sets group goals based on them. He then speaks to each learner and decides on individual priorities. He writes his scheme of work, incorporating the group needs and the individual needs.

COMMENT 9.9

Teacher A has a 'pre-prepared' syllabus, which means she doesn't have to start from scratch in her planning, but there may be questions over just how appropriate to the learners this syllabus is and this may be a reflection of institutional constraints. The degree of success she has in producing a course which truly manages to address both 'group' and 'individual' needs will be highly dependent on the accuracy of the initial placement procedures – otherwise she may find herself in the position of trying vainly to organize a wildly disparate group of individuals into a coherent class. She also appears to have been given very little time to conduct tutorials with individual learners.

Teacher B is, of necessity, following a more individual-centred and process-based pathway. The difficulty here will be around finding sufficient and appropriate 'group' goals for the class to work on together: this may involve a continual process of negotiation, together with a high degree of perceptiveness, tact and diplomacy on the part of the teacher. This will inevitably require a large allocation of time to tutorials and this teacher's success may well depend on how much time is actually available for this. Additionally, 'negotiation' may itself be problematic, it may be unwise to take all ESOL learners' negotiation of 'goals' at face value.

This approach tries to make a virtue of the disparate nature of mixed-ability teaching, though, and is open-ended enough to address changes of circumstance, group membership, and learners' perception of their own needs as they arise.

Teacher C's tactics are a compromise between the two approaches above. He neither starts with the 'group' as Teacher A does, nor with the 'individual' as Teacher B. Instead he attempts to triangulate between a curriculum level and the individuals in his class to produce a scheme of work that balances individual and group perspectives. As with Teacher A, this will be highly reliant on accuracy in the placement process. As with Teacher B, this approach makes considerable demands on the sensitivity and perceptiveness of the teacher.

Additionally, all three teachers face a further, and critical, difficulty – that of negotiating course content, or conducting tutorials, with learners whose level of English may be extremely low. Unless translators are available, it may simply not be possible to adequately obtain the learners' viewpoints and perspectives.

It is important to emphasize that, in any of the approaches above, this is a *cyclical* process. Once a course is planned and a scheme of work produced, the teacher doesn't just teach it for the rest of the year. 'Online planning', mentioned above in relation to lesson planning, applies equally well to course planning. A good scheme of work should be subject to constant review, evaluation and reflection, and learners should be, whenever possible, deeply involved in this process. We can, once again, apply Kolb's learning cycle.

Figure 9.3 provides an example of one possible 'order' for elements in the cycle:

Figure 9.3 A possible order for elements in the learning cycle

Another key point is that each element of *this* cycle can itself be subject to Kolb's experiential learning cycle. In other words, teachers and learners can consider each element of the cycle from concrete (teaching), evaluative, reflective and planning perspectives; each item is subject to a critical process which offers us the opportunity to critique or 'stand outside' the procedures and routines of educational practice. This in turn should offer us flexibility. We may wish, for instance, to re-order the elements of the cycle in Figure 9.3, or drop some of them, or introduce new elements.

It is important to recognize that at each stage, assessing learners' needs, or evaluating which goals and targets have been met, should not lead us to take a 'deficit' view of our learners' abilities:

> A traditional understanding of needs is that which underpins a 'needs analysis' approach commonly used in ESP and development work. 'Experts' use well-honed tools for finding out people's needs in clearly defined areas. Needs here are pre-defined by experts – categories of needs are presupposed by set approaches to analysis that depend on a predetermined set of questions. In needs analysis for language learners this is often closely linked to college and government agendas such as what they as providers can offer and what they think people need to learn in order to pass assessments which will attract further college funding or to job-seek and join the workforce. A methodology is used which can compartmentalise and decontextualise needs by narrowly focusing on language learning needs and with a narrow view of language as grammar, lexis and socially appropriate language, with no reference to how other types of more social needs may interplay with these. This approach also

suggests a decontextualised deficit view of people's 'needs' being problems that have to be sorted out rather than seeing these needs within the context of valuing what resources and skills people already have. It is a view which suggests people have to be told what their needs are by others and that the only way of addressing their needs is through the intervention of 'experts' as though people have no resources to draw on themselves.

(Roberts et al. 2004: 40)

As well as *needs*, learners have wants, desires, ambitions and impulses; these all need to be addressed if a tutor is to avoid putting learners in such a deficit position – in other words, this is akin to patients who need to be cured of their (linguistic) illnesses by (linguistic) treatment.

Individual learning plans (ILPs)

ILPs and tutorials

Before discussing ILPs – which at the current time are a central element of the planning process – in any detail, it is probably useful to differentiate between ILPs and tutorials. Tutorials are an opportunity for teachers and learners to reflect on the process of language learning, to talk *about* learning rather than to actually do it. Though ILPs will often be used or referred to during tutorials, they are not one and the same; the ILP is an actual document that is intended to be *owned* by the learner.

Tutorials may often, and very usefully, be conducted on a one-to-one basis by the teacher and learner. However, in many learning contexts, time often mitigates against tutorials on this sort of basis being conducted anything other than very infrequently. In this case, tutorials may often be conducted on a group basis within regular class time. This is not entirely without value, for instance learners can be asked to:

- Compare progress over a period of time.
- Review the content of recent lessons and decide what needs further work or clarification.
- Work on study skills – e.g. dictionary work, file organization.
- Compare the language-learning work they do outside the class.
- Decide what they would like the content of future lessons to be.
- Compare ILPs.
- Compare their experiences of using English outside the class.
- Discuss barriers to learning.

ILPs and SMART targets

Research indicates that when learners feel more involved with, and take control of, their own learning they learn better and faster. One aspect of placing the individual, as opposed to classes/groups of, learners at the heart of the learning process is the use of ILPs. A good ILP should facilitate a learner's involvement with, reflection on and, crucially, *ownership of* the act or process of learning.

However, the use of ILPs for ESOL learners has to surmount two crucial difficulties. ILPs are typically produced in the target language itself thus the learner has to reflect on, and set goals for, their learning in the language they are trying to acquire. Further, to do this they may well have to also acquire a whole new metalanguage – the language of talking about language and language-learning. At Entry 1, this may simply not be possible (or merely counterproductive) without translation into their first language or interpreter help.

The second difficulty is to do with the nature of language learning itself, which as we have noted is a messy and unpredictable process that cannot easily be broken down into a series of steps:

> In fact, there is a view that learners often begin to communicate using unanalysed chunks of language, which they later try to analyse. At this later stage, they may appear to become less accurate or fluent and thus seem to regress, whereas in fact they are in the process of developing a deeper understanding of the grammar of the language. This phenomenon, if observed in learners, is likely to cause immense difficulty for teachers obliged to record step-by-step progress
>
> (Sunderland and Wilkins 2004)

At the time of writing the current orthodoxy in the learning and skills sector – particularly with reference to inspection regimes – is an expectation that tutors will use SMART targets when they draw up ILPs with learners.

SMART is an acronym standing for Specific, Measurable, Achievable, Realistic and Time-related. The argument goes that learners should be encouraged to set and work towards targets that have these characteristics. Undoubtedly, such targets may sometimes be of value to learners; one can readily set study objectives that fit this paradigm. For instance, learners might:

- Complete a set of exercises on punctuation within a timescale.
- Watch a series of TV programmes and note down language features.
- Practice diphthongs or another problem sound a set number of times each day in front of the bathroom mirror, etc.

Unfortunately, although these may be valuable as *study* objectives, they all have considerably less meaning as *learning* objectives. The weight of SLA research tells us that language learning, far from being SMART, tends to be CASUAL:

C   *Cyclical* – language isn't learnt step by step; items and skills need continual revisiting and review.
A   *Asymmetrical* – different skills and aspects of language may develop at different paces. 'Spiky' profiles, where a learner might have, for instance, advanced speaking and listening skills, but only intermediate reading, and elementary writing skills, are the norm rather than the exception.

S   *Social* – language learning is a social process rather than a measurable set of competencies.

U   *Unpredictable* – how exactly learning takes place, and under what circumstances it occurs is still very mysterious. Learners do not all follow the same path.

A   *Affective* – language learning involves the whole person – their emotions and identities affect and are affected by aspects of the language learning process.

L   *Local* – language learning is highly context-bound, both in terms of what is learnt, and how it is learnt.

TASK 9.10

The question we should ask is what sort of ILPs would be of most use to ESOL UK learners. *How do you think learners and teachers could apply* Kolb's learning cycle *to the ILP process?*

Concrete experience

Observation and reflection

Active experimentation

Abstract conceptualization

COMMENT 9.10

Learners would probably benefit from an ILP process that allowed or encouraged them to engage with each of the stages in this cycle. Their 'concrete experience' of using language, and of life both inside and outside the classroom, would be the raw material that they engaged with. With regard to this, learners could be asked to:

- Keep diaries of their language use.
- Record language used by themselves or others in their daily lives.
- Record (or keep) texts they encounter.
- Keep a record of specific linguistic items they have 'noticed'.

All this material and data, recorded or simply experienced, provides a basis for reflection. Learners often enjoy talking about their experiences of using or encountering the language they are trying to learn and this process can be of great benefit to them. Teachers, simply by discussing with learners their use of language in the 'real world', can help learners make sense of linguistic encounters, texts and social realities that were perhaps initially perplexing.

This sort of reflection on experience should enable ILPs to become sites of concept formation, or hypothesis making, the third stage of Kolb's cycle. Learners here are getting ready to go out and try new ideas. These might range from alternative ways of handling social encounters to trying out new grammatical understandings or intonation patterns. This naturally leads on to the fourth stage of Kolb's cycle, the actual testing/trying out of these ideas in new situations and it is here that it is possible for teachers and learners to set meaningful 'targets' in the ILP. Learners might, for instance:

- Try making their next, e.g., dental appointment over the phone.
- Interpret attitudes from body language/intonation of 'real-life' interlocutors.
- Try out a set of lexical chunks in a social setting.

These would not simply be 'targets' to be 'ticked off' – the concrete experiences they provoke would be the raw data of the next turn of the cycle, to be reflected on and discussed by teacher and learner.

Part 3

Inclusive learning

10 Differentiation

Mary Weir

Imagine going with a group of hungry friends to a restaurant where there was no choice on the menu, just a 'take it or leave it' option of, say, roast beef and Yorkshire pudding with greens and potatoes and sherry trifle for pudding. Some in the group will really enjoy their meal and feel well nourished after it, but what about the vegetarians or the guy with a wheat intolerance? What about the girl who loves fruit but hates cream and custard? What about those who don't drink alcohol?

A lesson without differentiation is like the 'take it or leave' option in the restaurant – great, perhaps, for some, but only partially suitable for others.

It is likely that whatever the teaching circumstances, to plan lessons and schemes of work teachers have to work within the framework of a curriculum and the targets of an exam or qualification syllabus. Courses and lessons planned within this framework alone are unlikely to work; knowledge of the learners is a vital element in planning for success.

Differentiation involves focusing closely on *who* you are teaching as well as *what*. It involves seeing 'the class' as a group of individuals and considering every one of them at the planning stage, during teaching and throughout the course. No two people and no two learners are identical. Teachers who differentiate well place the learners, and a wealth of knowledge about them, at the centre of their preparation. They are also sensitive and responsive to change in individuals and can adapt their teaching accordingly. Spiegel and Sunderland (2006) see '... differentiation as the awareness of commonalities, strengths and differences within a group and the subsequent impact of this awareness on assessment, planning, teaching and the evaluation of learning.'

Why is differentiation important?

> It is not enough to be to be doing very well with most learners and failing a few. As teachers we must reach all of the learners, all of the time.
>
> (Perry 2003: 22–3)

This point is hardly contentious, it is one with which any committed teacher will surely agree as an underpinning philosophy. Perry continues: 'Differentiation is seen as an effective way of responding to diverse learning needs, overcoming potential barriers and setting suitable challenges for all learners, whatever their abilities.' This comment refers to learner differences in terms of needs, barriers and abilities.

TASK 10.1

Think of groups of ESOL learners you know. How many factors can you list that differentiate the learners from one another? You should be able to find at least ten.

COMMENT 10.1

What did you come up with? Here are some:

- Age.
- Gender.
- Nationality.
- First language.
- Oher languages they use.
- Previous educational experience.
- Level of literacy in first language.
- Study skills.
- Expectations of the class.
- Reasons for being in UK.
- Reasons for coming to ESOL classes.
- Attendance pattern.
- Confidence.
- Motivation.
- Personality.
- Learning style.
- Learning difficulties.
- Health.
- Disabilities.
- Contact with English outside the class.
- Spiky profiles[1].
- More temporary factors such as mood or tiredness ...

This list is not exhaustive. It is arguable that a group of ESOL learners can be one of the most diverse classes anywhere. Baynham (2006) refers to the 'hyperdiversity' of ESOL learners. It is possible to have learners at different points on a spectrum of all of the categories above in one single class. Some classes, particularly where provision is limited, have a wide range of learner levels in the group ranging from Entry 1 in some skills to Level 2 in others. Differentiation in a group such as this is vital. On the other hand, some teachers will say: 'I'm teaching work-based learning in a factory. All my learners are from Poland and they are all working towards Entry 2. How and why should I differentiate?' Well, yes, some ESOL classes are more homogeneous than others, but even in a relatively homogeneous group there will be differences to be taken into account such as motivation, purposes for learning English, previous experience of education, attendance pattern, speed of learning, interests, personality and variable temporary influences such as mood. All of them have an impact on learning and so need to be taken into account; recognizing this helps us to help our learners to progress.

In a superficially homogeneous class it is also unlikely that the whole group will all be working at the same level on each of the four skills of listening, speaking, reading and writing. They will have spiky profiles (see section on language skills in Chapter 2) and even spiky profiles within broad *Adult ESOL Core Curriculum* levels. For example two learners working towards Entry 2 may both be able to write a comprehensible note to the teacher when their children are absent from school, but one may write in clearly punctuated sentences with inaccurate spelling while the other spells well but does not use capital letters appropriately. If the teacher is to help each leaner to progress, then these differences need attention. Differentiation in any classroom is good practice and, as Perry (2003) notes, a lack of differentiation is a factor in many inspection reports on unsatisfactory provision.

Autonomy, identity and investment

Another reason for differentiation is to allow learners some control over their learning, to develop their autonomy as learners and to draw on their experiences and identity.

Norton (1995) is interested in the concept of the good language learner and how teachers can support learners in becoming good language learners. In her study, 'Social identity, investment and language learning' (1995), she concludes: '... the second language teacher needs to help language learners claim the right to speak outside the classroom. To this end, the lived experiences and social identities of language learners need to be incorporated into the formal second language curriculum' (1995: 26). The concepts of drawing learners' personal experiences into the classroom and fostering ownership of and investment in classroom discourse by learners are fundamental aspects of differentiation. If learners have some control over classroom talk and can initiate classroom conversations it may support them outside the classroom in defining an identity, in increasing motivation and in becoming better language learners.

When teachers draw on the lived experiences and social identities of learners in class they are making links between the classroom and life outside: 'bringing the outside in'. Baynham et al. (2006) identify this as an important element of effective practice.

What approaches can we use to differentiate between our learners?

> Given that learners start at different points, learn in different ways and progress at different speeds, one-size-fits-all strategies will clearly not do.

> (Perry 2003: 22–3).

Perry's point underlines the need for a range of approaches in any one class to meet the 'hyperdiversity' that we have identified here and in Chapter 1. She outlines five broad approaches for differentiation as identified in Ofsted's *Handbook for the Inspection of Schools*. These are differentiation by:

1 Outcome, where learners can respond at different levels to open-ended activities.
2 The speed at which learners work through tasks.
3 Enrichment or extension where learners are given further tasks to deepen their skills beyond the basics.
4 Resources where there is a range of materials available for learners to use.
5 Task or activity within a common theme.

TASK 10.2

Consider the list above for a moment. What do these approaches mean to you? Do you already use any of them? Have you seen other teachers use them? Can you give examples? Which of the above is used in the following classroom activity:

> Talk to your partner about your neighbour. Describe your neighbour and tell your partner whether you like your neighbour or not, and why.

COMMENT 10.2

Each approach merits some exploration.

1 *Differentiation by outcome, where learners can respond at different levels to open-ended activities.* This is the approach used in the example. Learners can say a little or a lot, they can describe the physical and or personality traits of their neighbour. Whether they are working at Entry 1 or Level 2, they can respond in some way to this question. The same question could be a written task and still elicit open-ended responses. The stimuli for similar activities could be a discussion of pictures, newspaper headlines or perhaps a TV programme. This kind of activity can offer learners opportunities to work together even if they are at different levels; they draw on personal experience or

responses to stimuli beyond simply linguistic challenges. The differentiation here is subtle and can help a group of learners to work together in spite of significant differences.

2   *Differentiation by the speed at which learners work through tasks.* This appears to be an easy way to embark on differentiation as it allows learners to work at their own pace. Learners may all start the same task but almost always they will finish at different times. The key here is that once they have completed a task learners need something to progress to, something which is a little more difficult and challenging, not simply more of the same. This is, in effect, the next approach.

3   *Differentiation by enrichment or extension, where learners are given further tasks to deepen their skills beyond the basics.* Differentiation by speed and by enrichment depends on careful and detailed planning by the teacher. These strands present an important opportunity for individual learning to take place, for learners to work at their own pace, but there is a risk that the class may spend a disproportionate amount of time on individual tasks at the expense of group work. Perry explains:

> While there is a role for learners to work individually, especially on specific weaknesses, differentiation by progress can lead to 'death by worksheets', an approach much criticized by OFSTED and ALI. Here the danger is that learners work in isolation from the group, concentrating on a narrow range of skills and missing out on language development gained through social interaction.

> (Perry 2003: 22–3)

4   *Differentiation by resources where there is a range of materials available for learners to use.* This also involves careful planning and preparation. Learners choose from or are directed to a range of resources. Work on a grammar point could be computer-based, a card-sort activity, a listening task, from a page from a grammar book or a deductive task designed by the teacher to raise awareness of the point. This choice can cater for learners' different learning preferences and skills. It can also include learners choosing their own task.

In terms of classroom management these approaches can present challenges:

- How do you avoid 'death by worksheet'?
- At what point and how do you check answers or progress?
- Do you review all the work individually?
- At what stage do you bring the whole group together and highlight specific learning points?
- And what about the learner who feels anxious because all those around him or her have moved on to the next exercise or task?

One response to the challenges here is to encourage learners to compare and discuss their answers as they finish work. This strategy will lead to pairs or small groups of learners working together according to the speed at which they work. Once two learners have agreed on their answers they can then compare with another pair, and so on. This will encourage collaboration, discussion of work and an exploration of language. It will also give the teacher the freedom to support learners selectively according to their needs and give him or her time to spend with the anxious, slower learners or to stretch the more advanced. Small-group work such as this can be scheduled to run up to a break so that a phased end to activities can take place or the teacher can specify at the start of small-group work the time that it will finish. The teacher should also ensure that learners understand from early on in the course that the purpose of such an activity is to focus on their individual development.

5   *Differentiation by task or activity within a common theme. This can include mixed ability, pair or group work, with learners taking on different roles according to their abilities, aptitudes and needs.* Learners might take different roles in a simulation, for example: a receptionist or patient at the health centre making appointments; or one of a panel of interviewers or the interviewee in a selection process role-play. It could involve different tasks in the production of a class website or newspaper, or being the scribe in a group brainstorm activity while others contribute ideas orally. Roles and tasks could be assigned to learners according to their strengths, interests or the skills they need to develop.

This last approach is not without potential problems however. If different learners have different tasks the result can be that the weaker ones become de-motivated when they see that they have less challenging tasks. Sensitive planning and class management are required to avoid this. Learners need opportunities to draw on and display their strengths as well as work on their areas of weakness.

Task 10.3

Look again at the summary of the five approaches. For each one, think of one more example that you could use with your learners. What planning is involved for your chosen activity?

Planning

Planning for differentiation can be daunting, especially for a class with very mixed levels. The amount of information about learners that teachers gather formally and informally over time is invaluable. It should inform classroom practice, but the sheer quantity and complexity can be overwhelming. It would be counterproductive if, as a result, learners spent a disproportionate amount of time on individual work or if teachers spent a disproportionate amount of time on preparation. The following ideas are ways in which we can achieve some differentiated activities while keeping extra preparatory work manageable.

Use IT

Create worksheets on a computer and save them where they can be edited to suit different groups of learners. Editing could involve changing font size; deleting certain sections and questions; or adding supplementary tasks and questions. It is quick and easy to create differently gapped texts from one original on a computer. Some published materials available online and on CDs can also be edited in this way and then printed off, even if it cannot always be saved. For example, you can change the fonts and texts on the DfES *Skills for Life* (2001a) and *Citizenship Materials* (2006d).

Edit manually

You can also customize worksheets using Tippex and highlighters, glue and scissors, or simply by strategic folding. For example, with a gapped text the missing words can be supplied at the bottom of the page; weaker learners can be allowed to see and choose from the words from the start, while for stronger learners the paper is folded under the words and they are only allowed to look at them when they get stuck or when the teacher wants them to check their work.

Share

Teams of teachers should have opportunities to share ideas and materials. While there is a lot of useful material available on the Internet to share, locally produced materials which are based on and reflect local communities are invaluable. A bank of well-made, collated and indexed materials (which can be added to) should be available in a central resource area. These resources could include laminated pictures of the local area, tapes, local maps and telephone directories, stories from local newspapers and local radio. They might include realia and materials specific to work-based learning groups, but could also include more general realia such as empty medicine packets and bottles, or shopping. Suggestions for how to use the materials with different groups of learners can be included along with copies of any worksheets, tasks and questionnaires that individual teachers have prepared. Local, institutional online materials can also help to reduce the isolation of tutors working part-time or in outreach centres who may have little contact with other colleagues.

Strategies for differentiation based on listening and speaking tasks

Listening materials can be exploited for use in a class where there is a wide range of levels and backgrounds, and can act as a source for a range of literacy and speaking tasks.

When teachers use a recording with a group of learners, circumstances usually dictate that everyone listens at the same time, otherwise the tape is distracting for those working on other tasks and the listeners may be distracted by noise from others. However, differentiation can still take place if we ask learners to respond in different ways to the recording and complete different tasks. Learners should always have some sort of task before the tape is heard for the first time in order to help them tune in to what they hear. This should include questions to focus on the gist of the recording such as:

- How many people are speaking?
- What is the relationship between the speakers?
- What are they talking about?

Before the recording starts, it is possible to differentiate by asking specific learners to listen for the answer to a particular question. Nominating people in this way allows weaker learners to build confidence by getting things right in whole-group phases, and challenges more advanced learners from the start. When the responses are taken, it is vital, therefore, to ensure that the teacher asks the designated learners for the answers and that classroom discipline is such that others respect this. If conflicting answers are given by learners it isn't necessary to correct at this stage, as they can be asked to check by listening again and then discussing any uncertainties.

The same approach can be taken as the focus moves from listening for gist to listening for more detailed information and then on to work on speaking or writing skills. These activities can be conducted orally and interactively, and need not be worksheet-based. Some paper-based work can be useful, however, for example listening for key words and filling them in on a gapped transcript of the recording. Again, different groups of learners can have copies of the transcripts with different words missing. Some might focus, for example, on discourse markers, others on irregular past-tense forms while a third group focus on topic related vocabulary. As a follow-up, learners can liaise to check their answers using their different versions of the text. This strategy promotes collaboration and interaction alongside differentiated work.

The recording can be played again in short snippets with learners asked to repeat a phrase, focusing on intonation, pronunciation or stress, for example. This is an opportunity to target pronunciation issues specific to the first language of different learners.

TASK 10.4

Take the following transcript of two short dialogues. Devise questions and activities appropriate for a mixed-level class. Include activities to focus on: meaning, phonology, lexis and form.

A: Hello, Fitzalan High School. Can I help you?

B: I'm just ringing to let you know that my daughter, Sara Ibrahim in Year 8, can't come to school today. She fell over yesterday and she has twisted her knee and hurt her arm.

A: Thank you for letting us know.

C: Oh hello, Cecilia. It's Suzanne here.

D: Hi Suzanne.

C: I'm not coming in to work today. I didn't sleep well last night. I had a terrible toothache. So I've got an appointment to see the dentist.

(Adams 2007)

COMMENT 10.4

Look at the activities the tutor devised for her class in Appendix 1 at the end of this chapter. Published worksheets that came with the course were used with learners working on literacy skills at Entry 1. These include a picture of a person. Learners simply highlight the part of the body they hear mentioned on the tape.

Phonological work included asking all learners, but particularly the Chinese learners, to notice and repeat the elisions and weak forms in:

... I'm just ringing to let you know ...

... twisted her knee and hurt her arm ...

... I've got an appointment ...

Some Chinese, Punjabi and Arabic speakers worked on the stress in:

o 0   0 o   0   o 0
She can't come to school today

And practised substituting this phrase with:

o 0   0 o   0   o 0
He can't come to work today

o 0   0 o   0 o 0
I can't come to class today

Further differentiation for learning preferences involved demonstrating stress and intonation patterns visually (as above) as well as aurally and kinaesthetically (by clapping rhythms and miming intonation patterns).

Follow-up work included practice of phoning school, college or work about an absence. Learners working at the higher levels for speaking and writing role-played the part of the receptionist taking calls from different learners. They had to record the information and write a message for each call.

Learners working towards Entry 2 and 3 for speaking skills played the role of a parent phoning school, a husband phoning his wife's workplace or themselves phoning college, as appropriate to their circumstances. Reasons for absence were changed: cues were given on picture cards or learners could make up their own reasons. Some also played the role of the receptionist and filled in a prepared memo. Choice of pairs for role-play was based on mixing the first language of the pair, how well they knew one another and their confidence.

Further literacy work at Entry 1, 2 and 3 was based on writing an absence note to school; writing an email to the class teacher; or filling in a return to work form. Literacy work at Level 1 and 2 was a continuation of work from previous weeks on writing CVs and letters of application. It could also have been a more discursive task such as a letter to a friend about being off work.

A session such as this depends on careful planning as well as sensitive pairing and grouping of learners during the class. The pairs and groups the teacher plans for may not be possible on the day if any learners are absent or if there are new learners in class – so flexibility and spontaneity are also important.

The example above shows how differentiated work on listening, speaking and writing can arise from one source – in this case a listening task. It drew particularly on approaches 1, 2 and 5 discussed by Perry. It shows how source material, in this case initially aimed at beginners, can be adapted to whole groups and pair work for learners at different levels, with different languages and purposes for learning. The differentiation did not result in an overemphasis on individual literacy work – indeed, it promoted many opportunities for learners to interact, to negotiate meaning, to initiate talk and to draw on their own lives and experiences.

Tension between group work and differentiation

It is important to bear in mind that there can be a tension between group work and differentiation; resolving this is a real challenge for teachers. There is a risk that, if differentiation is taken to its logical conclusion, the language-learning class becomes a workshop where learners all work on individual tasks. This outcome runs counter to research, teacher knowledge and experience of how best to foster good language learning, and learning generally. Interaction is an important part of developing a wider range of skills and understanding: a collaborative and productive group ethos is an important element of any class, not just a language class. Recent ESOL case study research concluded: 'An emphasis on individualised teaching and learning may not support the needs of adult ESOL learners. Talk is work in the ESOL classroom and the most significant mode of learning for ESOL learners is through group interaction and opportunities to practise speaking and listening' (Roberts et al. 2004).

Differentiation in teacher talk

Many strategies stem from the way in which teachers talk to their learners. These don't fit neatly into Perry's (2003) categorization, can be very subtle and may be largely intuitive on the part of the teacher.

Pronunciation

Teachers can help learners to improve their pronunciation in many ways (see Chapter 4 and above). These vary according to the learners' first language and the different problems learners have with English phonology. Whole-class oral work may involve speakers of several different first languages but differentiated work can take place, for example, as new vocabulary is learned. As Kenworthy (1987: 114) points out: '… there are several aspects of pronunciation that can easily be integrated into vocabulary work: sounds, stress patterns, linkage and simplifications, sound/spelling correspondences, and clusters of sounds.' The teacher can also correct and give visual reminders to individual learners about phonology during whole class work, using gestures, for example, to indicate rising or falling intonation or contracted forms.

Thus, different learners can be selected for different reminders, correction and feedback according to their particular needs.

Error correction

Teachers employ a range of techniques for dealing with learner errors; indeed, the first decision to be made is whether to acknowledge the error at all or whether to allow the discourse to continue. The teacher may well respond differently to the same error in one class depending on who makes it and when. He or she may choose to react in one way when a confident learner working towards Entry 3 who wants to work on improving accuracy says – 'I go to London yesterday' – he or she may raise an eyebrow, or refuse to understand – 'Sorry?' – and elicit a correct version from the learner. Or he or she may reformulate the sentence him- or herself and move on – 'Oh you went to London yesterday did you? Tell us about it'. However, when a shy learner working towards Entry 1 says – 'I go to London yesterday' – she may well ignore the error and say – 'Really? Tell me about it …'

This is an example of spontaneous differentiation informed by the teacher's knowledge of the learners' abilities, short-term goals, personality and reactions. It shows how we can subtly vary the extent to which we are 'a sympathetic native speaker' within whole-group work (DfES 2001b).

Speech modifications by teachers: modification and elaboration

Teachers frequently adjust their own use of English according to the level of understanding of the learners. Chaudron (1988) noted that in class, teachers tend to speak more slowly, simplify or exaggerate their pronunciation, use a more basic vocabulary, repeat themselves more often and use less subordination. Nunan (1991: 191) suggests that teachers do this because they believe that the modifications aid comprehension and foster acquisition. If teachers modify their talk in different ways for different learners within the class according to the learners' ability to understand, then here again is an opportunity to differentiate. It is particularly important in classes where there is a wide range of levels. All of these techniques can be used to correct an error in understanding. Nunan (1991: 191) suggests that teachers' elaborating their talk, by including *repetition*, *paraphrase* and *rhetorical markers*, is more valuable for learners than teachers simplifying their grammar and vocabulary.

Open or closed questions and tasks

Closed questions involve a restricted choice of responses, perhaps just 'Yes' or 'No'. Within oral work, learners at lower proficiency levels can be involved in whole-group work by answering more closed questions and a restricted range of open questions, whereas other learners can be asked to respond to open questions. This strategy provides opportunities to differentiate listening and production skills, and falls into the category of differentiation by outcome identified by Perry (2003).

Display or referential questions

Display questions require the learner to provide information that is already known to the questioner, whereas referential questions seek information that is not known by the questioner. A teacher might hold up a photo of a football match and ask learners: 'What are they doing?' This is a display question: the teacher knows the answer but wants to know if the learner has the vocabulary. The question, 'Do you enjoy watching football?', is a referential question because the teacher doesn't know the answer. While referential questions are much more common in natural communication outside the classroom, display questions frequently dominate language classrooms:

> That the use of known-information or display questions in the classroom generates discourse which is fundamentally different from everyday discourse is an important consideration for language teachers. An increased use by teachers of referential questions, which create a flow of information from *learners* to teachers, may generate discourse which more nearly resembles the normal conversation learners experience outside the classroom.
>
> (Brock 1986: 49)

This reference to language outside the classroom echoes Norton's (1995) study and the 'lived experiences' of learners. Brock (1986) and Swain (1983 in Brock 1986) suggest that the production of the learner's own messages in the target language, 'may be the trigger that forces the learner to pay attention to the means of expression needed to convey his or her intended meaning' (Swain in Brock 1986: 56). This could be seen as differentiation; the teacher's selection of a question may stretch an individual to supply his or her own information in language at his or her own level and disposal. In Brock's (1986) study, referential questions also promoted longer and more syntactically complex responses from learners. Referential questions promoted more speaking turns on the part of learners and the use of more connectives 'to make explicit the links between the propositions they expressed' (1986: 55). Thornbury (1996: 282) suggests that responding to referential questions requires more effort and greater depth of processing from the learner. He also suggests that asking referential questions 'prompts a greater effort and depth of processing on the part of the teacher.' Leading and facilitating this kind of oral work is indeed a skilled process; it takes time and practice for teachers to accomplish.

Feedback: the Initiation–Response–Follow-up cycle

The differences between display and referential questions and the interaction they promote is developed in research into the I–R–F (Initiation–Response–Follow-up/ Feedback) cycle. This term describes classroom interaction where the teacher initiates a question, a learner responds and the teacher gives feedback on the response or follows up with a supplementary question which re-starts the cycle.

The example of the cycle below is taken from Cullen (2002: 117). Learners are looking at a picture; the teacher asks a series of display questions and gives evaluative feedback of learner responses.

T	What's the boy doing?	**I**
S	He's climbing a tree.	**R**
T	That's right. He's climbing a tree.	**F**

Evaluative feedback could also include correction or elicitation of a correct form if an error has occurred.

Discourse which relies more on referential questions and elicitation of learners' own ideas can stimulate richer interaction and language development. Here is an example from a classroom in the *ESOL Effective Practice Research* (Baynham et al. 2006):

T:	what about, I mean, what about the child? Does your child want to do that? Are they happy to do that?
L:	yes, yes
T:	yeah? They are.
L:	my mum
T:	did you look after her or did she look after you?
L:	yes

> T: or did you look after each other?
> L: each other [xxx]
> T: it's quite a difference
> L: but it depends, you know how is the er you know very old, no child can look after her, the mum goes, not grandchildren, the old people, I look after her when very old, but when it's a normal person
> S: in my country it's
> L: when she's sixty or fifty five she's quite young still but she needs some help so she got grandchildren, they help her

In this extract we see that given time and sensitive prompts and questions by the teacher the learners express complex ideas and experiences in their own words in extended utterances.

The focus is on communication and allowing the learners to take ownership of the topic. This is an aspect of differentiation in action; the learners involve themselves on their own terms. The teacher decides how to respond to each particular learner in the midst of a whole group activity. The decision may involve whether and how to correct errors. Being able to make these 'on-the-spot judgements' and balancing the needs for feedback on form or content-based follow-up 'are skills language teachers need to deploy constantly in almost every lesson they teach' (Roberts et al. 2004: 86).

Wait time and learner initiated talk

How long should we wait after asking a question in class? How much time should we give learners to respond before intervening to ask another learner or to re-phrase the question? Wait time is another aspect of differentiation. If the teacher allows each learner a reasonable time to respond without losing the momentum of the class it may give the shy, the slower or the more reflective learners more chance to participate. Of course, sometimes the teacher can adopt a less sympathetic attitude and deliberately reduce wait time in order to put stronger learners under more pressure to respond quickly.

Thornbury (1996) also refers to studies which showed that an increase of wait time from one second to three or four tended to stimulate longer responses and encouraged more learners to respond. There was also an increase in learner-initiated questioning. He comments, 'A high proportion of learner-initiated questions would suggest a healthy distribution of the "ownership" of classroom discourse, which in turn would tend to promote more "investment" on the part of the learner' (p. 282).

That learners should feel free to be actively involved in initiating interaction in the classroom is a fundamental part of a communicative classroom according to Kumaradivelu (1993: 14). Negotiation of meaning involves the learners in, 'clarification, confirmation, comprehension, requesting, repairing and reacting. Above all, the term negotiated means that the learner should have the freedom to initiate interaction not just react and respond to what the teacher says.' This freedom, I would argue, is another aspect of differentiation that the teacher can foster in the classroom for learners to use, as they choose.

This exploration of oral work underlines how complex and subtle differentiation can be. Indeed, while this aspect of differentiation is potentially very effective, the subtleties can be lost on observers who are not language teachers and/or do not know the learners in the class very well. When, as teachers, we are required to demonstrate how we differentiate, it is important that we ourselves understand these complexities and are able to articulate them as well as practise them. Our tacit knowledge may need to be more explicit.

Conclusion

Effective differentiation can only occur if teachers have access to:

- Initial and diagnostic assessment of learner language skills.
- Information about learners' goals, purposes for learning and backgrounds.
- Some knowledge of learners' first languages.
- An awareness of learning styles.

What teachers know about their learners will increase over time. There will be long-term and day-to-day changes that teachers need to take into account and respond to. Differentiation also relies on careful planning as well as the ability of the teacher to make spontaneous and sensitive responses to learners' contributions to class. The wealth of information that we accumulate about our learners and the multiplicity of their goals may sometimes seem overwhelming. We need to synthesize it all into coherent lessons and courses in which a balance between group and individual goals is achieved.

So, let us also end with a health warning. While we have explored many routes to differentiation here, any attempt to incorporate all of them into one lesson would be time consuming and counterproductive. We can, however, take simple steps towards increasing our repertoire of differentiation techniques; with experience and practice many will become intuitive.

Appendix 1

Take the following transcript of two short dialogues. Devise questions and activities appropriate for a mixed-level class. Include activities to focus on: meaning, phonology, lexis, form.

    A: Hello, Fitzalan High School. Can I help you?
    B: I'm just ringing to let you know that my daughter, Sara Ibrahim in Year 8, can't come to school today. She fell over yesterday and she has twisted her knee and hurt her arm.

> A: Thank you for letting us know.
>
> C: Oh hello, Cecilia. It's Suzanne here.
> D: Hi Suzanne.
> C: I'm not coming in to work today. I didn't sleep well last night. I had a terrible toothache. So I've got an appointment to see the dentist.

Here are some possible initial activities for students with a range of listening and literacy skills:

1 Learners working at Entry 1 are given a published picture of a person which accompanies the tape. They highlight the part of the body mentioned in each dialogue.
2 Learners who can read at Entry 2 use the following multiple choice questions and then a gap fill.

LISTEN

1 Circle the best answer:

A) Tariq is not coming to   **work** / **school** / **college**   today.

B) He has got   **toothache.** / **a headache.** / **a cough and a cold.**

C) Suzanne is not coming to   **work** / **school** / **college**   today.

D) She didn't   **eat** / **sleep** / **work**   last night.

E) She had a terrible   **headache.** / **toothache.** / **tummyache.**

2 Now listen and fill in the gaps:

S   Oh hello Cecilia, _____ Suzanne _____.

C   Hi Suzanne!

S   I'm _____ coming into work today because I _____ sleep last night. I _____ a terrible toothache so _____ _____ an appointment to _____ the dentist.

---

3   Learners at Entry 3 could have comprehension questions. They could also focus on vocabulary and language forms:

Task – Listen to the tape again. Underline the differences between what you hear and this text:
- Hello, Fitzalan High School. Can I help you?
- I'm just calling to tell you that my daughter, Sara Ibrahim in Year 8, can't come to school today. She fell down yesterday and she has injured her knee and bruised her arm.
- Thank you for telling us.

4   Learners at Level 1 and Level 2:

Task – You are the receptionist at Fitzalan High school. You take two messages. Listen to the tape twice.

- Write a note for the class teacher in message 1.
- Suzanne in message 2 works in the school canteen. Write a note for her line manager.

Note

1   Spiky profile is the term used to describe the different levels in listening speaking reading and writing that one student may have. Their receptive skills may be stronger than their productive skills; their oral skills may be stronger than their literacy skills, or vice versa.

11   Inclusive learning

Marina Spiegel and Efisia Tranza

When I first started teaching ESOL I hardly ever heard anyone talk about disabled learners or how to support them. They were somehow invisible, even though we'd all had disabled learners in our classes at some point ... people with physical disabilities as well as other kinds. I taught a small group of disabled ESOL learners in an outreach centre but some teachers said it wasn't our job, that we were language teachers, not special needs.

(Marie, retired ESOL teacher)

Introduction

Marie's experience was, until fairly recently, quite widespread. Many ESOL organizers and practitioners felt unprepared and lacking in expertise when it came to the subject of disabled bilingual learners. There was often a sense of embarrassment about what to do. With one or two notable exceptions,[1] there were few publications that looked at how to teach bilingual learners with any kind of cognitive or sensory disability or mental health difficulty. Disabled learners were invisible. This feeling that they were 'someone else's responsibility' was compounded by the fact that TESOL teacher-education programmes rarely gave trainee teachers an opportunity to discuss any of the issues facing disabled learners from a different culture living and studying in the UK, and to explore their impact in the classroom.

This chapter will briefly explore some key issues around disability and culture, as well national legislation and policy changes in the teaching and learning sector, which have made disability visible and inclusive learning a shared responsibility. It will reflect on the experiences of both teachers and learners, and focus on some practical applications based on these experiences.

Disability and ethnicity

The situation facing disabled learners from other cultures in the UK is complex and at times contradictory. Some recent research and publications[2] have begun to provide powerful insights into the relationship between disability and ethnicity, too often disability and learning difficulty are regarded as culturally neutral concepts and the aims and needs of learners with a disability or learning difficulty from different ethnic groups are assumed to be exactly the same as those from other sections of society.

(DfES 2006a)

Terminology and definitions

It is important to realize that in Europe the concept of disability was born out of particular historical events and circumstances in the last century, and that in many non-technologically developed countries disability as a social identity is only just emerging. In many societies, 'disability' as a recognized category does not exist (Ingstad and Whyte 1995).

Different cultures have different ways of defining disability,

> The Western term 'learning difficulty', in particular, has no easy translation in many languages. A study of South Asian communities in Birmingham and Tower Hamlets in London (Maudslay 2003) found no direct translation for the term. Work in the Turkish community (Section 3 of this document) showed no translation for the concept of 'moderate learning difficulty' while 'severe learning difficulties' were defined in terms of mental health rather than learning.
>
> (DfES 2006)

It is important to realize that terminology and definitions are not static, they change over time within particular societies, as concepts and attitudes evolve,

> In Eritrea prior to the war of independence the most common word used to describe physical disability was the Italian word 'balidi' which had derogatory connotations. However, after the war the new indigenous term 'akale-senkool' was popularised out of respect for war veterans who had become disabled in the independence struggle.
>
> (DfES 2006a)

TASK 11.1

Can you think of ways in which disabilities and disabled people are described in societies you are familiar with? Has terminology changed over time? If it has, consider some actual examples and reflect on the changes.

Social versus medical models of disability

Currently in the UK there is considerable debate around the ideologies that underpin the language we use to think, talk about and act towards disabled people. Two prevalent models exist: the medical and social models of disability.

In the medical model disabled people are described as leading lives which are restricted by their impairment. They are seen as needing care and treatment. This care is often delivered in residential institutions and hospitals by medical professionals. This way of thinking is criticized for disempowering disabled people. They are seen as 'the problem', and experts are authorized to determine whether disabled people have treatment or not and to decide how and where they spend their lives.

The social model of disability, originally created by disabled people themselves, is a challenge to this. It describes disability not as a medical issue but as one where disabled people face daily barriers in society, for example, from the way we design and build our towns and cities, the way we organize our education system or social activities and in the attitudes that we perpetuate, which favour non-disabled people over disabled people. The social model analyses the daily discrimination and exclusion faced by disabled people as a consequence of prejudice, even when this prejudice springs from well-intentioned motives. In the last decade, changes to the way professionals in education consider their role in relation to disabled learners have been very considerably influenced by the social model of disability.

Policy and legislation

The Tomlinson Report – Inclusive learning

In 1996 the Further Education Funding Council (FEFC) Learning Difficulties and/or Disabilities Committee chaired by Professor John Tomlinson produced a very important and influential report called *Inclusive Learning*. This report followed the first national inquiry in England into FE provision for learners with disabilities and/or learning difficulties. It was based on evidence from learners, parents, carers and providers, and proposed a new vision.

The report found that the 'old' approach which makes learners with learning difficulties and/or disabilities different from other learners did not work. It recommended a new approach – 'inclusive learning' – which focuses on the institution's capacity to understand and respond to the needs of individual learners rather than locating the difficulty or deficit within the learner. This requires moving 'away from labelling the learner and towards creating an appropriate educational environment' (FEFC 1996).

Inclusive learning requires that the whole process of learning and assessment be redesigned to fit the needs of all learners. In this way, meeting the needs of learners with learning difficulties and disabilities would be part of the institution's usual procedures, not something additional or different. As discussed in Chapter 7, disability and health-related matters are part of the range of factors that influence our approach to differentiation. Inclusive learning means seeing learners with disabilities and/or learning difficulties first and foremost as learners. It is about trying to provide the best match between the learning environment and the individual needs of the learner.

TASK 11.2

Consider the example below and think about what inclusive learning might mean in practice:

> Learner X is dyslexic[3] and finds abstract grammar concepts and 'rules' quite difficult to process and retain if they are not presented in context and personalized.

How might you meet his individual needs when planning for the group as a whole?

COMMENT 11.2

You could meet Learner X's needs by ensuring that:

- Grammar points are presented through dialogues, stories or narratives.
- The content is discussed and learners are asked to express opinions and share views and experiences before examining and practising the specific grammar point.
- Learners have opportunities to do role-plays using the particular grammar point.
- You give the rule to those learners who find this helpful but encourage Learner X to use more personalized strategies, for example inventing a mnemonic or creating a visual representation of the grammar point to help him remember it.

The Disability Discrimination Act Part 4

One of the most far reaching acts in relation to the rights of disabled people is the Disability Discrimination Act (DDA) 1995. For the first time, discrimination on the basis on disability became unlawful. The DDA gives rights to disabled people in employment (part 2 of the Act), provision of goods and services (part 3 of the Act) and, since 2001, education (part 4 of the Act).

The DDA Part 4 has two areas: pre-16 education and post-16 education. The Act states that post-16 education providers:

- must not treat learners with disabilities 'less favourably' for any reason related to their disability, and
- must make 'reasonable adjustments' to ensure learners with disabilities are not placed at a substantial disadvantage in relation to a learner who is not disabled.

These duties apply to all staff within the institution.

Who the Act covers

The Act protects learners, potential learners and applicants who fit the definition of disability given in the Act. The legal definition of disability in the Act is: 'a physical or mental impairment which has a substantial and long-term adverse effect on your ability to carry out normal day-to-day activities'. This is quite a broad definition and can include people with physical and sensory impairments, those with physical conditions such as epilepsy, cancer, HIV, multiple sclerosis, people with learning difficulties and those with mental health difficulties.

In 2005 new legislation was passed to amend the DDA. The changes mean that more people are covered by the Act. Originally mental health conditions were required to be 'clinically well recognised'; this is no longer necessary. Also cancer, HIV and multiple sclerosis are covered from the point of diagnosis not from when the condition begins to affect normal day-to-day activities. This is because of the stigma that can be attached to individuals who have these conditions.

The Act gives a list of 'responsible bodies'. These organizations are covered by the legislation and include, for example, higher and further education institutions, adult and community education, and sixth form colleges. From September 2007 general qualification awarding bodies have also been included.

TASK 11.3

Do you think these learners are protected by the Act?

1. Mohammed's right leg was amputated (up to the knee) after injury resulting from a land mine. He has a prosthetic limb and has, so far, not experienced difficulties getting about in his college.
2. Sara is 49 years old. She did not have the opportunity to go to school and has no literacy in her first language. Her spoken English is Entry 3 level but she is finding her ESOL class very difficult because of her limited literacy skills.
3. Abdi was in a motor cycle accident and broke his right arm and shoulder. His arm is in plaster and he is unlikely to be able to use it for three to four months.

COMMENT 11.3

Mohammed is the only one covered by the Act as his disability could have a substantial and long-term adverse effect on his ability to carry out normal day-to-day activities, including learning.

What are 'reasonable adjustments'?

Education providers must make 'reasonable adjustments' to alleviate disadvantage faced by a learner with a disability. A reasonable adjustment might involve changing admission or examination procedures. It may include changing course content, teaching arrangements or providing additional teaching. Offering information in alternative formats, for example Braille or providing additional support are also adjustments that might be appropriate.

The duty to make reasonable adjustments is a duty to disabled individuals generally not just to an individual. This means that providers must anticipate what sort of adjustments may be necessary for disabled individuals and make adjustments in advance.

TASK 11.4

What kind of adjustments could be made for these learners?

1   Abdi applies to the local adult education institution to enrol for an ESOL class. He has rheumatoid arthritis and misses his ESOL classes when the pain is particularly severe. Also walking is slow and painful. The adult education institute is based in a listed Victorian house. The ESOL classes are on the second floor and there is no lift.

2   Fahim has been hard of hearing since he was a child. He attends an Entry 2 ESOL class but is finding it difficult. He can hear well when working in a pair or when the teacher works directly with him but cannot hear the teacher well when she explains something to the whole group or when there are whole group discussions.

3   Amina has medication for anxiety and depression. In class she responds when questions are directed at her and occasionally takes part in whole-group discussion spontaneously. She finds it difficult to follow instructions directed at the whole class but is generally able to complete individual tasks well when clear about what is required. Amina prefers to work alone or with one other learner, and becomes anxious when asked to work in small groups or to take part in activities that make her the focus of attention (e.g. presentations). At times Amina finds it difficult to concentrate and tends to stare vacantly ahead, interacting very little with others.

COMMENT 11.4

What did you come up with? Here are some suggestions:

1   The class could be moved to a classroom on the ground floor.
2   A loop system could be employed to help bring Fahim into the discussions. A loop system is a device which helps deaf people who use a hearing aid to hear sounds more clearly because it reduces or cuts out background noise. For more information see *ESOL Access for All* (DfES 2006c: 23).
3   The teacher can give Amina individual instructions and check back discreetly that Amina is clear about what she has to do. She needs to be sensitive to Amina's 'absences' and not put pressure on her to interact when Amina does not feel able to engage. Opportunities for one-to-one support would be very beneficial to Amina.[4]

Taking reasonable steps

The DDA requires education providers to take reasonable steps to find out if a learner has disability-related needs. They need to be proactive in encouraging learners to disclose a disability. Examples of different ways institutions have attempted to do this include:

- Providing information about provision made for learners with disabilities and learning difficulties in different languages.
- Using interpreters.
- Simplifying questions on application and enrolment forms; providing opportunities at initial interview, in induction and throughout the course when learners can talk in private about needs they may have.

Generally, learners are more likely to disclose a disability when the atmosphere and culture within the institution is one which is welcoming and supportive to those who might have additional needs.

Once a learner discloses a disability or an additional need to one individual, the whole institution is deemed to know.

The Disability Equality Duty (DED)

December 2006 saw the establishment of a new duty to promote disability equality. This duty extends the existing requirement to anticipate and respond to the needs of disabled people. Education providers and other public sector bodies will be required to produce a disability equality scheme with an action plan to show how they are meeting the new duty.

Teachers and learners

Identification and formal assessment

A common question raised by ESOL teachers in relation to learning difficulties and disabilities is how to identify learning difficulties/disabilities which are not visible and which the learner may not have disclosed or may be unaware of. The short answer is that it is often difficult to formally assess whether a learner has disability-related needs. Some difficulties, dyslexia, for example, may not have been identified previously and so the learner will not realize they have a disability to disclose. The stigma attached to other disabilities, for example mental health difficulties, may make it harder for individuals to disclose the disability. Also, as has already been suggested, many bilingual learners may not understand the terminology or the concepts that currently underpin terms such as 'learning difficulty' in the UK. They may not have equivalent terms in their language and might not define themselves according to Western models of disability. Clearly, this is not what a number of institutions really want to hear. Many practitioners fear that without straightforward assessment tools educational institutions will be unable to put in place the support that a learner may need.

It is important to recognize that assessment of literacy and learning performance is a complex process, particularly for bilingual learners. For example, learners' skills may be weak because they did not have access to education or experienced a disrupted education or have limited literacy in their first language. Also, features of the learners' first language may influence the way they approach English and these might be misinterpreted, for example a learner used to writing a language which is phonetic may have weak visual memory, which is important for spelling in English. Further, those with very little spoken English may not be able to complete assessment tasks without the aid of interpreters, which might impact on the results. It is not easy to separate out these factors in the assessment process. Good practice in assessment requires time and a coordinated approach so that practitioners with different expertise (ESOL, dyslexia, learning difficulties) work together. In many institutions, this kind of collaborative practice is an aspiration rather than a reality.

Teachers' voices

Many ESOL teachers have worked very successfully over considerable periods of time with learners suffering from the effects of trauma and loss, either through forced exile or migration. Other practitioners have considerable expertise in working with learners with cognitive learning difficulties. Many of these learners have not been formally assessed or diagnosed as having a disability or a learning difficulty. Below are excerpts from interviews conducted with two ESOL teachers, recounting their experience.

Interview 1

Philip has taught in a community-based adult learning centre for a number of years. He is responsible for a relatively small ESOL/basic literacy group which meets twice a week. Many of his learners are asylum seekers.

Interviewer: What advice would you give a new ESOL teacher working with bilingual learners who might have mental health difficulties?

Philip: I'd say, just be a good teacher. People with mental health difficulties function pretty much OK a lot of the time. It's about group dynamics and the relationships you help learners build up. If the class feels safe, and someone isn't feeling well on a particular day, has a crisis, but the relationships between them as people are strong, then everyone will be able to accommodate what's going on. If someone's upset and leaves the class and you go out for a few minutes to see that they are alright, the rest of the group would accept and understand. That's my experience of how it works. Learners get to know each other pretty well, particularly when the groups are small. They know each other's stories and what's led up to things.

Interviewer: Does it help you with your planning to know if a learner is receiving treatment for a particular mental health difficulty?

Philip: Hmm … maybe, but … not sure it does necessarily. I don't think I'd sit down and consciously do something differently; it would just become part of the way I differentiate on the basis of knowing them as individuals. I hate to label people. Everyone has strengths and weaknesses, whether they are suffering from trauma or not. It's in part about being flexible, responding sensitively. Some days some learners don't concentrate too well or may want to be left alone to work, other times they need you to work with them. It goes back to what I said before, if people feel comfortable with you and with others, they'll ask if they need something. I guess what you need is confidence.

Interviewer: How can teachers become more confident, less fearful about working with learners with mental health difficulties?

Philip: I think getting to know the learners as people is really important. Tutorials pay big dividends, I know they were set up for ILPs and all that, but really they've created great opportunities for learners to talk to you, say how things are affecting them, what they need.

Interviewer: What about staff development?

Philip: Well yes, it probably can help … basic approaches about how to relate to learners come … from life experience and contact with people. It's about picking up signals and knowing how to respond. You can't upset people by listening to them.

Interviewer: What kind of support can the institution offer teachers and learners?

Philip: A lot, I think for learners with psychotic difficulties, for support from your line manager and the institution as a whole is incredibly important.

Interview 2

Joanna Williams works in a large FE college. She has considerable experience as an ESOL teacher and teacher-trainer. She has worked with learners with learning difficulties and co-wrote *Making it happen.*[5]

Interviewer: What advice would you give an ESOL teacher working with learners with learning difficulties in their class?

Jo: Well, the context is absolutely crucial, which it is in all ESOL classes. It possibly needs to be more concrete with learners with learning difficulties. It helps if contexts are very immediate for learners, for example situations in the college, shared experiences of living in London, homes and families – supported by visits in the local area, to the canteen, learners' own photographs from home or in the local area. It wouldn't be sensible to say 'imagine …' This might not be meaningful. The context needs to be personally relevant, the more relevant the better.
               Also … taking great care to make sure everyone is on board … you need to take care about pace, because learners may be focusing in different ways, maybe concentrating in different ways.
               The learners I worked with were very perceptive and very aware of atmosphere in the class. They would pick up atmosphere very quickly … So, you have to be really in there, being very focused, keeping people on board and helping people feel safe. Taking care of the learners in terms of making sure they're not struggling. Structure and focus is very important … giving a sense of feeling contained instead of lost.
               … giving positive feedback … you can't say 'That's good but …' you have to think very carefully about the use of language so that you really are identifying the good bit and then, in thinking about the area to work on, making it clear that it's not a problem … just the next step … so thinking a lot about the feedback is important.

Interviewer: Does it make a difference to know a learner has been formally assessed as having learning difficulties?

Jo: No … I wouldn't think it makes any difference because you're getting to know your learner … like you get to know any learner … you're getting to know what their experiences are, what their areas of interests are, what their strengths are.
               I think if someone was on medication it might help to know that in case the learner isn't able to concentrate for long.

In fact, I think one of the problems is seeing learners with learning difficulties as people who have a sort of problem that can be assessed and somehow that will ... I don't know what ... help you teach them? But it's just like anybody ... it's just having differences of approaches. And, in fact, I think it's really important to not stress the assessment thing because it stops people actually thinking this is an interesting person ... I wonder what their experience is ... I wonder what they need language for. It's like seeing people as a case rather than just the same as anybody else.

Interviewer: What support can the institution offer teachers?

Jo: I think that thing about positive feedback is incredibly important because learners have very often not had a lot of positive feedback to things that have happened in their lives and they've probably had a lot of negative feedback ... So it's very important that the tutor has the training to be able to identify skills. For example, in teaching reading and writing, if someone is a beginning writer it's important that the tutor can identify the skills that learners have so they're not actually thinking this person can't write. If you haven't had training in working with beginner readers and writers you can't identify what are skills ... you need the training so you can go back to thinking about what it feels like to be a beginning reader and writer, and then think how incredibly successful someone is to be able to hold a pen, form words, create their own text. So when you're feeding back on a learner's strengths you're not just saying 'oh good' to make someone feel better, you're actually identifying the skill that they've used.

Another thing is getting support with working with a support worker because very often the tutor is given no help with how to work together. The institution needs to give time for the support worker and tutor to look at the lesson plan and think about what they are each going to do in the lesson. And time to feedback on what worked in the lesson. Also training to see what the expectations are of each other's role so that there's not assumptions being made about roles that are unhelpful ... so that the support worker knows what her remit is and the ESOL tutor knows what their remit is ... and respect for each other's roles.

Finding out from learners what works for them

People with disabilities are as diverse as any other group in society, whether the disabilities are visible or not. Take learners who are blind or who have visual impairments:

Some learners will have been born blind or with visual impairments. A far larger number acquire visual impairment in later life. There are many myths around blindness. Many people assume that there is a distinct line between seeing clearly and seeing nothing at all. In fact, visual impairment covers a whole spectrum from people who are only slightly affected to the very small proportion who are totally blind and cannot distinguish light from dark. Also everyone experiences deteriorating vision with advancing age. ESOL learners may have lost their sight through trauma, as a result of war or through disease rather than gradually deteriorating over time. Sensitivity in exploring the reason and how learners are taught must reflect the root cause of the sight loss.

(DFES 2006c)

Many bilingual learners with disabilities overcome considerable barriers and not only learn English but go on to complete vocational and academic courses and have successful and fulfilling careers.[6] Below are two brief case studies of learners with visual impairments. They highlight just how individual people are, and the importance of discussing with all learners, but disabled learners in particular, what helps them with their learning.

Case study 1

Kabara is an articulate Somali man in his twenties, who as a child began to lose his sight and has now lost 70 per cent of his field of vision. He has very restricted tunnel vision. He cannot use Braille but can write in English though quite slowly in a large, sloping cursive hand. His education in Somalia was restricted by both the political upheavals in the country and his disability. He is, however, literate in Somali. He has been in the UK for five years and is making good progress in English. He is in an Entry 3 class at a large college in London. Kabara says that at first he really struggled with reading but many things have helped him and he now enjoys his classes. Good light is really important. The college have purchased a special desk light which he uses when reading. It does not help him if print is enlarged, rather the opposite as it just takes longer for him to access and get through the text. He says that when he first began attending classes it would have been helpful to have had a buddy to read aloud to him and help him steer his way around the building. He found getting around rather intimidating, with a lot of pushing and rushing, and this sapped his confidence. However, his teachers were extremely supportive and asked him what he thought would help him with his studies. He asked them to keep to a particular classroom layout so that he could move about without fear of crashing into things. He also asked for one-to-one help with reading, which he receives on a weekly basis as in-class learning support. Kabara says that his classmates have been great and include him in everything. He has been on an IT course at the college which was specifically set up for visually impaired learners. It is staffed by specialists who, after conducting specialist assessment, train the learners to use a range of voice-activated, voice-recognition and screen-reading software.[7] This has been a revelation for Kabara. He is now expert at using the software, and finds that being able to dictate texts and hear texts read out to him on screen helps him with revision and reinforcement of grammar and vocabulary. He has learnt to touch type and does so with considerable speed and accuracy. He enjoys surfing the Web and, thanks to one of his teachers, has joined the national blind five-a-side football league.

Case study 2

Jazria is a single Kurdish woman from Iraq and is in a mixed-level class at an adult learning centre. She was severely injured by a bomb, lost her left eye, her right hand and has very reduced vision in her right eye. She was a teacher in Iraq and is literate in English and Arabic. She has been attending classes for a number of years and despite ongoing health problems she has great determination and loves attending her twice-weekly ESOL class. Her sister comes to class with her and acts as her interpreter and note-taker. Larger print helps, she likes handouts in sans serif font (e.g. Arial) and her optimum font size is 22 point. She finds it easiest when key information is kept to the right hand side of the page, so she asks her teacher to format text this way. She finds diagrams and tables very difficult to decipher and interpret. She always needs more time for everything but enjoys multisensory activities, playing tactile games and doing matching activities. Jazria asked her teacher to put everything they do in class on tape, and she finds this really helps her. Jazria likes talking things through and working with other people. She found discussions very difficult at first, but now knows to raise her hand or clap when she wants to contribute. Her class mates also now invite her to give her point of view and she really appreciates how her teacher has helped her to integrate. Jazria went on a class outing to the Houses of Parliament and kept a bilingual audio diary of the visit. She is currently learning to use an adapted computer and has started to use email.

Classroom implications

Integrating learners with visual impairments

TASK 11.5

Read through the Entry 3 activities for the class Kabara attends. Consider what you might need to do to ensure Kabara is fully integrated into the activities. Make notes and then compare your thoughts with the ideas in the task answers.

Entry 3 activities around expressing your point of view on diet and healthy living and linked critical reading task

1   Learners work as a whole group to do a 'find someone who' activity with questionnaire, e.g.:

Find someone who:
- *likes to swim and goes to the pool at least once a week*
- *plays football twice a week or more*

- *eats chips most days*
- *thinks s/he has a good diet*

2 Teacher splits class into small groups and asks them to decide what constitutes a healthy diet and way of life. Each group is asked to agree three key points. Teacher facilitates and monitors.

3 Learners are asked to reassemble into new groups and exchange and share the three key points from their original group. Teacher monitors and makes notes on discussions.

4 Teacher brings the whole group back together, clarifies any new lexis that has emerged, e.g. *fast food, obesity,* summarizes small group discussions and key points. Asks for recommendations for healthy living from each group and notes them down, asks group to copy these down for future lesson.

5 In pairs, learners read a short article on children's diet in the UK written by a McDonald's spokesman, defending fast food.

6 Teacher checks gist and comprehension of key terms in text with whole group.

7 Teacher sets comprehension questions for pairs: what is the author's point of view? What is his purpose? Why is it written in this way?

8 Pairs exchange views and answers with other pairs. Teacher monitors.

9 Whole group feedback and wider discussion on how they might respond to the article.

10 Homework task: doing an exercise to ensure they understand the topic-specific lexis, e.g. matching lexis to definitions or multiple choice on possible definitions.

COMMENT 11.5

1 Pair Kabara for the 'find someone who' activity (1) with a buddy who will do the activity with him and can read the statements aloud out to him before starting out. Ensure that it is safe for Kabara to move around (no bags on the floor, etc.) and that you have prepared a clear space in the room for this mingling task. Alternatively, if the classroom is small, ensure there is a clear path around the room.

2 For (2), the teacher assigns Kabara a physical space in the classroom, at the front, for the small group work. The teacher will need to monitor this activity closely to ensure that Kabara is offered turns in the discussion and that he is involved in the free discussion later on.

3 For (3), Kabara does not move from his physical space, others come to him.

4 The teacher records the summary of the discussion for (4), recommendations and new lexis on a CD or tape for Kabara to use as out of class reinforcement. Kabara may want additional time to use the voice-recognition programme he is familiar with to dictate new lexis to his PC or laptop.

> 5   The text and questions are put on CD or audio tape so that Kabara can participate in the critical reading activity (5). He can listen individually while the others are reading in pairs, or he can be listening as part of a small group who all listen to the tape and read simultaneously.
> 6   Teacher makes sure that Kabara's buddy reads the comprehension questions (7) aloud to him.
> 7   Teacher asks Kabara's buddy to work on the homework task (10) with him. Ensures they have agreed a time and place to do this.

Integrating learners with learning difficulties

There is no such thing as a typical disabled learner, least of all a typical learner with learning difficulties; each individual will have their own specific strengths and areas of difficulty. However, focusing on one particular learner will help us identify some of the key issues when working with learners with learning difficulties in general.

We can begin by considering this pen portrait of Imresh, a learner in an ESOL Entry 1 class:

Background

Imresh is a Punjabi speaker who came to England from north India as an adult. She is now in her mid-50s and lives with her husband and their three children. She did not have a good experience of school; her teacher complained that 'she had something wrong with her head'. Imresh soon stopped attending and stayed home to help her mother with household duties. Imresh has lived in the UK for many years but did not join an ESOL class before because of family commitments and lack of confidence. She now attends a support group organized by Social Services. The social worker encouraged her to enrol on an ESOL class at the local college; she attends an Entry 1 class twice a week.

Strengths and areas for development

Imresh can understand a lot of English if the context is clear and familiar. She can communicate in English using familiar key words and actions. She is making slow but steady progress in speaking and understanding. She has found developing reading and writing more difficult. She can recognize some key, personal whole words and can write her name independently. She copies slowly but accurately.

Aspirations and interests

Imresh enjoys the ESOL class and values the opportunity to interact with other learners. At home she is busy with running the home and looking after her family. She enjoys cooking and watching Indian films.

Setting objectives

One of the key elements in developing an inclusive approach to teaching involves setting realistic goals, which will enable Imresh to develop and gain a sense of achievement. This is likely to mean setting different learning outcomes for different learners. You might like to refer to *Making it Happen*,[8] which gives advice on setting differentiated outcomes, for example:

> Asking for food in the canteen:
>
> ...
>
> - some learners say the name of one food they would like to ask for, with some accuracy/clarity;
>
> - some learners ask for foods using the phrase 'Can I have some rice and chicken ... Thank you'.

(DfES 2006b)

TASK 11.6

Look at the group outcomes the ESOL teacher has planned, using the context of *'where we live'*.

LEARNING OUTCOME(S) OF THE SESSION: (*What you expect* learners *to be able to do during and after the session*)

1 Listen to a dialogue on tape and obtain specific information about what there is in the area.
2 Talk about their area and make use of: What's it like? Is there a ...? There's a ...
3 Read and understand a short text about the area where the ESOL class is based and obtain specific information:
     - What it has or doesn't have (e.g. post office, park, etc.).
     - What it's like (e.g. noisy or quiet).
4 Write a short text to describe their area using a model.

Consider how you could differentiate these outcomes so that there is an outcome that all learners will be able to achieve (including Imresh) as well as the more demanding outcome that some learners will reach.

COMMENT 11.6

The following are possible learning outcomes for all learners in the group:

1   Listen to a dialogue on tape for key vocabulary, e.g. post office, laundrette, park.
2   Answer questions about their area with yes and no.
3   Read a short text about the area where the ESOL class takes place and identify familiar key words, e.g. name of the area, post office, laundrette, etc.
4   Write a sentence 'I live in ...' with support (provide words for learner to copy) and begin to learn to spell the name of their area.

Developing activities and staging lessons

As highlighted in Interview 2, many of the features of good practice in ESOL teaching (for example, ensuring activities are embedded in contexts which are meaningful to learners) are especially important when working with learners with learning difficulties. Both *Making it Happen* (DfES 2006b) and ESOL *Access for All* (DfES 2006c)[9] provide us with guidance on some of the ways that learning difficulties may impact on learning and on strategies which can be used to enhance learning:

> When planning activities and staging lessons it is important to note that learners with learning difficulties may have difficulties with short term memory and with consolidating and retaining information. Strategies that can support learners with these difficulties include the use of multi sensory approaches, 'over-learning' (continuing to practise even after a learner seems to have learnt something) and systematic reviews. In addition, learners often have difficulty understanding abstract concepts and will, therefore, learn better by experience and in contexts that are interesting and relevant to them. They may also have difficulty with concentration and, again, using contexts of interest will help with this as will breaking tasks into small steps.
>
> (DfES 2006c)

TASK 11.7

1   Look at the activities for Imresh's class. These are some of the activities which focus on the speaking and listening outcomes (see Task 11.6 above).
2   Consider what you might need to do to ensure Imresh is fully integrated into the activities. Compare your thoughts with the ideas in the task answers.

Entry 1 speaking and listening activities. Context – where we live.

Vocabulary review

1 Teacher puts up visuals (park, post office, launderette, etc.) around the room.
2 Learners go around the room and say what the places are. Teacher checks and reviews pronunciation as necessary.

Listening

1 Teacher prepares learners for the listening text by explaining 'I've moved to ... and I'm talking to my friend about where I live.' Teacher plays tape twice.
2 Learners listen to the tape and tick the pictures of the places that are mentioned.

Speaking practice 1 'What's it like?' – question and response

1 Teacher uses visuals to elicit clean, dirty, noisy, quiet, etc. Drills adjectives.
2 Teacher presents the 'What's it like?' question and responses.
3 Learners repeat question and response – whole group, individuals and open pairs.
4 Learners work in pairs. They use visuals and take turns to ask, 'What's it like? and respond.

Talking about their area in pairs and small groups

1 Teacher organizes learners into small groups/pairs to talk about where they live. Monitors and supports.

COMMENT 11.7

Activities	Integrating Imresh
Vocabulary review	Use different activities to present, practice and review the language before listening and speaking. Other possibilities might be:
1 Teacher puts up visuals (park, post office, launderette, etc.) around the room.	
2 Learners go around the room and say what the places are. Teacher checks and reviews pronunciation as necessary.	• Arrange photos around the room. Ask learners to find particular places. • Ask learners to point to photos and name particular places. • Ask learners to find a partner with a photo of same type of places, e.g. pairs of photos of different places supermarkets, laundrettes.

Listening

1 Teacher prepares learners for the listening text by explaining 'I've moved to ... and I'm talking to my friend about where I live.' Teacher plays tape twice.

2 Learners listen to the tape and tick the pictures of the places that are mentioned.

- Use visuals to set the context of the listening. A photograph of the teacher talking to a friend (possibly another teacher that the learners will have come into contact with) will make clear who will be talking.
- A photograph of the area where the teacher lives (possibly an area that the learners know) can help learners predict the content.
- Imresh may need to demonstrate her understanding of the listening in a different way. Instead of completing a worksheet it might help to ask her to hold up the picture or point to the picture of the place she hears mentioned in the tape.
- Have visual prompts to support instructions.

Speaking practice 1 'What's it like?' – question and response

1 Teacher uses visuals to elicit clean, dirty, noisy, quiet, etc. Drills adjectives.

2 Teacher presents 'What's it like?' question and responses.

3 Learners repeat question and response – whole group, individuals and open pairs.

4 Learners work in pairs. They use visuals and take turns to ask 'What's it like?' and respond.

- Drilling might be stressful. Give Imresh time to respond. Consider the amount of accuracy she can achieve.

Talking about their area in pairs and small groups

1 Teacher organizes learners into small groups/pairs to talk about where they live. Monitors and supports.

- Put more support/structure in pair- and small-group speaking activities.
- In the conversation about learners' own areas, use set of photographs (market, etc.) to help structure the interaction, i.e. photographs act as prompts for questions.

Resources and technology

Technological advances have made an enormous difference to access to learning for learners with learning difficulties and disabilities. As Kabara's case study demonstrates, this is particularly true for learners who have physical or sensory impairments, though it has also had a considerable impact for those who are dyslexic or have learning difficulties.

A number of factors in the use of technology stand out:

- The appropriate match of technology and associated study strategies to the needs of the learner – effective assessment.
- The teacher's confidence in the use of a range of resources and technologies.
- Institutional support, through staff development and the employment of specialist technical staff who can maintain equipment, support effective assessment, train learners and staff in how to use technology effectively and troubleshoot as necessary.

What technology?

There is a wide range of technological resources and facilities now available to support learning.[10] Some of the *high-tech* resources include:

- Computers.
- Information learning technologies (ILT) – for example, electronic whiteboards, etc.
- Standard facilities on software programs – for example using the 'zoom' facility to magnify the onscreen text (usually found within the 'View' menu of MS Office programs).
- Assistive and enabling technologies – for example, text-to-speech software (screen readers), adaptive keyboards.
- Multimedia – for example, digital or video cameras.

Technology can be a very powerful and empowering tool. Many learners are highly motivated by its use, not least younger ones, and new and extraordinary resources are being developed all the time. Take the example of the Talking Tactile Tablet (www.talktab.org) designed for learners who are blind, it can benefit all learners. It combines a visual and tactile diagram with interactive audio experiences.

However, it should also be remembered that,

> technology is not always the answer for all learners. Some learners may experience difficulties in using technology. For example, older learners may never have used a computer before, and some may find it intimidating or difficult to remember how to use icons or sequence procedures to open programs. Learners who experience epilepsy may need regular breaks from a

computer screen. It is essential to be sensitive to situations like these when learners may experience difficulties in the use of technology.

(DfES 2006c)

It is therefore important to consider *low-tech* support and not to underestimate the usefulness of simple adaptations and materials:

- Providing a hand-held magnifier.
- Placing cardboard at the sides of a screen to alleviate glare.
- Triangular pens or pens with rubber bands around them to form a gripholder for dyslexic or dyspraxic learners with poor fine motor control.
- Printing handouts on coloured paper (ask learners for their preferred colour), using a sans serif font.
- Raising or lowering the height of chairs or of a computer.

TASK 11.8

Conduct a survey in your institution to find out:

- What technology learners find motivating and are familiar with.
- What high- and low-tech resources are available in your institution.
- What technology colleagues employ and would like further support in using.

Implications for institutions

Developing an inclusive approach impacts on the full range of services and facilities within an educational institution. Institutions are attempting to meet the challenges of inclusive learning in many different ways. Figure 11.1 opposite gives some examples of the strategies and policies that institutions have found to be particularly effective. You might like to consider your own institution in relation to these areas of provision and identify what is already in place as well as areas for further improvement.

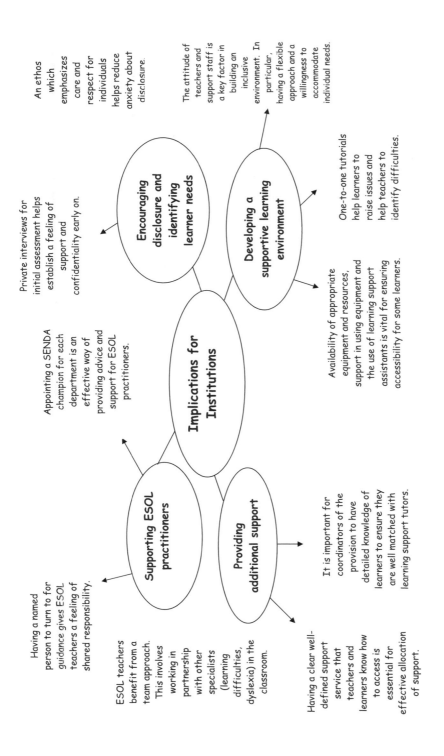

Figure 11.1 Some effective strategies and policies for inclusive learning

Notes

1 *Dyslexia and the Bilingual Learner*, by Sunderland et al. (1997), was a ground breaking publication examining the issues of dyslexia in relation to adult bilingual learners and giving practical advice about assessment and methodology.

2 See 'Overviews' in the Annotated Bibliography.

3 For more information around the subject of dyslexia and bilingual learners, see DfES 2006c: 45–51and case study pages 64–6.

4 For further information on working with learners with mental health difficulties, see DfES 2006c: 40–45 and the list of additional guidance boxes in part 2: 97–8, the bibliography and useful organizations and websites, (503–46).

5 DfES (2006b).

6 See 'I done it, innit!' Ali Amasyali's remarkable story, written by Alison Meek (2004) in *Language Issues* (2), Autumn/Winter.

7 For further information on the kind of software that is available and working with learners with visual impairments, see DfES 2006c: 15–18, 25–9.

8 DfES 2006b.

9 *ESOL Access for All* part 1 and 2 (DfES 2006c).

10 For a detailed discussion of technological resources for use with disabled bilingual learners and names of suppliers, see DfES 2006c.

12 ESOL issues for teachers in the lifelong learning sector[1]

Sue Colquhoun and Jo-Ann Delaney

Introduction

This chapter is aimed at those teachers in the sector who are untrained in teaching ESOL and who may have a number of second-language speakers in their classes learning other, often vocational, subjects to prepare them for the world of work in the UK. Up to one million people in England do not speak English as their first language and many of these may be the very learners whom you are likely to encounter in the learning and skills sector.

As illustrated earlier, there are many reasons for speakers of other languages to settle in the United Kingdom and their motivation for attending classes varies widely, but they are likely to bring a wide range of skills, abilities and experience from varying cultures and backgrounds as well as diverse languages. They will also include individuals highly qualified within their countries of origin as well as others who might have literacy or language needs in their first language. In addition to the demands presented by a particular subject specialism and/or vocational area, most ESOL learners will also face challenges of acquiring English language skills and accessing the dominant culture of the society in which they are now living.

Britain's multicultural heritage provides evidence of descendants from central and eastern Europe in the shape of the Romans, Normans and their Breton and Flemish allies as well as the first Africans who came as soldiers of the Roman army. Later, others such as the French Huguenots and Russian Jews fled religious pogroms to settle in this country and as a result of the two World Wars, refugees from Belgium, Spanish Basques, more Jewish settlers, Poles and Hungarians sought sanctuary here. At different times in the twentieth century refugees from all over the world – Uganda, Chile, Vietnam, Bosnia, Somalia, Eritrea, Afghanistan, Iraq, Zimbabwe and many other countries – have also made their home in the UK. In a survey conducted by the Refugee Council (1997), it was found that the majority of refugees were highly qualified, successful in their home countries, often coming from professional back-grounds with skills exceeding the levels of the general British population.

For centuries, then, people from all over the world have come to settle in the United Kingdom for a variety of reasons: some who seek a better life and more challenging opportunities; and others who fear persecution and are driven to escape danger and civil war in their own countries. The history of immigration provides a rich source of diversity and today's ESOL learners are no exception. Throughout Britain there are communities of people whose first languages range from Amaric, Bengali, Chinese, Farsi, Somali and Turkish to Urdu and many others. In more recent times, the expansion of the European Union has meant that there are groups of migrant workers coming to the UK to look for better employment opportunities. Learners in these groups can be quite knowledgeable about language, but lack the skills to speak and communicate with fluency. Those with very limited English language skills are likely to be placed within dedicated English language classes in the learning and skills sector, while others with more advanced English language skills may well be engaged in studying a variety of subjects or vocational areas alongside native speakers of English.

TASK 12.1

List all the ESOL learners in your class, noting their countries of origin, the languages they speak and their reason for coming to the UK.

Defining the terms

Some of your ESOL learners may be newly arrived asylum seekers or refugees with more secure rights, while others may be long-settled and well-established residents. Some may have come to join their spouse or other family members, others will have work permits and there may even be some second generation immigrants and younger people. The different terms used are sometimes very confusing and emotively charged, especially in debates in the media, so that within the context of inclusive education in the learning skills sector, it might be more helpful to disregard the definitions surrounding their residential status and to focus on their personal needs as speakers of other languages within your classroom.

Similar confusion sometimes reigns in the terms used to describe English language teaching, such as:

- ESL – English as a second language.
- EAL – English as an additional language.
- ESP – English for special/specific purposes.
- EAP – English for academic purposes.

However, in keeping with the currently accepted term favoured in post-compulsory education in the UK in the learning and skills sector, 'English for speakers of other languages', abbreviated to ESOL, is used throughout this chapter.

Another distinction that can cause confusion is that between ESOL and EFL – English as a foreign language. While both involve the teaching of English language, ESOL learners generally intend to take up permanent residence in an Anglophone country whereas EFL learners have chosen to learn English for pleasure, work or education, for example, au pairs living and working abroad for a year before returning to their own countries or business people who recognize English as an international language and feel they need it to succeed professionally.

Traditionally EFL both within the UK and abroad has been an important and lucrative market, largely in the private sector, focusing on the overseas visitor who is likely to be formally educated in their country, often but not necessarily of European origin. Groups of EFL learners will normally be expected to progress at roughly the same pace, and their reading and writing skills will be at a similar level to their speaking and listening skills. ESOL is based in the UK, predominantly within the state sectors though private training providers are becoming increasingly involved. There are many similarities between teaching EFL and ESOL. For both it is necessary to focus on the language systems that underpin our ability to communicate (grammar, vocabulary, discourse). English language teachers will develop their learners' communication skills in speaking, reading and writing, though this may be done in different contexts with EFL and ESOL learners. Chapter 9 outlines the impact of these different contexts in the selection of resources.

Theories of bilingualism and second-language acquisition

Many ESOL learners may be multilingual but described as bilingual; even though the term 'bilingual' strictly refers to fluency in only two languages, it can be used to indicate an ability to speak more than two languages. It is hoped that some recognition and understanding of the implications of some theories of second-language acquisition may be helpful in pointing the way for devising strategies to support ESOL learners and further suggestions for facilitating this will be made at the end of the chapter.

Early theories of second-language acquisition tended to make comparisons with learning a first language or mother tongue and to suggest that there were only certain levels of learning and knowing any two languages simultaneously; for example, that there was only a certain amount of space in the brain to cope with the acquisition of one language at a time! These theories have sometimes been presented diagramatically as a set of scales, with a second language increasing at the expense of the first language or in a sketch of two language balloons, showing the monolingual with one well-filled balloon in his or her head, while the bilingual has two half-filled balloons (Baker 2001).

Subconsciously, these ideas have been absorbed and repeated by many people and are often part of a 'common sense' understanding of what it means to be bilingual, namely two languages operating separately in a restricted space, although research has now shown it is wrong to make these assumptions (Baker 2001). They have sometimes encouraged a notion of first language interference that has negative implications for acquiring additional languages. In challenging this notion, Jyoti Nayar (2004) draws on memories of her own experience and describes how children learn a first language easily and naturally so that 'by the age of three we children used three languages separately and without mixing'.

There are a good number of differing theories of second language acquisition. Research has thrown up many issues to consider and for ESOL teachers there have been various 'methodologies' that are suggested by different theories. The general consensus is that we do not know exactly how languages are learned, but we can certainly identify factors that will impact on language learning. It is these factors that will be useful for any teacher with second-language learners in their classroom.

One view of second-language acquisition investigates theories of first-language acquisition and the sequence or patterns of how this development takes place and concludes that, 'the further the child moves towards a balanced bilingualism, the greater the likelihood of cognitive advantages' (Baker 2001). In other words, at the first level of learning when (both) languages are inadequately developed, there may be negative cognitive effects, but as language proficiency advances in at least one of the languages, the cognitive effects will be balanced until greater competence is achieved in two or more languages so that there are positive advantages for the cognitive development of bi/multilinguals over monolinguals. The implications of this 'thresholds theory' are relevant to teachers and they have been explored by Cummins (Baker 2001) in terms of two distinct levels of language acquisition, namely, basic interpersonal communicative skills (*BICS*) and cognitive/academic language proficiency (*CALP*).

BICS refers to everyday language of survival which is 'context embedded'. With this ESOL learners may function at a basic level of communication, drawing upon face-to-face cues, verbal and non-verbal support in everyday situations. In contrast, CALP, is 'context reduced' and specific to academic situations which require individuals to apply higher thinking skills, such as analysis, synthesis and evaluation (Baker 2001). Very often in the learning and skills sector those ESOL learners who have transferred from dedicated ESOL classes to mainstream vocational courses might well have achieved BICS, but not yet CALP, so that they are likely to appear ready to be taught in the second or other language, but they may find it much more challenging to understand the content of the curriculum and/or to engage in higher order cognitive processes of the classroom, such as synthesis, discussion, analysis and evaluation.

In recognizing this distinction between BICS and CALP, teachers are able to acknowledge that ESOL learners' linguistic knowledge and understanding may be highly developed, even though they are not in a position at a particular point in time to produce language which is beyond the level of BICS. If they are to achieve CALP, it is essential that they are exposed to new language structures and that teachers and others in the class model and provide opportunities for them to put these language skills into practice. This theory also underpins the importance of considering how assessment is carried out with learners. Second-language speakers may need more time and guidance in formulating answers as they will have the subject knowledge but not necessarily be able to express this in analytical language.

There are other theories to bear in mind that can be of relevance when teaching second-language speakers. Krashen has proposed that one of the most powerful factors in learning a second language is the lowering of the *affective filter* (or anxiety barrier) so that we are relaxed and acquiring new language more easily (Krashen

1982). For some ESOL learners this anxiety can be a result of personal circumstances and their situation in a new society. In the classroom it is important to emphasize strategies that encourage learners to contribute in a safe environment. This can be particularly relevant when teachers are setting up group or class discussions. Often the embarrassment of speaking in front of a large group will impede the learners' ability to gather the language necessary to express themselves. One solution is to allow a generous amount of time for preparation. It is also useful to actively monitor any negative feedback from other learners about accent or ungrammatical expressions.

An important area of recent research is based on a language project run by Prahbu in Bangalore. In this project, learners' language skills were significantly improved by focusing on tasks which were not related to language (Brumfit 1984). This has led to a methodology known as 'task-based learning'. In mainstream subjects where the focus is not language, learners are in fact being given an ideal opportunity to develop their language skills. However, one important aspect of task-based learning is that the task activity is followed by some focus on language. For this reason a mainstream class where there is some support from an ESOL specialist offers the ideal opportunity to pursue task-based learning. If teachers are working in an environment where they have access to ESOL teaching resources, a good way to use this is as a follow up to a subject-specific task carried out in the non-ESOL lesson.

TASK 12.2

Can you think of any different strategies which you could use in your teaching to encourage the development CALP in your class?

COMMENT 12.2

You may have suggested some of the following:

- Setting a rich and relevant context.
- Using non-verbal cues to aid communication.
- Use of visual aids such as pictures, realia and videos to support understanding.
- Classroom or workshop demonstrations of key techniques as well as or instead of oral descriptions.

Any, or all, of these strategies might play a part in aiding the transition from BICS to CALP for your ESOL learners, and might actually support the learning of all your learners.

Language skills and spiky profiles

Teachers of ESOL classify the acquisition of knowledge of English language in terms of four skills, namely, speaking, listening, reading and writing. It is common for learners to be slightly more advanced in the 'receptive' skills of listening and reading than in the 'productive' skills of writing and speaking. However, it is not uncommon for ESOL learners to demonstrate varying levels of achievement in each of these skills simultaneously – for example, an individual ESOL learner may be highly competent in reading and writing with less developed skills in speaking and listening, or alternatively, they may be confident and articulate in speaking and listening, but lack skills in reading and writing. These uneven language skills are sometimes referred to as 'spiky profiles' and indicate those particular skills that would need urgent attention and support if individuals are to progress and achieve in their subject specialist areas.

Spiky profiles may be attributed to the role of the first language in the acquisition of an additional language or to other factors related to self-esteem, confidence, previous experience and/or formal education. In gaining these skills, ESOL learners may demonstrate fluency over accuracy or vice versa. Very often the learner's previous education and experience of language learning will determine whether fluency or accuracy is more developed. Personal factors such as lack of confidence or a desire to produce only perfect language can lead to an overemphasis on accuracy, whereas a strong preference for engaging in social communication can lead to the development of fluency at the expense of accuracy. Each individual should be encouraged to develop both accuracy and fluency. However the specific demands of the subject specialism are likely to determine the priorities given to error correction in this respect. For example, for a clinician or pharmacist being able to distinguish the difference in speech between 'fifty' and 'fifteen' might have life-threatening repercussions, while for a mechanic it might cause minor inconvenience. Similarly, having competent writing skills may be more important in some occupations, such as journalism rather than others, such as bus driving. Decisions about what to correct in terms of accuracy and fluency will depend on the requirements of the subject specialism and intended vocational/professional directions. Nevertheless, it is important to see the ESOL learner as more than just the subject they are learning or the vocational/professional pathway they have chosen. The bus driver will also be a parent and may need highly developed writing skills to communicate with their child's school. It is usual to consider the learner, not to just consider their language goals for their working life, but to also look in a more holistic way at developing their language skills for full participation in society.

Valuing multilingualism, belonging and identity

Whatever seems most relevant to your situation, it is important for teachers to value multilingualism as an asset to learning and cognitive development, and to recognize the complexity of the process involved in acquiring an additional language with its implications for motivation, self-esteem and identity as well as for personal development and growth in confidence. Language is inextricably linked with personal history and individual identity, and there are connections between citizenship, identity and belonging. Identity is about who we are as individuals, our distinctiveness, our very selves; about how securely we face the world and how confidently we manage and express ourselves through language, recognizing a sense of belonging to a particular group of people joined together by any number of factors, such as geography, race, ethnicity, gender, religion or language. For ESOL learners it may be difficult to feel a sense of belonging within the classroom and it would be the ultimate achievement of the inclusion agenda to secure that sense of belonging for each learner within the classroom. This may present particular challenges for teachers of ESOL learners who need to take into account unfamiliar aspects of their cultural identity, languages, previous education and experiences.

Within this context it is perhaps worth noting the mismatch in power relations between any teacher and his/her learners and the way in which this may be accentuated by the ability of those who control the classroom discourse through language, simultaneously acting as 'gatekeepers' to the social goods and services of the dominant community (Mitchell and Myles 1998). All learners are subject to this, but ESOL learners may be even more susceptible, so that to establish an inclusive environment based on social justice and equality within the classroom will present challenges.

Furthermore, implicit assumptions about bilingualism referred to earlier may need to be recognized and addressed. These may be expressed in a number of ways, such as, making negative judgements about an ESOL learner's intellectual ability based upon his/her inability to express him/herself in English. This might lead to low expectations and/or even as misinterpretation as signalling a deeper-seated learning difficulty; using simplified, pidgin English and/or speaking very loudly in a patronizing fashion; making the assumption that bilingual learners need to deny their own origins and culture and to become monolingual in order to succeed (Smyth 2003). At best, while these responses may be described as well-intentioned, they illustrate a deficit view of bilingualism which is negatively defined by its failure to conform to a white, middle-class, monolinguistic 'norm' of the dominant culture.

Beyond these wider issues of social context, it is important to find out what you can about your individual ESOL learner, and although a list of practical suggestions follows, it should be stressed that there are no simple, 'quick fixes' or shortcuts to getting to know your individual learners and their needs, and encouraging in them a sense of belonging and identity. For those feeling inexperienced, untrained or unsupported in working with ESOL learners, it may be helpful to recommend some starting points, bearing in mind that each learner is unique and what works for one, may not for another. While it is inevitably a time-consuming process of ongoing discovery and learning that doesn't always have a final destination, there are some basic guidelines for supporting ESOL learners, many of which would constitute good practice for supporting *all* learners.

Strategies and approaches to support ESOL learners and foster inclusion

Beyond the wider issues of social context mentioned above, it is important to find out what you can about your individual ESOL learner. Information, such as the name by which he or she prefers to be called and how that is pronounced, first language and other languages and competence in each might be a good starting point. In addition, information about previous formal education (if there was any), length of time in the UK, details of family, friends or relatives, future intentions and aspirations might provide insights into the kind of support that would be appropriate. Some of this information may be readily accessible, but the ESOL learner may be reluctant to disclose other aspects and his or her reasons should be respected and treated with sensitivity. Sensitivity and tact are of utmost importance in eliciting personal details from your ESOL learners and gaining their confidence. It may be helpful in establishing a positive relationship to learn how to say 'hello' or 'thank you' in their language and/or to display some of this language in the classroom, personally valuing their identity and cultural origins.

Another way of valuing ESOL learners is to draw on their knowledge and experience of other languages and cultures, and to create opportunities for them to share and demonstrate this within the context of the subject specialism. This would enhance the multicultural and multilinguistic nature of the class without falling into the trap of tokenism. The way in which small-group activities are set up should enable ESOL learners to demonstrate what they know and can do, rather than exposing their weaknesses in English language. For example, the ESOL learner may be practically adept but not confident in reporting back or writing up on flipchart paper what has been observed, so these tasks could be shared out, encouraging collaboration among group members.

TASK 12.3

In response to Sir Claus Moser's (1999) landmark report, *A Fresh Start*, in which it was claimed that up to seven million adults in England could not read or write at the level expected of an 12-year-old, the government launched its Skills for Life initiative in 2001, setting out a national strategy for improving the standards of adult language, literacy and numeracy skills. This involved setting ambitious targets, linked to funding and the development of the adult core curricula in ESOL, Literacy and Numeracy. The introduction of the adult ESOL core curriculum in 2002 has clearly laid out levels of achievement, starting at Entry 1, 2, 3 to Level 1 and 2 which correspond to the national curriculum levels for curriculum levels for schools. These indicate what ESOL learners should be able to demonstrate in the different skills of speaking, listening, reading and writing at each level and they may provide helpful guidance for teachers about what to expect from their learners and also how to support their needs on different programmes as well as applying appropriate criteria when interviewing and selecting individuals for particular courses.

> Refer to the ESOL core curriculum and identify the language functions that all your learners should be able to demonstrate at the beginning of your course.

Embedding ESOL

Although teachers may be primarily concerned with their own subject specialism, it is possible to address language issues within the subject content they are delivering. When this is done formally it is described as 'embedded' learning. In an embedded course the subject specialist and the ESOL teacher work together when planning the lessons, and the language that comes up in the main subject is addressed by the ESOL teacher. For example, on a catering course where the content was related to food hygiene, the ESOL teacher might focus on structures around cause and consequence:

- **If** you store X at X degrees, **it can** be kept until …
- X must be put in an air tight container **so that** it doesn't …

Collaboration between the teachers is vital to ensure that the ESOL learners are well supported.

Furthermore, in planning curriculum activities, it is useful to analyse the language needed in terms of functions, structures and specialist vocabulary so that potential problems may be pre-empted before they occur. The way in which this might be done is illustrated in Table 12.1 below:

Table 12.1 Language analysis of functions, structure and vocabulary in different subject areas

Curriculum activity or Subject specialism	Function/s	Structure/examples of language	Specialist vocabulary
Scientific experiment	Observing, identifying, comparing, hypothesizing, predicting, reporting.	Passive structures e.g. water is placed in a beaker. Conditionals e.g. if the heat is reduced, then the water stops boiling, etc.	Beaker, bunsen burner, pipette, etc.
Leisure/tourism	Advertising, persuasive language.	Language of brochures and use of adjectives (descriptive words) e.g. glorious, sun-drenched beaches; quaint, cobbled streets, etc.	Bed & breakfast; double room; twin room; self-catering, etc.

Curriculum activity or Subject specialism	Function/s	Structure/examples of language	Specialist vocabulary
Hairdressing	Customer care	Language of politeness & questions, e.g. 'Would you like ...?' 'Did you mean/want ...?'	Hair gel, conditioner, shorter? Curlier? Straighter? Longer?
Child care	Story-telling	Narrative discourse, e.g. Once upon a time; They all lived happily ever after.	Narrator, personal history, empathy and identification, emotional development, etc.
Plumbing	Fitting a washer	Imperative (giving an order), e.g. adjust the spanner; twist clockwise; insert washer, etc.	Spanner, washer, wrench, etc.

TASK 12.4

Think of different curriculum activities in your own subject specialist area and then complete the table below for each one:

Curriculum activity or Subject specialism	Function/s	Structure/examples of language	Specialist vocabulary

In those institutions where ESOL specialists and resources are available, it is helpful to consult language specialists and to enlist their assistance in analysing the language of your subject specialist area in more detail to raise awareness of how this can be presented and practised and to consider how it is embedded (and often taken for granted) within the subject specialism. This is usually called a language audit. Language audits might include a detailed analysis of syllabus used, assignments set, handouts, materials, course book/s, exam papers and assessment tasks as well as the language used in the vocational context and requirements for conversing with customers and so on. A helpful starting point might be to consider samples of successful learner writing or tape recordings of oral work and use these as benchmarks for identifying and illustrating appropriate standards and levels of the language required for the particular subject specialist area.

Recent research and case studies on embedded language conducted by the National Research and Development Centre (Casey et al. 2006) show that when there is collaboration between vocational teachers and basic-skills specialists, learners find this motivating, retention is improved, achievement is enhanced and quality is improved for all learners. There is not one prescribed way of doing this, but a variety of modes of delivery in which vocational teachers can gain insights into language and literacy needs while language specialists equally gain knowledge of the vocational area. In order to secure embedded language learning into your subject teaching, you need to work backwards from the language requirements of the course. Furthermore, where individual ESOL learners are supported by language-support workers, it would also be helpful to liaise closely with them so that their work with these learners either within or outside the classroom relates directly to the requirements and needs of your own subject specialist area.

Another approach to enhancing learning is the use of an ESOL learner's own language, particularly if it is shared with another member of the class, when it might be applied in certain situations and prove an asset in securing the learning of a difficult concept as well as the English language. Many teachers who don't share the ESOL learners' first language may feel a little uncomfortable and insecure in not being able to control a dialogue in which they are unable to participate, but it might be illuminating if they see it as putting themselves in a similar position to the ESOL learner of not always being in control linguistically. This is about creating a space for individual learning and the development of trust which serves to value their identity, build confidence and self-esteem and brings us back to a point already mentioned, namely, about encouraging a sense of belonging within the classroom.

Practical suggestions for supporting ESOL learners

As you will note, many of the following suggestions would also constitute good practice for all learners.

Use plain English

1   Avoid idioms, figurative language and colloquialisms, for example, 'jot that down', 'give me a bell', 'have another go'.

2 Be aware of similar sounding works, such as, fringe/fridge, cheap/chic, thirty/thirteen, particularly when they are key to understanding the subject you are covering in the lesson.

3 Avoid digressions: learners may find it hard to distinguish them from the actual subject matter.

4 Explain technical and subject language and check understanding *before* you begin explaining or demonstrating. A second language speaker will focus on the words they do not understand and the rest of your explanation will be lost.

5 Avoid long complicated instructions and explanations.

6 Become more aware of the speed of your own delivery by taping/videoing a lesson and listening to it.

Repeat key vocabulary and concepts and summarize

1 At the beginning of each lesson or activity define the purpose of the lesson and say what you are going to do in relation to the last session.

2 Work out beforehand the key concepts you want students to learn and remember; repeat them frequently as a lesson progresses and possibly provide a key concept handout for your ESOL learners in advance.

3 Summarize more frequently as this gives students a second chance to pick up key information.

4 When talking, be explicit about the information you are giving: for example, 'first' – with number 1 written on the board or indicated by hand gesture, 'second', etc.

5 Write key words on the whiteboard or OHT, but remember that you may need to check all learners understand the key words.

6 Staged lessons – tell students very clearly when you are moving from one stage of a lesson to another. Reinforce this with written/graphic instructions on the whiteboard.

Note

1 Many of the ideas mentioned here were first used in a chapter on ESOL in the *FE Lecturer's Guide to Diversity and Inclusion* (Wright et al. 2006) but it is hoped that they will provide useful guidelines for those teachers encountering ESOL learners in their classes for the first time.

Annotated bibliography

Further reading

ESOL teaching and learning

Carter, R. and Nunan, D. (eds.) (2001) *The Cambridge Guide to Teaching English to Speakers of Other Languages*. Cambridge: Cambridge University Press.

This is a guide to the central areas of applied linguistics and language studies with particular reference to English language teaching (ELT). Each of the chapters looks in detail at a different area of ELT and draws lessons from applied linguistics – it is helpful as an introduction but also goes into great depth looking at both the history of various topics and future trends.

Cooke, M. and Simpson, J. (2008) *ESOL: A Critical Guide*. Oxford: Oxford University Press.

This book takes a critical standpoint in its account of the pedagogic, social and political contexts of teaching ESOL to adult migrants in countries where English is the dominant language. Multiple quotes from students and examples of effective practice drawn from Cooke and Simpson's research work bring the book to life.

DfES (Department for Education and Skills) (2004) *ESOL Exemplars for speaking and listening, reading, writing from Entry 1 to Level 2*. Nottingham: DfES publications.

A collection of learners' speech, writing and reading texts linked to the National Standards with detailed comment from experts, the *ESOL Exemplars* provide detailed guidance about the standards learners are expected to reach at each level of the national curriculum in reading, writing, speaking and listening.

Harmer, J. (2007) *The Practice of English language Teaching*, 4th edn. London: Pearson Education.

Scrivener, J (2005) *Learning Teaching*, 2nd edn. London: Macmillan.

Both of these texts are practical and comprehensive guides to the most recent ideas in methodology and language theory. They cover the full range of areas addressed in intial-teacher-education programmes and provide detailed guidance for beginning teachers and material for reflection for those with more experience. The latest edition of Harmer's book also has a DVD.

Hedge, T. (2000) *Teaching and Learning in the Language Classroom*. Oxford: Oxford University Press.

This is a reference manual with a reflective approach, frequently used on inservice teacher education courses. It is particularly valuable for its indepth yet practical treatment of language skills and systems.

Reference books about language

Thornbury, S. (1997) *About Language: Tasks for Teachers of English* (Cambridge Teacher Training and Development). Cambridge: Cambridge University Press ELT.

Teachers of English need not only to have a good productive command of the language, they also need to know a good deal about the way the language works. This book asks: 'What is it that a teacher needs to know about English in order to teach it effectively?' It leads teachers to awareness of the language through a wide range of tasks which involve them in analysing English to discover its underlying system. Throughout the book, the language is illustrated wherever possible from authentic sources.

Celce-Murcia, M. and Olshtain, E. (2000) *Discourse and Context in Language Teaching*. Cambridge: Cambridge University Press.

A discourse perspective has a potentially transformative effect on the way teachers look at language. This book introduces the fields of discourse and pragmatics and goes on to show how a knowledge of these areas can be applied to various aspects of teaching.

Carter, R. and McCarthy, M. (2006) *Cambridge Grammar of English: A Comprehensive Guide to Spoken and Written Grammar and Usage* (edition with CD-ROM). Cambridge: Cambridge University Press.

This reference grammar uses language research to offer clear explanations of spoken and written English based on real everyday usage. It has two sections: the first gives attention to lexico-grammar and other language areas that tend to be neglected in grammar references; the second covers traditional grammatical categories such as tense, clause structure and parts of speech.

Parrot, M. (2000) *Grammar for English Language Teachers*. Cambridge: Cambridge University Press.

This text sets out to help teachers develop their overall knowledge and understanding of English grammar, and also provides a quick source of reference in planning lessons and clarifying learners' problems. The book encourages teachers to appreciate the range of factors which affect grammatical choices, but also introduces the 'rules of thumb' presented to learners in course materials. It includes a 'typical difficulties' section in each chapter, which explores learners' problems and mistakes and offers ways of overcoming them.

Swan, M. (2005) *Practical English Usage*, 3rd edn. Oxford: Oxford University Press.

This popular and accessible grammar is often recommended on initial training courses. Over 600 concise articles, arranged in alphabetical order, explain and illustrate points of grammar, usage, vocabulary, idiom, style and pronunciation.

Schmitt, N. (2000) *Vocabulary in Language Teaching*. Cambridge: Cambridge University Press.

This text offers a comprehensive introduction for language teachers to the way vocabulary works. The chapters include teaching applications, exercises and suggestions for further reading. The appendices include a word list of academic vocabulary and a vocabulary test.

Kelly, G. (2000) *How to teach Pronunciation*. London: Longman.

This is a practical and accessible guide to key aspects of pronunciation, with ideas for teaching strategies. There is an accompanying CD with spoken examples of sounds, words and utterances.

Underhill, A. (1994) *Sound Foundations*. London: Macmillan.

Sound Foundations is an introduction to the English phonological system. The first half of the book is a description of the phonological system. In it, Adrian Underhill discusses the sounds of English and describes how they are physically produced. The second half consists of practical classroom activities for use with students to enable them to acquire more comprehensible pronunciation.

Second-language acquisition

Ellis, R. (1997) *Second Language Acquisition*. Oxford: Oxford University Press.

This is a very thorough guide through the field of SLA divided into seven major sections: (1) research and theoretical issues in second-language acquisition; (2) issues of maturation and modularity in second-language acquisition; (3) second-language speech and the influence of the first language; (4) research and methodology and applications; (5) modality and linguistic environment in second-language acquisition; (6) the neuropsychology of second-language acquisition and use; and (7) language contact and its consequences.

Basic literacy

Spiegel, M. and Sunderland, H. (2007) *Teaching Basic Literacy to ESOL Learners: A Teachers Guide*. London: LLU+, London Southbank University.

This is essential reading for teachers who are new to basic-literacy teaching, and also a valuable source of both theoretical knowledge and teaching strategies for those who are more experienced at working with ESOL literacy learners.

History of ESOL

Rosenberg, S.K. (2007) *A Critical History of ESOL for Adults Resident in the UK 1870–2005*. Leicester: NIACE.

This book traces the development of ESOL provision in the UK, giving a detailed and critical context in which to locate current practice. Multiple quotes from students and examples of effective practice drawn from their research work really bring the book to life.

Other references

Adams, H. (2007) *Listening for Beginners*. Cardiff: Cardiff County Council.

Allwright, D. and Bailey, K. (1991) *Focus on the Language Classroom*. Cambridge: Cambridge University Press.

Anderson, A. and Lynch, T. (1998) *Listening*. Oxford: Oxford University Press.

Atkinson, S. and Mather, J. (2003) *Learning Journeys: A Handbook for Tutors and Managers in Adult Education Working with People with Mental Health Difficulties*. Leicester: NIACE.

Auerbach, E. (2002) The power of writing, the writing of power: approaches to adult ESOL writing, *Language Issues*, 14(1) Spring/Summer. (Reprinted in R. Bhanot and E. Illes (eds) (2009) *Best of Language Issues*. London: LLU+).

Baker, C. (2001) *Foundations of Bilingual Education and Bilingualism*, 3rd edn. Cleveland: Multilingual Matters Ltd.

Barton, D. (1994) *Literacy: An Introduction to the Ecology of Written Language*. Oxford: Blackwell.

Barton, D. and Pitt, K. (2003) *Adult ESOL Pedagogy: A Review of Research, and Annotated Bibliography and Recommendations for Future Research*. London: NRDC.

Baynham, M. (1995) *Literacy Practices: Investigating Literacy in Social Contexts*. London: Longman.

Baynham, M. et al. (2006) *ESOL Effective Practice Project*. London: NRDC.

Baynham, M., Roberts, C., Cooke, M. et al. (2007) *Effective Teaching and Learning: ESOL*. London: NRDC.

Bignall, T. and Butt, J. (2000) *Between Ambition and Achievement*. Bristol: Joseph Rowntree Foundation/Policy Press.

Block, D. (2003) *The Social Turn in Second Language Acquisition*. Washington, DC: Georgetown University Press.

Boud, D. and Miller, N. (eds) (1997) *Working with Experience: Animating Learning*. London: Routledge.

Bray, K. (2004) *Our Rights, Our Choices*: Disability Rights Commission. Available at: www.drc.org.uk

Breen, M. P. (2001) The social context for language learning: a neglected situation?, in Candlin, C. N. and Mercer, N. (eds), *English Language Teaching in its Social Context: A Reader*. London: Routledge.

Bremer, K., Broeder, P., Roberts, C., Simonet, M. and Vasseur, M-T. (1996) *Achieving Understanding: Discourse in Intercultural Encounters*. London: Longman.

Brock, C. (1986) The effects of referential questions on ESL classroom discourse, *TESOL Quarterly*, 20(1): 47–59.

Brooks, G. et al. (2007) *Effective Teaching and Learning*: *Reading*. London: NRDC.

Brumfit, C. (1984) The Bangalore procedural syllabus, *English Language Teaching Journal*, 38: 233–41.

Bygate, M. (1987) *Speaking*. Oxford: Oxford University Press.

Candlin, N. and Mercer, N. (eds) (2000) *English Language Teaching in its Social Context: A Reader*. London: Routledge.

Carter, R. (2002) The grammar of talk: spoken English, grammar and the classroom, *Language Issues*, 14(2).

Carter, R. (2004) *Introducing the Grammar of Talk*. London: QCA.

Carter, R. and McCarthy, M. (1997) *Exploring Spoken English*. Cambridge: Cambridge University Press.

Casey, H. et al. (2006) *You Wouldn't Expect a Maths Teacher to Teach Plastering*. London: NRDC.

Chamba, R., Ahmad, W., Hirst, M., Lawson, D. and Beresford, B. (1999) *On the Edge*. Bristol: Policy Press.

Chaudron, C. (1988) *Second Language Classrooms: Research on Teaching and Learning*. Cambridge: Cambridge University Press.

Chen, S. (1997) Error correction in written work & learners' foreign language acquisition, *Language Issues*, 9(2) Autumn/Winter.

Cline, T. and Shamsi, T. (2000) Language needs or special needs? Research Report No 184, DfEE, London.

Close, R. A. (1992) *A Teacher's Grammar*. Hove: Language Teaching Publications.

Collie, J. and Slater, S. (1995) *True to Life: Elementary Class Book*. Cambridge: Cambridge University Press.

Cooke, M. and Dudley, K. (2007) *Turning Talk Into Learning: Working With Learner Talk in the Esol Classroom*. London: NRDC.

Cooke, M. and Roberts, C. (2007) *Developing Adult Teaching and Learning: Practitioner Guides – ESOL*. London: NRDC/NIACE.

Cope, B. and Kalantzis, M. (eds) (1993) *The Powers of Literacy: A Genre Approach to Teaching Writing*. Sussex: Falmer Press.

Cope, B. and Kalantzis, M. (eds) (2000) *Multiliteracies: Literacy Learning and the Design of Social Futures*. London: Routledge.

Crick, Sir B. (2003) The new and the old; Report of the Life in the United Kingdom Advisory Group, Home Office, London.

Crystal, D. (1997) *A Dictionary of Linguistics and Phonetics*, 4th edition. Oxford: Blackwell.

Crystal, D. (1998) *Discover Grammar*. Harlow: Longman.

Crystal, D. (2003) *The Cambridge Encyclopedia of the English Language*. Cambridge: Cambridge University Press.

Cullen, R. (2002) Supportive teacher talk: the importance of the F-move, *ELT Journal*, 56(2), April: 117–27.

DfEE (Department for Education and Employment) (2001a) *Skills for Life: the National Strategy for Improving Adult Literacy and Numeracy Skills*. London: DfEE.

DfES (Department for Education and Skills) (2001b) *Adult ESOL Core Curriculum*. London: DfES.

DfES (Department for Education and Skills (2002) *Success in Adult Literacy, Numeracy and ESOL Provision: A Guide to the Common Inspection Framework* (Ref: DfES/GCIF02/2002). London: DfES

DfES (Department for Education and Skills) (2004) *Differentiation in ESOL Teaching* (video and notes). London: DfES.

DfES (Department for Education and Skills) (2005a) *ESOL Exemplars*. London:DfES.

DfES (Department for Education and Skills) (2005b) *Skills for Life*. London: DfES.

DfES (Department for Education and Skills) (2006a) *It's Not as Simple as You Think: Cultural Viewpoints Around Disability*. London: DfES.

DfES (Department for Education and Skills (2006b) *Making It Happen: An Inclusive Approach to Working with People with Learning Difficulties Who Have ESOL Needs*. London: DfES.

DfES (Department for Education and Skills) (2006c) *ESOL Access for All*. London: DfES.

DfES (Department for Education and Skills) (2006d) *Citizenship Materials for ESOL Learners*. London: DfES.

Eckert, P. and McConnell-Ginet, S. (1992) Think practically and look locally: language, gender and community-based practice, *Annual Review of Anthropology*, 21: 461–90.

Ellis, R. (1997) *Second Language Acquisition*. Oxford: Oxford University Press.

Essential Communication (n.d.) Spelling. *Essential Communication*. London: MCH Publications.

FEFC (Further Education Funding Council) (1996) *Inclusive Learning: Principles and Recommendations: A Summary of the Fndings of the Learning Difficulties and/or Disabilities Committee*. Coventry: FEFC.

Fowler, E. (1997) Developing independent readers, *Basic Skills*, April/May: 6–19.

Gass, S. (1997) *Input, Interaction, and the Second Language Learner*. New Jersey: Lawrence Erlbaum Associates.

Grief, S., Meyer, B. and Burgess, A. (2007) *Effective Teaching and Learning: Writing*. London: NRDC.

Halliday, M. A. K. (1975) *Learning How to Mean*. London: E. Arnold.

Hamilton, M., Barton, D. and Ivanic, R. (eds) (1994) *Worlds of Literacy*. London: Multilingual Matters.

Hardi, C. (2005) My Children, *Poems on the Underground*. Maryland: PublishAmerica.

Harmer, J. (2001) *The Practice of English Language Teaching,* 3rd edn. Harlow: Longman Handbooks for Language Teachers.

Harris, R. (1997) Romantic bilingualism: time for a change? in C. Leung and C. Cable (eds), *English as an Additional Language: Changing Perspectives*. Watford: NALDIC.

Hedge, T. (2000) *Teaching and Learning in the Language Classroom*. Oxford: Oxford University Press.

Hedge, T. (2006) *Writing*, 2nd edn. Oxford: Oxford University Press.

Hiller, Y. (2002) *Reflective Teaching in Further and Adult Education*. London: Continuum.

Holmes, J. (2001) *An Introduction to Sociolinguistics*. Harlow: Longman.

Home Office (2005) Controlling our borders: making migration work for Britain. Five year strategy for asylum and Immigration, Cmnd. 6472, 7 Feb. Home Office, London.

Hussain, Y., Atkin, K. and Ahmad, W. (2002) *South Asian Disabled Young People and Their Families*. Bristol: Joseph Rowntree Foundation/Policy Press.

Ingstad, B. and Whyte, S. R. (eds) (1995) *Disability and Culture*. California: University of California Press.

Ivanic, R. and Tseng, M-I. L. (2005) *Understanding the Relationships between Teaching and Learning: An Analysis of the Contribution of Applied Linguistics*. London: NRDC.

Johnson, D. W. and Johnson, F. P. (1996) *Joining Together: Group Theory and Group Skills*, 6th edn. Boston, MA: Allyn and Bacon.

Kelly, G. (2000) *How to Teach Pronunciation*. Harlow: Longman.

Kenworthy, I. (1987) *Teaching English Pronunciation*. Harlow: Longman.

Kolb, D. A. (1984) *Experiential Learning*. Englewood Cliffs, NJ: Prentice Hall.

Kolb, D. A. and Fry, R. (1975) Toward an applied theory of experiential learning, in C. Cooper (ed.), *Theories of Group Process*. London: John Wiley.

KPMG (2005) *Review of English for Speakers of Other Languages*. London: DfES/Learning and Skills Council.

Kramsch, C. (2002) Introduction: how can we tell the dancer from the dance?, in C. Kramsch (ed.), *Language Acquisition and Language Socialisation: Ecological Perspectives*.

Krashen, S. (1976) Formal and informal linguistic environments in language acquisition and language learning, *TESOL Quarterly*, 10(2): 157–68.

Krashen, S. (1978) The Monitor model of adult second language performance, in M. Burt, H. Dulay and M. Finocchiaro (eds), *Viewpoints on English as a Second Language*. New York: Regents.

Krashen, S (1982) *Principles and Practice in Second Language Acquisition*. New York: Prentice-Hall,

Kumaravadivelu, B. (1993) Maximising learning potential in the communicative classroom, *ELT Journal*, 47(1): 12–21.

Lave, J. and Wenger, E. (1991) *Situated Learning: Legitimate Peripheral Participation*. Cambridge: Cambridge University Press.

Leech, G. and Svartvik, J. (2002) *A Communicative Grammar of English,* 3rd Edn. London: Pearson Education Ltd.

Lewis, M. (1993) *The Lexical Approach*. Hove: Language Teaching Publications.

Lewis, M. (1997) *Implementing the Lexical Approach: Putting Theory into Practice*. Hove: Language Teaching Publications.

Lightbrown, P. and Spada, N. (1999) *How Languages are Learned*. Oxford: Oxford University Press.

LLU+ (2006) *'I came to England'* (video /DVD), (Skills for Life Quality Initiative). London: LLU+, London South Bank University.

Losey, K. (1995) Mexican American students and classroom interaction: an overview and critique, *Review of Educational Research*, 65(3): 283–318.

LSC (Learning and Skills Council) (2005) *Priorities for Success: Funding for Learning and Skills, 2006–2008*. Coventry: LSC.

LSC (Learning and Skills Council) (2006) *Annual Statement of Priorities: Raising Our Game*. Coventry: LSC.

LSDA (Learning and Skills Development Agency) (2004) Taking the work forward, *Project 9: Disability and Ethnicity*. Available at: www.lsda.org.uk/DDA

Maudslay, L., Rafique, A. and Uddin, A. (2003) *Aasha: Working with Young People with a Learning Difficulty from a South Asian Background*. London: Skill, National Bureau for Learners with Disabilities.

Maybin, J. (1994) *Language and Literacy in Social Practice*. London: Multilingual Matters / OU.

McCarthy, M. J. (2001) *Issues in Applied Linguistics*. Cambridge: Cambridge University Press.

McNamara, T. (2000) *Language Testing*. Oxford: Oxford University Press.

Miles, M. (1992) Concepts of mental retardation in Pakistan: towards cross-cultural and historical perspectives, *Disability, Handicap and Society*, 7(3).

Mir, G., Nocon, A., Ahmad, W. and Jones, L. (2000) Learning difficulties and ethnicity, Valuing People Materials, Department of Health, London.

Mitchell, R. and Myles, F. (1998) *Second Language Learning Theories*. London: Arnold.

Mitchell, R. and Myles, F. (2004) Second Language Learning Theories, 2nd edn. London: Arnold.

Moore, A. (2005) *The Good Teacher: Dominant Discourses in Teaching and Teacher Education*. London: Routledge Falmer.

Morton, T., MacGuire, T. and Baynham, M. (2006) *A literature Review of Research on Teacher Education in Adult Literacy, Numeracy and ESOL*. London: NRDC.

Moser, C. (1999) *A Fresh Start: Improving Literacy and Numeracy for Adults* (the report of the working group chaired by Sir Claus Moser). London: DfEE.

Moss, W. (1999) Talk into text: reflections on the relationship between author and scribe in writing through language experience, RaPAL Bulletin No. 40, Winter.

Murphy, R. (2004) *English Grammar in Use*, 3rd edition. Cambridge: Cambridge University Press.

Nattinger, J. and De Carrico, J. (1992) *Lexical Phrases in Language Teaching*. Oxford: Oxford University Press.

Nayar, J. (2004) A study of individual's languages and literacies, *Language Issues*, 16(2), Autumn/Winter.

NIACE (National Institute of Adult Continuing Education) (2003) *New Rights to Learn: A Teacher Guide to Teaching Individuals with Disabilities in Adult Education to Reflect DDA*, Part 4. Available at: www.niace.org.uk.

NIACE (National Institute of Adult Continuing Education) and LLU+ (Language and Literacy Unit, London South Bank University) (2005) *Citizenship Materials for ESOL Learners*. Leicester: NIACE.

NIACE (National Institute of Adult Continuing Education) Committee of Enquiry (2006) *More than a Language*. Leicester: NIACE.

North of England Refugee Service/DfEE (1996) *Refugees: Real Assets* (video: out of production). London: DfEE.

Norton, B. (1995) Social identity, investment and language learning, *TESOL Quarterly*, 29(1): 9–31.

Norton, B. and Toohey, K. (2001) Changing perspectives on good language learners, *TESOL Quarterly Language Review*, 35(2), Summer: 307–21.

NRDC (National Research and Development Centre) (2006) *Embedded case studies: Phase 1 and Comparing embedded and non-embedded teaching of literacy, language and numeracy for learners on vocational programmes: Phase 2*. London: NRDC.

Nunan, D. (1991) *Language Teaching Methodology*. London: Hemel Hempstead/Prentice Hall.

Nunan, D. (2008) *Syllabus Design*. Oxford: Oxford University Press.

Perry, D. (2003) Differentiation–policy and practice, *Language Issues*, 15(1), Summer: 22–3.

Peter, M. (1985) *Spelling Caught or Taught*. London: Routledge.

Pitt, K. (2005) *Debates in ESOL Teaching and Learning: Cultures, Communities and Classrooms*. London: Routledge.

Refugee Council (1997) *Credit to the Nation: A Study of Refugees in the UK*. London: The Refugee Council.

Roberts, C. and Campbell, S. (2006) *Talk on Trial: Job Interviews, Language and Ethnicity*. DWP.

Roberts, K. and Harris, J. (2002) *Disabled People in Refugee and Asylum Seeking Communities*. Bristol: Policy Press.

Roberts, C. and Baynam, M. et al. (2004) *ESOL Case Studies of Provision, Learners' Needs and Resources*. London: NRDC.

Roberts, C. et al. (2005) *Embedded Teaching and Learning of Adult Literacy, Numeracy and ESOL: Seven Case Studies*. London: NRDC.

Rogers, A. (2002) *Teaching Adults*, 3rd edn. Buckingham: Open University Press.

Rogoff, B. (1990) *Apprenticeship in Thinking: Cognitive Development in Social Context*. Oxford: Oxford University Press.

Rogoff, B. (1995) Observing sociocultural activity on three planes; participatory appropriation, guided participation and apprenticeship, in J. V. Wertsch, P. del Rio and A. Alvarez (eds), *Sociocultural Studies of the Mind*. Cambridge: Cambridge University Press.

Rosenberg, S. K. (2007) *A Critical History of ESOL for Adults Resident in the UK, 1870–2005*. Leicester: NIACE.

Roskvist, A. (2002) 'and stuff like that': informal spoken language. What should we be teaching and how can we do it?, *Language Issues*, 14(ii).

Rutter, J. (2000) Refugees: a long history, *Language Issues*, 12(1): 4–8.

Saxena, M. (1994) Literacies among Panjabis in Southall, in M Hamilton et al. (eds), *Worlds of Literacy*. Clevedon: Multilingual Matters.

Schmitt, N. and McCarthy, M. (eds) (1998) *Vocabulary: Description, Acquisition and Pedagogy*. Cambridge: Cambridge University Press.

Schön, D. (1983) *The Reflective Practitioner*. New York: Basic Books.

Schumann, J. (1978) Social and psychological factors in second language acquisition, in J. Richards (ed.), *Understanding Second and Foreign Language Learning*. Rowley, MA: Newbury House.

Scrivener, J. (2005) *Learning Teaching*, 2nd edn. London: MacMillan.

Slayen, S. and Osmaston, M. (2000) e-mail project, *Language Issues*, 13(1), Spring/ Summer.

Smyth, G. (2003) *Helping Bilingual Pupils to Access the Curriculum*. London: David Fulton Publishers.

Soars, L. and Soars, J. (2009) *New Headway English Course: Intermediate*. Oxford: Oxford University Press.

Somerville, W. (ed.), (2006) *Working in the UK: Newcomer's Handbook*, 2nd edn. London: Centre for Economic and Social Inclusion.

Spiegel, M. and Sunderland, H. (1997) *Friends, Families and Folk Tales*. London: Language and Literacy Unit, Southwark College.

Spiegel, M. and Sunderland, H. (2006) *Teaching Basic Literacy to ESOL Learners*. London: LLU+, London South Bank University.

Street, B. (1995) *Social Literacies: Critical Approaches to Literacy in Development, Ethnography and Education*. London: Longman.

Sunderland, H. and Wilkins, M. (2004) ILPs in ESOL, *Reflect*, 1. Available at: http://www.nrdc.org.uk/content.asp?CategoryID=539&ArticleID=462

Sunderland, H., Klein, C., Savinson, R. and Partridge, T. (1997) *Dyslexia and the Bilingual Learner*. London: Language and Literacy Unit.

Swan, M. (2005) *Practical English Usage*. Oxford: Oxford University Press.

Sylvester, R. (1998) Blair's chat show accent is defended, *Daily Telegraph*, 4 June.

Target, F. (2003) *Working in English Language Teaching*, 2nd edn. London: Kogan Page.

Taylor, C. (2007) *ESOL and Citizenship: A Teacher's Guide*. Leicester: NIACE.

Tennant, M. (1997) *Psychology and Adult Learning*, 2nd edn. London: Routledge.

Thornbury, S. (1996) Teachers research teacher talk, *ELT Journal*, 50(4), April: 279–87.

Thornbury, S. (1997) *About Language: Tasks for English Language Teachers*. Cambridge: Teacher Training and Development, Cambridge University Press

Thornbury, S. (1999) *How to Teach Grammar*. Harlow: Longman.

Thornbury, S. (2005) *Beyond the Sentence*. London: Macmillan.

Thornbury, S. and Slade, D. (2006) *Conversation: From Description to Pedagogy*. Cambridge: Cambridge University Press.

Trask, R. L. (1999) *Key Concepts in Language and Linguistics*. London: Routledge.

Tribble, C. (1996) *Writing*. Oxford: Oxford University Press.

Ur, P. (1996) *A Course in Language Teaching*. Cambridge: Cambridge University Press.

Van Lier, L. (2000) From input to affordance: social-interactive learning from an ecological perspective, in J. Lantolf (ed.), *Sociocultural Theory and Second language Learning*. Oxford: Oxford University Press.

Wallace, C. (1992) *Reading*. Oxford: Oxford University Press.

Weir, M. (2004) ILPs: a trivialisation of teaching and learning?, *Reflect*, 2.

Wertsch, J. V. (1998) *Mind as Action*. New York: Oxford University Press.

Willis, J. (1996) *A Framework for Task-Based Learning*. Harlow: Longman/Pearson Education.

Willis, D. (2003) *Rules Patterns and Words: Grammar and Lexis in English Language Teaching*. Cambridge: Cambridge University Press.

Wright, A. Colquhoun, S., Speare, J., Abdi-Jama, S. and Partridge, T. (2006) *An FE Lecturer's Guide to Diversity and Inclusion*. London: Continuum Publishers.

Zera, A. (2004) Getting on brilliantly (keynote address to Annual NATECLA Conference), *NATECLA News*, 75, Autumn.

INDEX

TEACHING ADULT LITERACY

Principles and Practice

Nora Hughes and Irene Schwab

Are you teaching or training to teach literacy to adult learners?
Do you want to update and deepen your practice?
Yes! Then this is the essential book for you!

In this book, the authors offer friendly guidance on how to work with adult learners to develop their literacy skills and practices. They challenge the negative view of adult literacy learners as social 'problems', often described in terms of their deficits. They promote an alternative view of people who have rich resources and skills in many areas of their lives which they can bring to the learning process.

The contributing authors have a wealth of experience as practitioners and researchers in the field. They pull together a wide range of current theory and research on adult literacy, offering new perspectives on theory and applications to everyday practice.

Key features include:

- Case studies of real student experiences
- Samples of learners' writing with commentary and analysis
- Application of linguistic theory to literacy teaching
- Practical suggestions for teaching, planning and assessment
- Guidance on supporting learners with dyslexia and global learning difficulties
- Reflective tasks, encouraging readers to develop and apply their knowledge

This book is an invaluable resource for trainee teachers studying on literacy specialist courses leading to teaching qualifications, as well as for experienced practitioners wishing to update and deepen their practice.

Contents: *Introduction – Section one: Adult literacy and society – Literacy in its social context – Who are the learners? – Section two: Language awareness for literacy teachers – How language works – Language variety – Student profiles and sample texts – Section three: Teaching and learning literacy – Reading – Writing – Speaking and listening – Assessment and planning – Section four: Inclusive learning – Dyslexia – Literacy learning for adults with global learning difficulties – Embedded literacy*

2010 368pp
978-0-335-23736-4 (Paperback) 978-0-335-23735-7 (Hardback)

TEACHING ADULTS 3e

Alan Rogers

'I recommend this book to teachers of any experience ...It is an easy book to read and the illustrations/diagrams make the points mean-ingful. In addition, the book has a comprehensive bibliopraphy, for those who wish to read more about any topic in the book.'

National Association for Staff Development in the Post 16 sector

How can we make our teaching of adults more effective?

In the 3rd edition of this bestselling text, Alan Rogers draws upon a range of recent work on adult lifelong learning to address this key question, by looking at what is distinctive about adult learning and teaching. Based on nearly 40 years of practical experience in a variety of contexts in the UK and overseas, the book discusses what it is that makes helping adults to learn different from teaching younger students. It is concerned with both basic principles and useful hints for teachers and, as such, it will be of value to teachers and programme organisers, to students on adult education courses, to policy makers and to administrators. The emphasis throughout is on the practice of teaching through greater understanding of what it is that we are doing – and the author speaks with involvement and from experience.

There is much that is new in this revised edition. It provides a comprehensive and up to date handbook for students and practitioners with important insights into contemporary understandings of how adults learn both formally and informally, and how they can be helped to learn. Its overall theme – that of making the natural and largely subconscious learning which all adults do both more conscious and more effective – resonates with current thinking and has received much support from the growth of interest in adult learning outside formal learning situations. An invaluable resource for lecturers and trainers, this book will also appeal to those such as health visitors and clergy who are primarily engaged in other activities.

Contents: *Introduction – Before you start – A contract to learn – Definitions – Adult students – The nature of learning – Learning and teaching – Pause for thought – Goals and objectives – Adult learning groups – Roles and the teacher – Teaching – Content and methods – Pause for more thought – Blocks to learning – Evaluation – Participation – Conclusion – Bibliography – Index*

2002
978-0-335-21099-2 (Paperback)

ADULTS LEARNING 5e

Jenny Rogers

- How do adults really learn?
- How do I handle the first class or session?
- How can I get my material across in a way that will interest and excite people?

Completely revised and updated throughout, the new edition of this friendly and practical book is the guide on how to teach adults. Written in an accessible style, it unravels the myths of teaching adults, while explaining why it is both a rewarding and a complex task.

Using case studies and examples from a wide range of sources including higher education, adult education and management development, *Adults Learning* answers questions such as:

- How do I deal with a group of mixed ability?
- How can I can I manage the conflicts that may arise in a group?
- Which teaching methods work best and which are least effective?

The author includes new chapters on problem-based learning and action learning, updated and extensive new material on handling groups, and a revised chapter on coaching, providing plenty of points for further discussion.
Adults Learning is a must-read for anyone involved in teaching adults.

Contents: *Introduction – Adult learners: what you need to know – The first session – Giving feedback – Understanding your group – Facilitating – Action learning – Problem-based learning – Coaching – Role-play and simulation – Delivering information: lecturing, demonstrating and blended learning – Design for learning – Evaluating*

2007 272pp
978-0-335-22535-4 (Paperback)